Playing with Lines

Child Drawing and Modern Literary Experience

ENGLISH ASSOCIATION STUDIES, 17

English Association Monographs: English at the Interface

Established in 1906, The English Association is the oldest established association in the UK for all those interested in English at all levels, from primary to higher education. Its aim is to further knowledge, understanding and enjoyment of the English language and its literatures and to foster good practice in its teaching and learning at all levels. The English Association's flagship journal, *English*, is published four times a year by Oxford University Press and its prestigious and innovative book series, *English Association Monographs: English at the Interface*, is published by Liverpool University Press.

English Association Monographs invites submissions that explore or represent English Studies at the interface with other languages, cultures, professions and disciplines from the medieval period to the present day. It also welcomes submissions that reflect on or contribute to interdisciplinary conversations, or which are the product of thinking across disciplines or across sectors, or which explore the intersections between English Studies, Digital Humanities, and the new technologies of any period. The General Editors and the Editorial Board will work with authors to produce books that are written clearly and eloquently, and represent the best and most exciting new work in English Language and Literature.

Also in this series:

The Life of Rachel Speght: 'A Forward Woman' by Helen M. Stringer

Proximities: Literature, Mobility, and the Politics of Displacement by John Culbert

Elizabethan Occult Poetics: Exploring Practice and Knowledge in English Poetry by Rachel White

Reading Place Writing: Geography, Form, Immersion, 2010–2020 by David Cooper

Multilingualism and the Early Modern City: Language and Society in Norwich (1500–1750) by Christopher Joby

THOMAS GOULD

Playing with Lines

Child Drawing and Modern Literary Experience

LIVERPOOL UNIVERSITY PRESS
THE ENGLISH ASSOCIATION

First published 2026 by
Liverpool University Press
4 Cambridge Street
Liverpool
L69 7ZU

British Library Cataloguing-in-Publication data
A British Library CIP record is available

ISBN 978-1-80596-015-7 (hardback)
ISBN 978-1-80596-022-5 (ePDF)
ISBN 978-1-80596-029-4 (epub)

The manufacturer's authorised representative in the EU for product safety is: Easy Access System Europe, Mustamäe tee 50, 10621 Tallinn, Estonia https://easproject.com (gpsr.requests@easproject.com)

Typeset by Carnegie Book Production, Lancaster
Printed and bound by CPI Group (UK) Ltd, Croydon CR0 4YY

Contents

Acknowledgments

This book and the research that went into it were made possible by a Leverhulme Trust Early Career Fellowship (2019–2023) at the University of East Anglia (UEA). The period 2019–2023 was a difficult time to be doing anything, but my mentor, David Nowell Smith, was immensely supportive and helpful throughout my fellowship. At UEA, I was a temporary and often absent member of the Legible/Visible research group, but I learned a lot from Jack Hartnell, Nick Selby, Rye Holmboe and Ed Krčma. Rye and Ed are both in this book. I first started thinking about *Playing with Lines* when I was at King's College London, specifically outside Ye Olde White Horse with Igor Reyner. Igor belongs to a rare type of person whose ways of thinking and seeing the world refract your own experience and change your life. I am grateful to lots of other people from King's: Benjamin Dalton, Patrick ffrench, Jo Malt, Nikki Ikani and Richard Mason. I am certainly missing some others. I am grateful to Anna Moser, Monica Kam, Olarn Chiaravanont, Andrew Hadfield, Timothy Richardson and John Bisset-Smith. I am grateful to Charlotte and Joe, Matilda, Edward, Sukie (for teaching me about drawing and string), Boonchai, Jintana, my parents, and most of all to Supradya.

Permissions

Parts of the Introduction and Chapter 4 are adapted and reworked from 'Dilection: On the Phenomenology of Child Drawing and the Genesis of Poetic Expression'. Copyright © 2021 Johns Hopkins University Press and Substance, Inc. This article appeared in *SubStance*, 50.3 (2021), pp. 162–183.

An earlier version of Chapter 6 appeared as 'Rhetoric and Rhythm: Derrida, Nancy and the Poetics of Drawing'. In *Paragraph* 44.2 (2021), pp. 157–175.

Four children's drawings are used in this book. Two drawings by 'Richard' are used with the kind permission of the Melanie Klein Trust. A drawing from Georges-Henri Luquet's *Children's Drawings*, by an unknown Dutch boy, is included with the permission of Alan Costall.

The drawing of a mule and jockey by Julio Gomez (or 'Giulio Gomez'), which was reproduced in *The Complete Poems of Marianne Moore*, is used by permission of Faber and Faber Limited and by permission of Viking Books, an imprint of Penguin Publishing Group, a division of Penguin Random House LLC.

Abbreviations

CD	*Children's Drawings*, Georges-Henri Luquet
CPP	*Child Psychology and Pedagogy*, Maurice Merleau-Ponty
GA	*Gesamtausgabe, Band 5: Holzwege*, Martin Heidegger
ILA	*Introductory Lectures on Aesthetics*, G.W.F. Hegel
LGR	*Love, Guilt and Reparation*, Melanie Klein
MB	*Memoirs of the Blind*, Jacques Derrida
NCA	*Narrative of a Child Analysis*, Melanie Klein
OC I	*Oeuvres complètes*, Vol. 1, Francis Ponge
OC II	*Oeuvres complètes*, Vol. 2, Francis Ponge
PD	*The Pleasure in Drawing*, Jean-Luc Nancy
PLT	*Poetry, Language, Thought*, Martin Heidegger
PP	*Phenomenology of Perception*, Maurice Merleau-Ponty,
PR	*Playing and Reality*, D.W. Winnicott
VT	*The Voice of Things*, Francis Ponge

Introduction

Why Child Drawing?

'At the dawn of civilization', Paul Klee wrote in his Bauhaus notebooks of the 1920s, 'when writing and drawing were the same thing, [line] was the basic element. And as a rule our children begin with it' (Klee 1992a, 103). The American artist Rembrandt Peale's popular early nineteenth-century drawing manual *Graphics: A Manual of Drawing and Writing, for the Use of Schools and Families* (1835) taught, similarly, that '[w]riting is nothing else than drawing the forms of letters' (Peale 1835, 6). More recently, Tim Ingold discusses precisely this idea in relation to Winnie the Pooh. He observes that, in A.A. Milne's *The House at Pooh Corner* (1928), Christopher Robin 'realizes that A is a letter, and that as such it is just one of a set of letters, called the alphabet [...] *But at what stage does he cease to draw letters and begin instead to write?* (Ingold 2016, 125; emphasis mine).

Children learn how to write first by marking and re-marking lines and learning how to make those lines conform to a code.[1] We can say that all literate people therefore experience, to some degree, the dynamic 'meaning-making process' of drawing before they experience the dynamic meaning-making process of reading and writing.[2]

Playing with Lines is an intervention into the literary study of

1 'As a rule', Klee says: such 'rules' are one of the conceptual sites in which nature and culture dissolve into one another.

2 Marit Holm Hopperstad writes that drawing, for children, is a 'meaning-making process in which children draw signs to express their understanding and ideas in a visual graphic form' (Hopperstad 2008, 134).

the relationship between words and images, with a central focus on the relationship between writing and drawing. Rather than studying the relationship between the written word and an art-historically sanctioned construction of drawing, *Playing with Lines* aims to explore a counter-discourse of 'child drawing'. The English language generally allows 'adult' as both a noun and an adjective, but 'child' is deployed almost exclusively as a noun. We say, 'adult behavior', 'adult content' or 'adult responsibilities'. For 'child', we rely more on the disciplining of adjectives like 'childlike', and related terms like 'infantile' and 'puerile'. With the conception of 'child drawing', the aim of this book is to resist this pejorative and othering tendency. Further, we start with the term 'child drawing' and not 'children's drawings' because our point of departure is less a material history of actual drawings by actual children, and more the discursive and imaginative investments that surround such graphic production and, behind that, the persistent cultural associations and connotative flows between drawing and childhood as mutually metonymic abstractions.

In other words, the point of departure for *Playing with Lines* is an idealized conception of drawing (crucially, not just drawings by children), linked to childhood or infancy, which provides a horizon for the work of writing among a wide selection of twentieth and twenty-first century poets, writers and philosophers. Whenever drawing is idealized (or, conversely, suppressed) within this expansive cultural context, it is linked metonymically to ideas and feelings of childhood. That is: to forms of expression that precede the mastery of the written alphabet; to supposedly *pure* ways and means of representing; and to an uncorrupted field of play that itself is metonymically connected to the figure of the child. When A.R. Ammons, for example, writes intricately lineated poems about drawing lines; when Jacques Derrida mourns his own childhood drawing from the 'inside' of writing; when Anne Carson conceives of her own writing practice as a form of 'complicated drawing', they are all writing implicitly toward an idea, image or posture of childhood. They are all playing with lines. The expansiveness of this book is deployed so that we might think expansively, and hopefully also a little playfully, about the inner child of literary experience.

With all that said, here is a provisional (rather than definitive) set of criteria for what distinguishes a children's drawing, as a cultural artifact, from other historical constructions of drawing, and makes it such a powerful object in the discourse of child drawing:

1. It is a simplistic and accessible form of graphic expression that does not overtly abide by artistic conventions or traditions.

2. It tends to consist largely of basic linear forms: squiggles or outlines; shapes, wandering lines.

3. It can shift fluidly, on the same page, between figurative or abstract imagery and calligraphic or dysgraphic squiggles, words or phrases.

4. It bears visible traces of the speed, motion or emotion with which it was made.

5. It suggests an urge to process and to express—often as if for the first time—perceived or imagined objects, using simple means, and possibly constrained by limited technical ability (though not necessarily so).

6. It is naive, in the sense that it proceeds *toward* a position of knowledge, rather than emanating from a center of knowledge.[3]

7. It does not fully cover the sheet of paper or material support, often leaving tracts or patches of white space that contribute to its meaning, effect or value.[4]

On this very last point, let us turn to Walter Benjamin. Benjamin is uncommonly sensitive to the formal particulars of the mode of drawing we are considering. Drawing, unlike more culturally codified forms of visual art, requires the presence of what Benjamin calls an unexhausted 'background'. For Benjamin in 1917, '[t]he graphic line marks out the area and so defines it by attaching itself to it as a background [...] The pure drawing will not alter the meaningful graphic function of its background by "leaving it blank" as a white ground' (Benjamin 1996,

3 Jean-Luc Nancy uses the metaphor of the bow and arrow. The line, he says, 'leaves the intention of the aim in order to enter into the tension of the gesture alone and its abandon' (PD 99).

4 Although Alexander Alland Jr. notes cultural differences here: his sample of Taiwanese children, for example, 'draw with compulsion to fill the page' (Alland Jr. 1983, 69), in ways that children raised in other cultures do not.

83). This feature contributes to the textuality of drawing, because texts depend upon the whiteness of the page for their significance.

Both the developmental and medial boundaries between writing and drawing are blurred. In literary studies, the relationship between drawing and writing is routinely figured as an unequal partnership between media that are bound together from birth.[5] Reflecting on the distinction in terms of legibility and visibility, Martine Reid calls drawing the 'timid counterpart' of the written text: its 'problematical opposite and unacknowledged twin' (Reid 1994, 1). My aim is to bring such literary-theoretical formal studies into dialogue with an interdisciplinary discourse of drawing and line-making. For the sake of this Introduction, the premise here is that, instead of 'ceasing' to draw letters and then 'beginning' to write, the somatic and psychical memories of drawing (of struggling to control lines, of being tempted toward squiggles, of choosing between one shape or another) remain as a shaky foundation for certain experiences not just of writing, but also of reading, even when (and sometimes *especially when*) those habits and histories of literacy are increasingly mediated or interrupted by screens.

Psychologists tend to think of the developmental shift from drawing to writing as simply a fact of growing up. As they grow up, children draw less. This is treated as an internal marker in the acquisition of literacy, an 'important moment of a child's development' (Longobardi et al. 2015, 1), with a free play of scribbles and shapes eventually yielding to the formality and convention of handwriting. In one of several prominent developmental studies of the 1980s, Howard Gardner sums up this view: '[o]nce writing mechanics and literary accomplishment have advanced sufficiently [...] the stage is set for the decline—or demise—of graphic expression' (Gardner 1980, 155). So drawing, apparently, leaves the stage for literary accomplishment. The undergirding logic of such studies is that studying child drawing, therefore, can teach us something about

5 An instructive case study is the poet Robert Grenier, whose work is invested precisely in re-tracking this question of when we cease to draw letters and begin to write them. While critics have read Grenier's drawing poems as an attempt to rearticulate Pound's ideogrammic method, a simpler way of viewing them is as an attempt to justify childhood experience. See my own chapter: Thomas Gould, 'The Hatred of Speech and the Poetics of Silence', in *Silence and Its Derivatives: Conversations Across Disciplines*, edited by Mahshid Mayar and Marion Schulte (Cham: Palgrave MacMillan 2022), pp. 199–213.

our forgotten existences as children—a cordoned-off past that is in subtle ways coextensive with a forgotten period of incipient literacy.[6] Contrary to the strict developmental view, we will approach child drawing as a form of textuality, a distinctive mode of relating to, expressing, and *sharing* a frontier between inner feeling and outward orientation on a material support. Child drawing provides a wide variety of models, fantasies and foils for literary experience; the variety of this book intends to account for the variety of those manifestations in a constellatory, modular approach.

What is Literary Experience?

I use the term literary experience, simply, to refer to what occurs when one reads or writes a text whose agreed or assumed primary purpose is not to communicate or to give information. I distinguish 'experience' from the critical term 'event', which is often used to characterize literary reading and writing as distinctive activities. Derek Attridge, for example, defines the 'literary work' as 'an act, *an event*, of reading, never entirely separately from the act-event (or acts-events) of writing that brought it into being as a potentially readable text' (Attridge 2004, 59; emphasis mine). In favoring experience over event, I aim to designate a continuum between drawing and writing (and therefore also reading), rather than the medium-specific singularity that Attridge is aiming for, but also to underscore the role of ongoing processes over circumscribed occurrences in meaning-making.

Literary experience, like child drawing, involves intertwined processes of *playing* and *forming*. It appropriates and manipulates practical elements taken or abstracted from lived experience, sets them aside, and re-combines them into new textual forms. I take this association between play and form from Alexander Alland Jr. who, in another influential text from the boom of developmental studies in children's drawing of the 1980s, defines child drawing precisely as 'playing with form' (an idea that I have adapted into my own title).[7] For Alland Jr., in fact (and this is a significant point for the present study)

6 As one study puts it: 'We need a society that can [...] recognize that perhaps their drawings may tell us much more about childhood than we ever imagined' (Anning and Ring 2004, 124).

7 In addition to Alexander Alland Jr.'s and Howard Gardner's books, see also

a child's developing proficiency in drawing responds to and registers their developing proficiency specifically in the metaphoric (or literary) functions of language. 'The extension of formal play into the visual symbolic realm', Alland Jr. writes, 'comes when children are taught that forms can be linked to content' (Alland Jr. 1983, 10). One of the most generative affordances of the discourse of child drawing is that it provokes us to examine how original experiences of *play* and of *form* are related.

This is in large part because the activity of play always requires formal demarcation. This is most literally the case when one thinks of a playground or a play area, but some kind of implicit or explicit formal demarcation is always necessary. Using the analogy of a picture frame, this is what Gregory Bateson calls the 'play frame' (Bateson 1985, 139). Play, that is, requires a frame, a form, or a page: it takes place in a bounded space in which the player or players acknowledge that normal rules, realities, selves and communicative functions are suspended. Play, we might say, is a kind of poetic absorption. On a related note, Howard Gardner writes that the 'young drawer' is 'preoccupied with the production of forms for their own sake' (Gardner 1980, 45). My claim is that this is already a kind of literary experience.

I also intend the term 'literary experience' to admit conceptual currents from more recent developments in literary theory: specifically cognitive literary studies and new materialism. By this, I mean that experience refers both to *embodied cognition in time* as well as a dynamic *material frontier* between a subject and an object. First, let's take an example from the 'cognitive turn'. Raymond W. Gibbs Jr. refers to the 'embodied dynamics of *literary experience*', arguing that 'reading, of all sorts, involves our imaginative, embodied engagement with texts', an engagement that 'shapes the very process by which linguistic meanings are interpreted' (Gibbs Jr. 2017, 221; emphasis mine). The thing about early years drawing is that it is an entry point into embodied experience directed towards a textual object, as well as being an entry point, as we have already discussed, into the 'processes' of linguistic meaning. The expanded focus afforded by the cognitive turn provides a further justification for returning to child drawing as a site of embodied engagement with the formation of meaning (perhaps not strictly linguistic meaning, but rather *textual* meaning). The vast body of psychological literature

Joseph H. Di Leo's *Interpreting Children's Drawings* (New York: Routledge 2013), first published in 1983.

on the expressive and formal activity of child drawing has so much to contribute, directly and by parallel association, to the growing field of cognitive literary studies.

Similarly, the new materialist turn can equally benefit, and benefit from, an expanded account of literary experience that considers the vivid material engagements of early graphic expression. Jane Bennett, whose 2009 book *Vibrant Matter* did much to ignite this trend, elevates her own obsessive doodling practice as 'enact[ing]' what she calls, after Walt Whitman, 'influx-and-efflux [...] that ubiquitous tendency for outsides to come in, muddy the waters, and exit to partake in new (lively/deathly) waves of encounter' (Bennett 2020, x). Experience, in this style of thinking, is the experience of a dynamic process of boundaries breached and reconstituted through contact, interpenetration and exchange. So, a new materialist framework like Bennett's is, again, interested not in aesthetic 'events', but in the interpenetrative matter of experience. We will re-consider such ideas, later, especially through the work of D.W. Winnicott and his thoughts on transitional experience, drawing and squiggling. For now, if literary experience is the experience of the prehension, permeation and penetration of matter by matter, then how is literary experience, in turn, permeated by our formative encounters of the 'influx and efflux' of graphic play? How is the experience of scribbling and squiggling, or carefully depicting, on a piece of paper recollected in the experience of wrangling with a poem?

A typical children's drawing is an 'image-text' (Bearne and Kress 2001, 90).[8] Alongside related activities such as reading picture-books, making drawings aids children in working through the gaps and overlaps between the legible and the visible.[9] Developmental psychology teaches us that drawings, for children, are texts because of the ways in which they operate socially, affectively and hermeneutically; they can be parsed and pored over, held and interpreted. Like all texts, their meaning depends on their contexts, on the signifying webs that surround them. As Hidemoto Makisa argues '[w]hat is drawn, the content of the

8 This term is taken from W.J.T. Mitchell's influential *Picture Theory* 1994, in which Mitchell seeks to replace the binary word/image with the dialectical figure of the 'imagetext' (see Mitchell 1994, 9).

9 Ellen Handler Spitz writes that picture-books are 'fascinating precisely because they are intended to span this "war-town" border [between word and image] just at the juncture in the lifespan when such bridges are being constructed' (Spitz 1993, 262).

drawing, is not connected with particular meanings but can be given meaning within the structure of relationships around it' (Makisa 2013, 371). Furthermore, they are read for the narratives, symbols and forms that they contain. In one recent study, a four-year-old child, Thea, is observed to say of her drawing, as she draws it: 'These are the fish. The shrimps are here. The shrimps have died ... But the fish were still alive' (Deguara and Nutbrown 2018, 11). Such children talk to and about their drawings as they make them and turn them into stories. The authors of the study observe as Thea and her friend Neal draw together, talking as they go, and 'they co-constructed and co-authored a complex and meaningful "collective social product"'(Deguara and Nutbrown 2018, 16). This case is obviously a prototype for literary experience. Thea, the study observes, plays '*at*, *in*, and *with* drawing [...] all of which were informed by the rich *content* of her own experiences and imagination, and taking the schematic *form* of enclosure, vertical and back and forth trajectories' (Deguara and Nutbrown 2018, 19). Note, in particular, that this description could be taken, too, as a basic description of what it is that poetic form does, right down to the formal particulars of the 'enclosure' of the page, and the vertical and back-and-forth trajectories of lineated scansion.

Of course, child drawing *does* patently demonstrate paths of development—of motor skills, of perception and cognition—and it is not my aim to deny this. Instead, my claim is that the linear, chronological account of development ought to be reconfigured through a return to the core premise of Freudian psychoanalysis that the early orientations and investments of infancy and childhood endure in profound ways in our grown-up lives. As Jacqueline Rose writes, childhood 'is something in which we continue to be implicated and which is never simply left behind' (Rose 1998, 12). Freud himself famously claimed in *Three Essays on the Theory of Sexuality* (1905) that 'there is no period in human life at which the capacity for receiving and reproducing impressions is greater than precisely during the childhood years' (Freud 2016, 36). The practice of drawing, as the French psychoanalyst Sophie Morgenstern argues, constitutes, during the childhood years, a simply unrivaled means for expressing that capacity for the reception and reproduction of impressions (see Morgenstern, 1927 and 1939).[10] According to this school of psychoanalysis, the materials of drawing are the medium through which the child makes tentative forays into expressing an individuated

10 We will discuss Morgenstern in Chapter 2.

experience.[11] Drawing is a field of expression in which *implications* and *impressions* are figured more directly and literally than through any other medium.

Writing Mourning Drawing

To be clear, *Playing with Lines* does not argue that childhood drawing is a universal form of proto-literature. Instead, we will focus on the ways in which the imagination of this inheritance haunts modern and contemporary conceptions of literary experience, and explore the ways in which the blurry connection between writing and drawing can enrich a theory of modern and contemporary poetics.

Let's begin by looking at an instructive case study: Jacques Derrida's *Mémoires d'aveugle: L'autoportrait et autres ruines* (*Memoirs of the Blind: The Self-Portrait and Other Ruins*), which was published in 1990. We will look at this book in depth in Chapter 7. For now, let us consider how, in *Memoirs*, Derrida suggests that his career-defining fascination with the primacy of writing stems, in fact, from a childhood disavowal of drawing (conceived as writing's other). Derrida's vignette is remarkably Freudian. As a child, Derrida recalls, his brother was better at drawing than him:

> I suffered seeing my brother's drawings on permanent display [...] Economizing on visible drawing, on drawing as such, as if I had said to myself: as for me, I will write, I will devote myself to the words that are calling me. And even here, you can see very well that I still prefer them: I draw nets of language about drawing, or rather, I weave, using *traits*, lines [...] and letters, a tunic of writing wherein to capture the body of drawing, at its very birth [...] [D]rawing always returns. Does one ever give it up? Does one ever get over drawing, is one ever done mourning it? (MB 37–39)

It is a kind of origin story. Derrida's self-aware 'I' turns to writing because he has to 'economize' (suggesting a trade-off, but also perhaps

11 Here, Norman Bryson, in art-historical context, refers to drawing as enabling 'transactions between the artist's inner and outer worlds': 'Perhaps no other medium possesses the quality of instant interplay that the drawn line involves, between active and receptive states' (Bryson 2003, 158).

a zero-sum game between the lines of drawing and the lines of writing). Note that Derrida's switch from drawing to writing is not ontogenetic (that is, relating to the development of the individual), but contextual. That is, he does not spontaneously turn to writing because that is the linear path of his own development, but because he sees and relates affectively to his brother's drawings. Child drawing, as elsewhere, is distinguished as a field of expression by the fact it typically implies the presence of others: a sibling who is better or worse, for example, or a parent or caregiver who is listening and watching.[12]

We should be wary of taking Derrida too literally here. Nor, for that matter, should we take him too literally anywhere. The deconstructive position does not trust the accurate recall of memory enough to be making such a literal autobiographical point. Perhaps the story of Derrida's brother is a form of what Saidiya Hartman calls critical fabulation—the stitching together and stringing out of a coherent narrative from the archives, in this case Derrida's own autobiographical archive (see Hartman 2021, 127–135). As for the wider question of why writing might always 'mourn' drawing, we find an answer in Tim Ingold's work. Using a similar figurative language of mortality, Ingold argues that writing announces the death of drawing: '[f]ully linearized, the line is no longer the trace of a gesture but a chain of point-to-point connections. In these connections there is neither life nor movement. Linearization, in short, marks not the birth but the death of the line' (Ingold 2016 155). A sheet of paper covered in sentences may resemble a sheet of paper covered in doodles. But they represent two entirely different approaches to line-making and to play.

In *Memoirs of the Blind*, like the Freudian repressed, drawing 'always returns'. It returns, crucially, at the level of *style*. Derrida's own circumlocutory and knotty style emerges here as an act of compensation for an irrecoverable scene of drawing. Writing becomes a generalized ekphrasis, a means of creating lines and outlines, of hatching and shading: of making drawing figuratively, in a contiguous (because graphic) and yet incommensurate (because grammatical and sequential) system of mark-making. This is what I call linework: the verbal description of linear graphic forms. Now, it would require a tremendous extrapolatory leap to turn Derrida's anecdote into a universal model. I

12 As an aside, note also that, for Derrida here, writing relates to drawing as a garment relates to a body: it is a cultural supplement and a veil (drawing, Derrida seems to be suggesting, is denuded, a-cultural).

do not wish to do that, nor do I wish to slip into Derrida's own fervor for locating (and then deconstructing) points of origin. My argument, instead, is that in *Memoirs*, Derrida is touching on very widespread experiences that find themselves given form in the drawing by children, and that can, and often do, shape in profound ways how literary texts are both written and read.[13]

Finally, Derrida's description of his own linework as a garment or meta-language ('I draw nets of language') complements contemporary perspectives on the role of drawing in developmental psychology. Children, as Joseph Di Leo points out 'are likely to talk as they draw' (Di Leo 2013, 4). A recent study into the drawings of children in a range of ethnic and cultural contexts (for example, Peruvian and Thai) uses the exact same figure as Derrida: the net. It argues that, regardless of the context, 'scribbles are pervasive with no evident individual production different among children [...] part of a rich communicative framework—*a general system of signs which bounds language and various verbal representations, a sort of semiotic net that children and adults interweave*' (Pinto et al. 2011, 440; emphasis mine). I am drawn to the spatial topography of this argument. It is not that drawing, as graphic expression, *precedes* the acquisition of 'verbal representation', but that it surrounds and bounds it as a kind of delineating perimeter or concentric circle. The drawing of very young children provides a horizon for, and step-ladder into, verbal nomination and linguistic play.

Note, for example, how often children will alter the direction or name of a drawing once they have decided to reject someone else's name for it. It is not a cloud, it is a sheep. It is not me, it is you. Howard Gardner calls this tendency for children to 'chatter' about their drawings 'romancing': 'effecting an extremely general link between the realm of drawing and the realm of language' (Gardner 1980, 46). Such cross-cultural developmental studies as those we have just considered allow us to formulate drawing as an original extra-linguistic field, a 'net' in which children

13 The image of the child's scribble certainly provides a fresh perspective on the deconstructive conception, in the *Grammatology*, of the absolute anteriority of the 'trace' (Derrida 1976). If the gesture of deconstruction is to show how internal tensions and contradictions of signifying systems are already set in infinite play, then (again) perhaps child drawing is the field in which that literal play of signification is first encountered and manipulated, in which we begin to enter playfully, imperfectly and intimately, into affective relationships with signs and communicative relationships with other interpreters of signs.

start to gain mastery of literacy and understand that their drawings can be referred to through language. An adult might ask the child what the scribble represents—what is it?—or proffer a potential interpretation: a wave, say. Perhaps the child accepts this name, or perhaps they challenge it; but either way the child returns to the drawing with a new name for what that drawing depicts, and a new idea of what it is that a wave is.

I read this kind of scene as a very early and formative form of what we might call a relationship with textuality. I am aided here again by Walter Benjamin. Benjamin knew how to write about children's drawings. He also produced his own 'hashish drawings', diagram-like sketches, during his hashish experiments in the 1920s and 1930s. In his 1917 fragment 'Painting and the Graphic Arts', Benjamin writes: 'consider children's drawings: viewing them vertically usually conflicts with their inner meaning [...] they have to be placed horizontally on the table [...] pictures are set vertically and signs horizontally' (Benjamin 1996, 82) Children's drawings are signs, not pictures, because (again) they are intended to be *read*, handled and talked through. In Benjamin's eyes, they constitute cultural objects whose principal function is not to impart information, but to circulate between people and generate a kind of shared experience.

The Tension of the Text

It helps to figure the relationship between writing and drawing in terms of tension. To expand this point, I will turn more to conventional literary scholarship. Peter Brooks argues, for example, that all written narrative is inherently tensional: 'plot starts [...] from the moment at which story, or "life", is stimulated from quiescence into a state of narratability, into a tension, a kind of irritation, which demands narration' (Brooks 1977, 291). Narration, he suggests, becomes tensional when it enters a mimetic relationship with life. And what keeps us *reading*, Brooks says, is the fact that texts 'stimulate' us as readers 'into a tension' (Brooks 1977, 291): an urge for resolution or discharge (note, again, the Freudian notes here).

'Tensional' also happens to be the word that Anne Carson uses, when she describes the poem as a 'tensional unit that reenacts the reality of which it speaks' (Carson 1999, 52). We will return to Carson, an inveterate player with lines, in the final chapter of this book. But, again, why are texts tensional? Unlike paintings and drawings, we can never perceive a literary work as a unity. As J. Hillis Miller argues, '[t]he linearity of a novel is always temporal' (Miller 1992, 5). It is as impossible to behold, in a state of simultaneous and integral completion, the totality of Ezra Pound's short Imagist poem 'In The Station at the Metro' as it is Proust's *Recherche*. 'Tension' provides a framework for thinking through the un-totalizable quality of the literary text. Literary experience, as Brooks and Carson help us to see, *is* tensional, insofar as it amounts to an activity of tracking and holding together, untenably, a chain of 'disseminations' (to use Derrida's term) as a single, straight line through time and space.

Since totalities are always spatial, in order to behold a Pound poem, or a Proust novel, as a referable unit, we must always reduce the text to a visual and linear analog of itself. I offer Pound as an example advisedly, since his yearning for an 'ideogrammic method' was motivated precisely by the desire to produce a synoptic literary object; that's the motive that underlies his 'ideogrammic method' (see Pound 1934, 7). As W.J.T. Mitchell puts it in relation to Imagism and the ideogrammic method, the Imagist poem is imagined as a 'synchronic structure in some metaphorical space' (Mitchell 1986, 25). Literary texts are only ever fantasies of objecthood, fantasies of totality in 'some metaphorical space'. Textual criticism and literary studies provide the literary object with a 'net' that sustains it, anchors and outlines it. This is not unlike the net we discussed in relation to the meta-language that is realized by a child's production of drawings.

Perhaps one of the reasons that writing relates mournfully to drawing, its graphic other, is because it yearns for the graphic totality that writing cannot be. When figures like Derrida describe writing as mourning drawing (which at the same time is coextensive with the mourning of a childhood), yet another way of interpreting this is as the affect that attends any experience of writing or reading that wishes to attend to a complete object, in much the same way that child drawing amounts to the expressive simulation of a complete object in intermediate space. In *Narrative of a Child Analysis*, Melanie Klein observes her child patient 'Richard' and notes: 'Richard produced a series of drawings. The way he made them was significant: he did not start out with any deliberate plan and *was often surprised to see the finished* picture' (NCA 17; emphasis mine). One psychological study notes the tendency of children 'to declare completion' (Pinto et al. 2011, 236), to take a moment, or a few moments, to behold in full, and perhaps with a sense of surprise, the satisfying totality of the complete text. Literary experience does not bring with it the same opportunity for surprised beholding of integral completion. Perhaps, bearing in mind this loss or absence, this order of mourning is constitutive of every experience of textuality, and is the same mourning that informs any fantasy of literary interpretation. Seen as such, literary discourse is predicated on the tension of having to hold together, in the mind's eye, the text as a single line.

Linework

'Linework' will be one of the recurring terms in *Playing with Lines*. In its conventional art-historical or architectural sense, linework refers to the use of lines to produce forms or textures, encompassing the quality, style and purpose of lines. I use the term to describe a mode of written description (or textual evocation) of linear formations that, like the Derrida passage from *Memoirs*, draws our attention, through syntactic or semantic means, to both the lines that are made by writing and the lines that are *not* made by writing. By mobilizing the term 'linework' (with the emphasis, here, on *work*) I aim to unsettle the familiar opposition between work and play in textual production. Drawing, as Alland Jr. tells us, is *playing* with form. Writing, by contrast, is often treated as notational, instrumentalized and professionalized and to those degrees it is bound to a notion of work. '[W]riting', Tim Ingold writes, 'is a notation; drawing is not' (Ingold 2016, 120).[14] That is why, for example, it is so hard to write about writers' marginal doodles, like those that populate the notebooks and manuscripts of Samuel Beckett.[15] We can subject the words in a manuscript to genetic criticism, as a record of the development of a literary text, but by contrast doodles frustrate and obstruct the same genealogical drive.

The division between work and play is yet another way of understanding the persistent division between writing and drawing.

14 Another anthropologist, Michael Taussig, published a book-length study of his own fieldwork notebooks, *I Swear I Saw This* (2011). This book tries to develop a theory of the role of drawing not just in anthropology, but in a broader relation to writing as such. Taussig's proposition, as he puts it, is that 'drawing intervenes in the reckoning of reality in ways that writing and photography do not' (Taussig 2011, 13).

15 I have tried. See Thomas Gould, "Legerdemain/Gaucherie: Doodle Theory with Barthes and Beckett". In *Paragraph* 45.2 (2022), pp. 233–247.

Texts that explore their proximity to drawing expose the instability of the work/play binary. They remind us how cultural constructions of childhood and adulthood are often mapped onto this very opposition. Let us turn to a contemporary example. The interdisciplinary American writer and artist Renee Gladman works consistently along the hinge between drawing and writing, producing dense and loopy, illegible calligraphic drawings or 'architectures' which bear resemblance to other 'asemic' or '*illisible*' graphic practices.[16] Gladman's drawings were exhibited, for example, in *The Dreams of Sentences* in 2022 at Wesleyan University, and published in *Plans for Sentences* the same year, alongside brief ekphrastic linework sentences that begin with the simple future tense phrase 'These sentences will [...]' (Gladman 2022, 3). As this all suggests, Gladman is interested in a certain *fantasy* of the sentence, a totally expressive sentence that can only be dreamt or planned, written *toward*, or, ultimately, visually represented by a drawing on paper.

Gladman is a practitioner of the kind of linework I have been describing. Gladman's diaristic 2016 book *Calamities* documents, through writing, her fascination with the affordances and possibilities of drawing: 'I wrote into the days, not drawing. I wrote not drawing and this was surprising to me [...] I would recognize myself not-drawing and would wonder what it meant, what this material was and did it have content' (Gladman 2016, 114). Writing, here, is 'not-drawing', impelled along by a recursive sense of discovery at its emergence from a graphic childhood that necessarily comes before it.

Throughout *Calamities*, Gladman's writing finds itself oscillating between one mode of graphic expression and the other: '[W]ould to stop writing so as to draw make drawing impossible', Gladman writes, 'since drawing was a way to think with the body and writing was the story of the body in thought?' (Gladman 2016, 90). Here, drawing is conceived as being more intimately or immediately connected to the desires and drives of a *thinking body*, whereas writing is a second-degree and structurally referential activity that can only represent that thinking to itself (as *thought*) from a displaced position, as narrative. The point of Gladman's practice is not to pick between writing or drawing, or to oppose them to one another, but to set them into oscillation, to lean back and forth between the corporeal presentism of drawing and

16 For the 'asemic', see Peter Schwenger, *Asemic: The Art of Writing* (Minneapolis: University of Minnesota Press 2019), or, in notably, the work of Argentine artist Mirtha Dermisache.

the retrospective flow of writing.[17] Gladman conceives drawing as the immediate state of being a 'thinking body' orienting itself in relation to its materials and means of expression. It is a fantasy condition of purity, immediacy and innocence. Writing, on the other hand, is conceived as a state of loss or displacement from an originally placed self, a sense of loss that is strangely coextensive with the production of literary texts.

'Linework' can designate any writing that calls attention to its own graphic linearity. That might be writing that describes the flow and duration of a line of thinking that thematically or formally reflects on the linearity of its syntactical divisions and durations, or that refers ekphrastically, from a second-degree position, to the drawing that writing is not (writing as 'not-drawing'). Gladman's *Plans for Sentences* is full of such linework. For example: 'These sentences will have vectors that enter where they edge and will go to hollows, will curve to void and cleave to edge; they will funnel fourteen times and void' (Gladman 2022, 69). Such sentences are linework, because they directly describe themselves in linear terms (curving and cleaving, etc.). One is left with a sense at the end of the sentence that it is drawing attention to its own incapacity as a signifying linear unit.

The Closest You Can Get to Not Doing It: Situating Child Drawing

In 1968, Philip Guston said of his penchant for drawing that '[i]t's the closest I could get to not doing it. [...] Like drawing with your finger, you might say. So then all you possess is the simplest and most archaic of means' (Guston 2022, 86). By that phrase, 'the closest I could get to not doing it', Guston means that drawing with a stick of charcoal is the merest form of mediacy between himself and the world that he can avail himself of. And to go further, the reduction of simplicity of means puts Guston in touch with a conceptual simplicity, or rather the simplicity of means is a more adequate approximation, in visual style, of how one thinks without having to show one's thinking. 'Through his hands', the art historian Henri Focillon writes, 'man *establishes contact with the austerity of thought*' (Focillon 1942, 157).

17 Evie Shockley reads Gladman's experimentations with drawing—'writing as drawing and drawing as writing' (Shockley 2019, 516), as she puts it—as an expression of 'black subjectivity in an era of colorblindness' (Shockley 2019, 524).

Drawing is austere. While writing and drawing play along a continuum, writing is much easier to define and codify because it relies itself upon a codified system. But let me offer some positive and definitive statements about the kinds of object that the discourse of child drawing refers to. Even though, as I asserted at the very beginning of this Introduction, we are charting a history and theory of drawing that is distinct from (and sometimes repressed by) the art-historical history and theory of drawing, art history can provide us with important conceptual resources.

Ed Krčma, for example, argues against universalizing conceptualizations of drawing. 'To conceive of drawing as both relationally configured and as historically contingent', he writes, 'is to unburden ourselves of the futile search for a final, immutable (while also non-arbitrary) definition' (Krčma 2007, 19). Krčma is explaining this as part of a study of twentieth-century practitioners like Robert Rauschenberg and Willem de Kooning. But the study of child drawing also benefits from the twin principles of historicity and relationality. First, child drawing is not transhistorical, however much one may be inclined, as Barbara Wittmann does, to think of it as something that has been 'always there: in the sand by the water, on the bark of trees, on stones and rocks' (Wittmann 2013, 125). We saw Paul Klee doing the same thing in my opening paragraph. *Playing with Lines* is concerned, not with a drawing from the dawn of civilization, but with twentieth and twenty-first-century discourses, constructions and contexts of child drawing.

Second, child drawing is not universal. While most children draw, not all children do. Different children draw differently, and different cultures describe child drawing with different emphases and nuances. In an analysis of drawings by Japanese and US children, Masami Toku concludes that the study of child drawing must take into account the early influence of what we might call aesthetic ideologies on the formation of childhood drawing practices: 'children tend to draw based on attractiveness, more than what they know or what they see. In other words, children imitate the way in which nature and figures are drawn in cultural media rather than how they are seen through their own eyes' (Toku 2001, 58). In the same way that the study of child drawing allows us to conceptualize entryways into sociability and communication, so too can it help us to conceptualize the effects of ideology on formative representations, and the cultural mechanisms by which we learn to find things beautiful or worthy of representation, or by which we choose or select what it is that we like (in addition, of course to what we do *not* like, or what scares us).[18] The study of child drawing provides a means through which we can understand how different cultural and ideological frameworks shape and socially reproduce aesthetic subjects.

While I am focusing on drawing through a psychoanalytic, phenomenological and developmental conceptual nexus, I will be aided by artistic and art-historical approaches to drawing, like Krčma's, as an established medium in the history of Western visual art. Artists and art historians think in theoretically developed and sophisticated ways about the histories and formal qualities of, for example, the graphic line, in ways that can directly inform my study. This is especially the case with artists and art historians who focus on the affordances of the drawing of children as naive practice. For example, the twentieth-century painter Jean Dubuffet was fascinated with children's drawings because, as he put it in a 1952 note on his work, they offered 'modes of representation of objects that borrowed not from some false position [...] but from the record of unconscious looks, of unintentional traces spontaneously inscribed in the memory of every *ordinary* human, and of the affective reactions that normally link each one to the things that surround them' (Dubuffet 2016, 52). We should note here that Dubuffet is valorizing drawing specifically because, for him, it provides a universal foundation.

Child Drawing Now

Playing with Lines intervenes in a resurgence of critical and popular interest in drawing (and aims to counteract the biases of that resurgence toward *institutional* lineages of drawing).[19] The historical role of technology—that is, technologies that both rend and reunite drawing and writing—is an important current informing this resurgence. Whereas the cultural hegemony of figurative painting (and the perspectival mode

18 One study reads environmental anxiety into an array of children's drawings (see Barraza 1999, 49–66).

19 In the United Kingdom, major exhibitions of drawings are now a regular occurrence. At the time of writing, most prominent is *Astonishing Things: The Drawings of Victor Hugo* at the Royal Academy in 2025. The country's first art fair dedicated to drawing was held at the Saatchi Gallery in 2019. In the US, the Menil Drawing Institute, a research center for the study of drawing, was established in Houston in 2018. We could go on.

of drawing underpinning it) met an epistemic challenge with the advent of photography (see, for example, Paul Delaroche's much quoted and apocryphal 1839 pronouncement that 'painting is dead'), drawing as a medium encountered a technological upheaval on an additional front. Since it shares its material supports and media with writing, drawing was caught up in the advents of print and type: the supersession of the felt expressivity of graphic writing by the standardization of type. For Heidegger, this advent had the status of a tremendous ontological event, nothing less than a 'transformation in the relation of Being to man (Heidegger 1992, 80). As much as it transformed our relation with writing, the epistemic shift from inscription to type equally altered our relation with paper, alienating writing from the material surface and thus from its close proximity, as an inscriptive mode of expression, to drawing. This alienation, and its attendant nostalgia, plays its own part in the theoretical stances of post-structuralism. To return to Derrida, he reflects in an interview from the 1990s, on the role played in his own thinking (or, rather, writing) by a 'nostalgia for the colour, the weight, the thickness, the resistance of a sheet of paper' (Derrida 1998, 20).[20] That is, for the sensory and phantasmatic investments of child drawing that are coextensive with—but not simply reducible to—writing; a nostalgia not just for manual writing, but also for the graphic situation of child drawing, where expression emerges from tactile exploration and experimentation.

More recently, this technological history has tilted toward tools like tablets, touchscreens and digital styluses—devices that approximate the simplicity and portability of pen and paper. These tools partly reunite writing and drawing while also, ironically, threatening to abolish them altogether.[21] In the late 1990s, the online emergence of the 'asemic' movement (which exists somewhere between drawing and writing),

20 See also Craig Dworkin's chapter 'The Logic of Substrate' in *No Medium* (2015), 1–34.

21 At the time of writing this book, there has been an explosion of commentary around what psychologist Jonathan Haidt calls the 'phone-based childhood' (Haidt 2024, 7). Haidt's argument—grounded in a formidable array of statistics—is that the 'rewiring' of childhood from largely play-based activity toward a screen-saturated existence has inflicted, and without major policy intervention will continue to inflict, a cascade of social, psychological and existential harms. I defer to much of Haidt's observations, but I also note some degree of skepticism at his implied and explicit valorizing of the *way things used to be.*

where technology served rather than suppressed manual graphic practice, is an instructive case. It is a turn that belies the somewhat outmoded critical tendency to dismiss as Luddite, sentimental, or 'somatocentric' any theoretical approach to the written word that makes serious claims on behalf of the manual and the graphic as entry points into the material and phenomenological geneses of expression.[22] As I have already tried to intimate, far from being somatocentric, my approach to the lingering effects of child drawing in whole fields of literary and philosophical writing is peculiarly psychical, since child drawing provides an early outlet for the psyche to make forays into the world and to begin to accommodate and adapt itself to that world.

The discourse of child drawing provides a means for thinking through the cultural persistence and functions of graphism in a way that is not merely sentimental or primitivistic, and which, more importantly, foregrounds the essential and formative kinship between drawing and writing as expressive comportments. In so doing I aim to make a contribution to the discussions in expression theory, in which it is commonplace to locate the origin of artistic expression in everyday communicative expression. Jenefer Robinson, for example, argues that 'expression and expressiveness have their home in ordinary life and then are extended to the arts' (Robinson 2007, 19). Taking this to its logical starting point, my focus, specifically, is on how the ordinary 'expressiveness' of child drawing extends into other modes of expression.

Robinson's reference to the 'home' of expression and expressiveness offers me a route into a brief illustrative reading of Elizabeth Bishop's 1960 poem 'Sestina' (Bishop 2011, 121). 'Sestina' is a powerful example of a poem that channels the energies and affects of child drawing. The poem depicts a child and grandmother in a kitchen, bound by unspoken grief and the repetitive, circling logic of memory and emotion. Through its strict sestina form, the poem evokes a world where language fails to contain feeling, and expression emerges instead through images, objects and the act of drawing. 'Sestina' looks back to a domestic scene as a cauldron of expression and dramatizes most of the central themes—child drawing, expressivity, the transactions between visualization and verbalization—that are the focus of *Playing with Lines*.

22 In reference to Roland Barthes' drawings (or 'scribbles'), Andrew Brown uses the word 'somatocentrism' as a way of characterizing Barthes' 'anti-technological ideology' (Brown 1992, 179).

In the fifth stanza of the poem, Bishop writes: 'With crayons the child draws a rigid house / and a winding pathway. Then the child / puts in a man with buttons like tears / and shows it proudly to the grandmother' (Bishop 2011, 121). Bishop exploits the recursive mode of the sestina form to create a lyrical equivalent to what the philosopher and psychologist Georges-Henri Luquet calls the 'internal model' of childhood drawing—which is the idea that children draw objects from a mental image by aggregating individualized parts into wholes. We will discuss Luquet's theories in detail in Chapter 5. Bishop selects a limited array of tangible elements with which to construct the visual world of the poem, relying on simple declarative clauses (for example, 'The iron kettle sings on the stove') to sketch a house populated by this 'stove', an 'almanac' and a 'kettle' (Bishop 2011, 121). The poem, as such, mirrors the child's drawing that it describes: it is an example of how the condensed visual grammar of child drawing may be refigured verbally and prosodically into the patterned expressiveness of a poem. The final line of the poem—'and the child draws another inscrutable house' (Bishop 2011, 122)—understands not just the repetition-compulsion of some childhood drawing, but more importantly, that here expression originates less in a will to communicate or transmit information than it does in a private wrangling with perceived phenomena.

Finally, coming to terms with the problem that expression originates in 'inscrutable' experience, my approach to child drawing seeks something in the vein of Giorgio Agamben's account of infancy as an ongoing *experience* of subjectivity. By infancy, Agamben refers to an extra-linguistic experience that sustains itself in speech: '*In terms of human infancy, experience is the simple difference between the human and the linguistic. The individual as not already speaking, as having been and still being an infant—this is experience*' (Agamben 1993, 50). While Agamben's account of infancy unfolds in the domain of speech, I will argue for a comparable persistence of graphic infancy in the domain of writing.

Overview

Before I give a detailed overview of the book, let us consider three additional contextual points. The first is to emphasize that, conventionally, literary studies that are concerned with the relationship between word and image—or the legible and the visible—tend overwhelmingly to draw from aesthetic and art-historical accounts of visual production. They often elide the kinds of visual practice that, as we have already discussed, most children in most cultures participate in to some extent during their youth.

As we've just considered her poem 'Sestina', I will take Elizabeth Bishop as a case study. Bishop was a great admirer of visual art, and many of her poems reflect the influence of a range of modern artists. There is a substantial critical bibliography that rightly explores the relationship between her work and the visual arts—see for example, Peggy Anne Samuels' *Deep Skin: Elizabeth Bishop and Visual Art* (2010), or Linda Anderson's essay 'Visual Art' in *Elizabeth Bishop in Context* (2021). I am not suggesting this kind of scholarship is mistaken, nor that there is a zero-sum opposition between a representation of 'real' art and a representation of child drawing. But the dominance of such studies does reflect a critical orthodoxy: when poetry engages dialogically with visual art, that engagement is typically framed in terms of sanctioned, institutional traditions, rather than with more diffuse, informal or developmental practices such as child drawing.

The second point is that, while many studies have examined the role and influence of children's drawings in the development of modern visual art, far less attention has been paid to their significance in literary, poetic, philosophical or theoretical contexts. Picasso, for example, is often noted to have remarked: 'When I was a child, I drew like Raphael. It has taken me all my life to draw like a child' (quoted in Ashton 1972, 104). Deanna Petherbridge similarly observes that 'drawings by children became a standard ploy in early twentieth-century manifestos, exhibition catalogues and journals' (Petherbridge 2010, 416). And perhaps the most comprehensive critical treatment of this theme is Jonathan Fineberg's *The Innocent Eye: Children's Art and the Modern Artist* (1997). *Playing with Lines* seeks to extend this conversation by exploring the underacknowledged impact of children's visual practices on twentieth-century literary and theoretical production through a selection of illustrative case studies.

Third, and finally, readers will notice that the book—beyond its early philosophical and psychoanalytically-oriented chapters—leans heavily on a combination of French (Maurice Merleau-Ponty, Francis Ponge, Jacques Derrida) and North American texts (such as A.R. Ammons, Marianne Moore and Anne Carson—though I note that Carson is Canadian!). There are a few reasons for this, and not all of them are methodological. The most immediate is my own academic positionality:

I work as a comparatist with one foot in francophone intellectual traditions and the other in North American poetry and poetics. Speaking generally, there are fruitful affinities and instructive tensions between these two loosely organized traditions, especially around questions of visual and graphic practice; I can indicate some examples in a footnote.[23] But to get back to my positionality and method: it is my intention in *Playing with Lines* to practice a kind of scholarship that enacts some of the affects and gestures of child drawing—above all, the tendency to become absorbed in a line of thought and to let these lines connect organically with other objects of fascination. (I'm thinking here of Walt Whitman's poem 'There Was a Child Went Forth', which we will turn to in Chapter 1.) In other words, I have tried to explore what academic criticism can itself learn from the discourse of child drawing. Anne Carson is, in fact, something of a lodestar here, since—as I will explore in the final full chapter of the book—her writing often binds scholarly inquiry and close reading to a passionate engagement with the formal playfulness of drawing.

More substantially, both French and North American modern literary cultures have found space for a valuing a conception of graphic production that is untutored, appealingly amateurish, spontaneous or childlike. This interest has deep pedagogical roots: in the nineteenth century, both cultures developed a fervent appetite for drawing manuals. I have already mentioned Rembrandt Peale's *Graphics: A Manual of Drawing and Writing*; on the French side, we might consider Marie Elisabeth Cavé's *Le Dessin sans maître, méthode pour apprendre à dessiner de mémoire* (1850). As Joyce Bernstein Howell notes in a study of Cavé's work, 'at the beginning of the nineteenth century a well-defined doctrine of drawing was a fundamental and accented part of the discourse and practice of art in France' (Bernstein Howell 2005, 223). A media-theoretical lens might attribute this to the ideological affinity and explore why two revolutionary republics might elevate a medium that privileges spontaneity, free expression and immediacy.

23 Some examples: Betsy Erkkila, *Walt Whitman Among the French: Poet and Myth* (Princeton: Princeton University Press 1980), Marjorie Perloff, *The Poetics of Indeterminacy: Rimbaud to Cage* (Princeton: Princeton University Press 1981), Tom Quirk, *Bergson and American Culture* (Chapel Hill: University of North Carolina Press 1988) and François Cusset, *French Theory: How Foucault, Derrida, Deleuze and Co. Transformed the Intellectual Life of the United States* (Minneapolis: University of Minnesota Press 2008).

But my inclination is toward a more intertextual and aesthetic reading. The transatlantic fascination with the drawn line derives not just from pedagogical or political imperatives but from a shared visual culture: the legacy of artists like Picasso, whose influence reverberated across continents; the gestural intensity of movements like Abstract Expressionism; and, crucially, poetries that explicitly foreground line-making as both a material and metaphorical act and stage poetry as a comprehensively and spontaneously graphic medium. In France, this includes figures like Mallarmé and Apollinaire; in North America, a diffuse but resilient tradition that extends from Walt Whitman and Emily Dickinson through to the visual and spatial poetics of the postmodern era.[24] It is within this confluence of thought, pedagogy and artistic inheritance that *Playing with Lines* positions its central questions.

Chapter 1, 'Philosophical Adults: The Forgetfulness of Drawing', maps the conceptual absence of child drawing in modern philosophy—the negative space my later readings will occupy. I argue that modern European thought has suppressed or 'quarantined' drawing, and show, through readings of Hegel and Heidegger, how drawing, to put it in Derrida's words, *always returns*. Chapter 2, 'Gifts and Strains: Psychoanalysis and Child Drawing', is a standalone chapter that explores the incredibly rich and various ways in which twentieth-century psychoanalytic theory and practice approaches, interprets and instrumentalizes child drawing, inside and out of the therapeutic encounter. Drawing is treated not merely as a symbolic product, but as a medium that bridges inner and outer reality—manifesting both the child's omnipotent fantasies and their need for orientation, compensation and communication. Across case studies and theories, the chapter maps how drawing functions as both a model and metaphor of literary experience.

Chapter 3, 'Snails and Whales: Marianne Moore and the Case of the *Colonias Infantiles*' traces how a child's drawing made during the Spanish Civil War found its way into Marianne Moore's 1953 poem 'Tom Fool at Jamaica', offering a specific example of how mid-century literary modernism absorbed the visual grammar of child art. By

24 In *Dickinson's Misery: A Theory of Lyric Reading*, Virginia Jackson refers to the reader's awareness, reading Dickinson, of an 'archaic moment of handwritten composition' that 'becomes essential to modern lyric reading' (Jackson 2005, 10).

situating Moore's marginal appropriation of a single drawing within the broader context of mid-century psychoanalysis, war trauma and poetic collage, the chapter argues that Moore models her poetic practice on the spontaneous, imaginative and formally inventive qualities of child drawing. In doing so, she both aestheticizes and estranges the drawing from its history, foregrounding a deeper analogy between literary form and the affective logic of childlike selection. Remaining in the mid-century, Chapter 4, 'Georges-Henri Luquet, Maurice Merleau-Ponty and Francis Ponge: Graphic Infancy' elaborates a 'phenomenology of selection' through the work of proposing that child drawing emerges not from a stable model of mimesis or pure expression, but from an affective process of perceptual choice. Drawing is theorized as an embodied, expressive act shaped by the material field of the page and the selective investments of the subject—what Ponge calls *dilection*. Across philosophy and poetics, the chapter develops 'graphic infancy' as a conceptual tool for thinking about drawing and writing as parallel practices of situated, material selection.

Chapter 5 and Chapter 6 dwell on the relationships between the poetic line and the graphic line. Chapter 5, 'A.R. Ammons: The Nature of the Line' examines Ammons' poetry as a sustained inquiry into the roles of expressive line-making in instantiating provisional boundaries between nature and culture. Focusing on poems from the 1960s, it argues that Ammons' linework aligns with the errant, processual and selective gestures of drawing. Building on this case study, Chapter 6, 'Jacques Derrida and Jean-Luc Nancy: Rhetoric and Rhythm', argues that the drawing exhibitions and accompanying catalogs staged by Derrida and Nancy illuminate the conceptual and formal stakes of both graphic and poetic lineation. Through close analysis of *Memoirs of the Blind* and *The Pleasure in Drawing*, the chapter develops a poetics of drawing.

Chapter 7, 'Anne Carson: Still Drawing', is a lengthy study of Carson's writing, and how it emerges from and engages with the practice and conceptual space of drawing. Beginning with the observation that Carson's early prose poems in *Short Talks* originated as drawings, it argues that her entire body of work, through to *Wrong Norma* (2024), stages a productive tension between drawing and writing, between embodied, playful mark-making and the felt demands of narrative and description. Drawing, for Carson, becomes a metaphor and method for resisting narrative closure and performing self-obscurement. Her texts consistently hover at a threshold between visual and verbal expression, channeling the impulses of child drawing to name, to imagine, and to play as a serious aesthetic strategy. Finally, the Coda dwells on the notion of traceability and reconsiders childhood as the state of having traceable forebears. Through readings of John Berger and Jorie Graham, it considers how drawing and linework become a way to both mourn and memorialize, to outline loss and trace relational identity, especially between parent and child.

While I am not aiming to write a history of child drawing as it appears in poems and philosophical texts, the book does follow a roughly chronological trajectory, beginning with the aesthetic philosophy of Hegel in the nineteenth century and concluding with the work of contemporary writers like Anne Carson. And I do identify some historical trends. First, as I explore in Chapter 2, the advent of psychoanalysis and the terror and war of the 1930s and 1940s combine to elevate the analysis of children's drawing, because writers and analysts alike were convinced that drawings could offer insight into both the psyche of the child and the psyche of communities experiencing war and violence. In Chapter 3 and 4—companion chapters on mid-century modernism—I consider how the cultural diffusion of psychoanalysis, the aftermath of war, and the influence of modern visual art further inflect, in the specific cases of Marianne Moore and Francis Ponge, the interest in adopting the positions or postures of a naive draughtsperson. We will also consider how more contemporary texts, with their implied and explicit valorizations and explorations of free play and embodied experience, take place in an age where childhood is increasingly associated with a withdrawal from both play and embodiment.

CHAPTER ONE

Philosophical Adults: The Forgetfulness of Drawing

Introduction

Child drawing, as we have discussed, evokes a metonymic association between childhood and drawing: children draw, and drawing is seen as an activity that is especially suited for children. A huge exception to this logic is the enduring art-historical tradition that elevates drawing as the most advanced, or most *intellectual*, visual form: 'the projection of the artist's intelligence in its least discursive form' (Alloway 1975, 38). In that tradition, drawing becomes, in Ingres' famous words, 'the probity of art' (quoted in Roque 1994, 48).

Tempting as it may be, we should not read this elevation of drawing in a fine art context as a kind of Freudian reaction-formation—as if the 'childish' or spontaneously expressive were repressed in favor of purified form. That would elide a whole history whereby drawing was developed as the architectural foundation of linear perspective. There is a gulf of difference between the drawings that children make and the history of drawing in Western art and thinking about art, although, as we have noted, many modern (and contemporary) artists turned to actual children's drawings, or an idealized field of child drawing, as a source of inspiration. The important point is that the 'childlike' drawing of a Klee, Picasso or Dubuffet is made *within* (and, sometimes, *against*) established artistic histories, methods and traditions.

In this chapter, we will probe how drawing is structurally and theoretically repressed by dominant frameworks in the modern philosophy of art, which privilege abstraction, reason and formal integrity.[1] We will turn, at length, to two of the most influential figures in modern aesthetics: Hegel and Heidegger. Their writings on art—unparalleled in shaping the values of twentieth-century, philosophically-inflected art-historical discourse—provide the backdrop against which child drawing has been repeatedly marginalized. We will consider how Hegel and Heidegger construct ideas about drawing in its absence. Our aim here is i) to elucidate and explore these philosophical ideas around art and ii) to consider the ways in which they 'quarantine' drawing, while also thinking about the resources they may yield for theorizing a counter-discourse of child drawing.

We will therefore consider the question of whether Western philosophy, broadly conceived, is inimical in structure and in disposition to ideas and affects of childhood. I rely upon two principal allies when I pose this question. The first is the American philosopher Gareth B. Matthews, who argued in the 1990s that children, of all ages, can *do* real philosophy. Matthews argued not only that children should be encouraged to think philosophically, but also that adults should pay more attention to how children think. In *The Philosophy of Childhood*, Matthews observes that children frequently pose pointed philosophical questions and offer creative, surprising, and—crucially—valuable answers. Most pertinently, Matthews suggests that philosophy itself may be 'an adult response to the questions of childhood' (Matthews 1994, 16). Matthews is not suggesting that there is something fundamentally ingenuous about pure philosophy, but rather that children are simply more inclined toward everyday inquiry. What I take from Matthews is that what we might call the philosophical position—asking fundamental questions about the nature of things and appearances—is not just compatible with a childhood disposition, but an all-too unacknowledged extension of it.

The second ally is Jean-François Lyotard, by all accounts a very different kind of thinker to Matthews. In *The Inhuman*, Lyotard starts

1 The problem is that child drawing is completely absent from dominant frameworks in the modern philosophy of art. Philosophers—unlike, I think, artists or art historians—are much more likely to pose directly and linger upon the Big Questions of what art is, or where it comes from, or what it's for, and in doing so they end up awkwardly inhabiting that gulf of difference between 'low' and 'high' drawing, because such Big Questions tend to naturalize high-coded cultural productions and thereby draw a veil over the kind of expressive productions that fall outside of their criteria.

off by writing of an enigmatic debt. It is a debt, he writes, 'which each soul has contracted with the [...] indetermination from which it was born and does not cease to be born [...] This debt to childhood is one which we never pay off. But it is enough not to forget it in order to resist it and perhaps, not to be unjust. *It is the task of writing, thinking, literature, arts, to venture to bear witness to it*' (Lyotard 1991, 7; emphasis mine). Lyotard is writing in 1988, but in terms that are germane (if, perhaps, rather portentous) for the present study. Childhood, here, is conceived not as an initial stage of life or consciousness, prior to education and acculturation, but as an ongoing submerged condition of infancy, weakness, muteness and indeterminacy. Western philosophy, Lyotard argues, has suppressed this condition of infancy. It is the role of the whole field of cultural production to try 'to bear witness' to it, to *see* it where others, historically, have failed to see it.

Despite their (very) different philosophical registers, both Matthews and Lyotard call for a renewed attention to a childhood conceived not as an ontogenetic phase, but as a set of conceptual and affective dispositions that are repressed by dominant cultural paradigms. Neither is suggesting that we simply pay more attention to literal children (or, at least in the case of Matthews, not exclusively). They are suggesting that we examine how our paradigms and valued methods of thought and representation either forget childhood or cast it as the outside of a constructed and ennobled rational state that is called adulthood. Indeed, Lyotard's idea of a 'debt' is a useful way of subverting the developmental paradigm that we discussed in the Introduction. Rather than casting childhood as something to be left behind or cast off, it is a condition to which we remain essentially beholden, which persists as a constitutive absence within 'adult' subjectivity, and one that continually unsettles pretensions of rational mastery and self-possession.

But how, we might ask, does philosophy set off to deny its debts to an inner child? A helpful analog may be found in the work of Luce Irigaray. Like Lyotard, Irigaray's post-structuralist work of the 1970s and 1980s sought to expose the areas of silence around the universal subjects of Enlightenment thought and its legacies. In the 1985 book *Speculum of the Other Woman*, Irigaray argued persuasively that Western thought forgets the woman and the figure of the mother. 'We can assume', Irigaray writes, 'that any theory of the subject has always been appropriated by the "masculine"' (Irigaray 1985, 133). Irigaray identifies a deeply rooted tradition of androcentric paternalism in the history of ideas, from Plato's cave to Freud's phallus. This is relevant for our discussion because the erasure of the feminine in philosophical discourse often carries with it a correlated forgetting of the child—not through a simplistic identification of women with motherhood, but because both figures threaten the standalone coherence of the autonomous, adult, male subject on which Enlightenment thought so often tacitly depends. If the feminine is cast as the excluded other of reason, so too is the child, as a conceptual other, cast as its prehistory, its excess or its failure.

Queer theory, in a different register, has been an instrumental resource in showing how dominant discourses construct childhood as a regulatory fantasy embedded in heteronormative, futurist logics. Theorists like Lee Edelman and, after him, Kathryn Bond Stockton have drawn attention to how philosophical and cultural frameworks construct the child in repressive and normalizing terms. For Edelman, 'the child' belongs to the political imperative of the straight family, embodying what he calls *reproductive futurism*: 'the image of the Child', he writes, 'not to be confused with the lived experiences of any historical children, serves to regulate political discourse' (Edelman 2004, 11). Stockton complicates this picture by exploring queer modes of 'growing sideways' (Stockton 2009, 3)—resisting the linear teleology that often defines developmental narratives. Across both accounts, the child becomes a future-oriented fantasy, deployed as telos rather than engaged as a subject.

Within these structures, the child is insistently externalized, serving as a symbolic object rather than a voice-bearing participant or as an enduring element of human subjectivity. The term I take from pedagogy and critical childhood studies for this structural exclusion is *adultism*: a mode of political and epistemic marginalization that casts children as objects of care or control, never as interlocutors in their own right.[2] Modern European thought is adultist: it tilts historically toward an always-to-some-degree masculinist and penetrative will to identify and sustain conceptual lineages and rational subjects. And this set of dispositions does, in its assumed subject position, identify with and construct a position of adulthood.

Reading or returning to works of canonical philosophy with a weather eye on their overt and covert attitudes toward representations

2 On 'adultism', see, for example, Bertrand et al. 'Challenging Adultism: Centering Youth as Educational Decision Makers'. In *Urban Education* 58.10 (2020), pp. 2570–2597.

of childhood is a revealing exercise. Let's briefly take Hegel's wider philosophical project as an example. Hegel does not write about childhood in the *Phenomenology of Spirit*, except that the figure of the child appears only in the discussion of the ethical order, where the child belongs to the natural unity of the familial sphere, but is not yet an ethical subject in their own right (see Hegel 1977, 273). To venture further, in the *Phenomenology*, one can interpret the early stage of consciousness known as 'natural consciousness' as analogous to a kind of epistemological infancy: a condition of immediacy and naivety, in which consciousness assumes its knowledge to be self-evident and unmediated. Hegel writes, 'Natural consciousness will show itself to be only the Notion of knowledge, or in other words, not to be real knowledge' (Hegel 1977, 49). This stage is marked by a lack of reflection, a presumed unity with nature and world, and a condition of incompleteness that must be overcome. Through a dialectical process of negation and development—what Hegel calls *Bildung*—Spirit moves beyond this immediacy. Childhood for Hegel is not just bypassed, but systematically overwritten by the dialectic's demand for maturity and conceptual development. The *Phenomenology* is a machine for constructing adulthood.

I will come back to Hegel shortly, before I turn to a discussion of Heidegger. I will not focus on their grander philosophical projects (we won't discuss the *Phenomenology* any further), but on their comparatively brief but still all-compassing observations on the nature of art. In the title of the chapter, I have called it the *forgetfulness of drawing*, a phrase I have adapted from one of Heidegger's well-known turns of phrase, in his 1946 'Letter on Humanism', where he describes the 'forgetfulness of Being' (Heidegger 2011, 158). Heidegger's argument there is that Western philosophy has historically neglected to think about the beingness of Being. I am not just cribbing the term, but the basic structure of its argument. Philosophers like Hegel and Heidegger have historically neglected to think about drawing when they think about art. Drawing is relegated to a kind of philosophical quarantine.

I am all too aware that this chapter, indeed, is not really about child drawing at all; it is a close reading of two German philosophers who, by contrast to the premise of this book, write very dense and difficult things about the nature of art. But in paying attention to the forgetfulness of drawing, we can—if only negatively—further understand the stakes of an attempt to rethink the roles, affordances and spectral presences of child drawing in literary culture.

Hegel's *Introductory Lectures on Aesthetics* was drawn from the notes for lectures delivered at Heidelberg in 1818 and in Berlin in the 1820s. Heidegger's famous essay 'The Origin of the Work of Art', was originally published in 1950. I mention these dates mainly to provide the background coordinates of our present discussion's periodization of modern art (of course, any periodization is contingent). Let me explain what I mean by this. First, Hegel's lectures anticipate, or set the stage, for modernism. When I say this, I am aided by Robert Pippin, who argues that Hegel's famous thesis of the historical end of art provides an ideal lens through which to view modernism 'because Hegel understands the claims made on us in any sensible embodiment of meaning [...] and because he understands artworks, by existing at all, to embody an assumption about the possibility of shared meaning' (Pippin 2014, 97). Heidegger's mid-century essay, meanwhile, stages a dramatic rupture with these assumptions, through and in the emerging wake of modernism.

It is not just the diminution of drawing that these texts have in common. First, as other critics have noted, there are local continuities and kinships between Hegel and Heidegger's philosophical systems.[3] Heidegger himself described Hegel's lectures on art as 'the most comprehensive reflection on the essence of art that the West possesses' (Heidegger 2011, 133). John McCumber argues that both philosophers see in a systematic approach to art an unrivaled 'paradigm of transformation' (McCumber 1999, 14). Most relevant of all is that both Hegel and Heidegger's writings on art exert a profound influence on the reception of continental ideas about art within the disciplinary framework of literary studies (the positionality that I mentioned in the Introduction). This is particularly visible in the influential seam of post-structuralist criticism in the 1960s and 70s that transmitted the thought of later continental philosophers and literary theorists who were themselves profoundly influenced by Hegel and Heidegger. For example, echoing Heidegger's praise of Hegel's system, the literary theorist Paul de Man argued that '[n]owhere else does the structure, the history, and the judgment of art seem to come as close to being systematically carried out' (de Man 1982, 762).

The enduring reputation of both texts within (at least a particular

3 See, in particular, *Endings: Questions of Memory in Hegel and Heidegger*, edited by Rebecca Comay and John McCumber (Evanston: Northwestern University Press 1999).

tradition of) literary theory is a corollary of the privileged status both systems grant to poetry within their respective hierarchies of art forms. Both Hegel and Heidegger, in different ways, position poetry as a bridge between art and philosophy. Both elevate the *word* as a conceptual medium ('the *Word*', as Hegel writes, 'whose import it is to indicate ideas and notions' [Hegel 2004, 95]). With this in mind, perhaps it was inevitable that the *Lectures* and 'The Origin of the Work of Art' would go on to resonate with a disciplinary position (literary studies) that selects language as its primary object of study, and which treats that object as carrying some kind of redemptive or revelatory potential, even if it is redeeming proof of radical instability. Studies like David Nowell Smith's excellent *Sounding/Silence: Martin Heidegger at the Limits of Poetics* bear this out.[4]

Line and Color

Before we get into the details of Hegel and Heidegger's texts, it is necessary to make a brief excursus through the history of the theoretical divisions between color and line. We can trace this distinction back at least as far as the Renaissance divide between *disegno* and *colorire*. Leon Battista Alberti, in a 1435 treatise on painting, was the first to codify the foundational functions of drawing as the means of delineating forms and constructing perspective.[5]

Disegno, in Renaissance thinking, does not just apply to the formal or geometric underpinnings of visual representation, but also to the imaginative and inventive capacities (*invenzione*) of the artist. Leonardo's astonishing array of drawings of, on one hand, exquisitely observed phenomena and, on the other hand, intricately imagined technologies, demonstrate this dual valence of *disegno*. In France in 1671, the relative merits of drawing and color—now expressed as *dessein* and *coloris*—became the subject of a much-noted quarrel at the Académie Royale

4 Nowell Smith charts Heidegger's engagement with poetry. He also draws some astute comparisons between Heidegger and Hegel on aesthetics: 'Like Hegel, Heidegger considers the death of art that moment when it loses its claim to proof [...] in which beauty is no longer considered a mode of beings' autodisclosure but merely as the object of a judgment of pleasure' (Nowell Smith 2013, 34).

5 See Rosand 2002, 25–27.

de Peinture et de Sculpture. On one side, the *poussinistes* insisted that drawing mattered most. On the other, the *rubennistes* favored color. A typical contention of the *poussinistes* was that color satisfied the ocular faculty, whereas drawing satisfied the intellect.[6] This gives a sense of the general inflection of the debate: color is associated with sensory perception, whereas line has a theoretical, quantitative or abstractive function. It is very often in opposition to sensual color that drawing acquires its conceptual connotations.

With these archaeological underpinnings, aesthetic theory evolved still freighted with debates over whether line or color had to be said to reign supreme at the exclusion of the other. In the intellectual scene of Hegel's time, partisanship of color was the vogue. Hegel's lectures participate in a wider colorist tendency that rippled among sections of early nineteenth-century German thought: notably Goethe's 1810 *Theory of Colours* and Schopenhauer's 1816 *On Vision and Colours.* Later, in the early twentieth century, Heinrich Wölfflin's 1915 proto-structuralist treatise *Principles of Art History* took up a version of the distinction to partition the whole history of Western visual art according to the two categories of the 'painterly' (emblematized, for Wölfflin, by Rembrandt) and the 'linear' (in the other corner, Dürer; incidentally, one of Heidegger's cited examples in 'The Origin of the Work of Art', and one of Hegel's favored draughtsmen).

'They are two worldviews', Wölfflin writes, taking neither side, 'differently oriented in their tastes and interests, yet both quite capable of producing a comprehensive picture of the visible' (Wölfflin 2015, 100). The linear worldview, for Wölfflin, 'presents things as they are', and the painterly worldview, shows things 'as they appear to be' (Wölfflin 2015, 102). Given the time of its publication, Wölfflin's strict cleaving of visual art according to these two categories seems strangely insensitive to the revolution in modern painting, initiated decades earlier by Cézanne, that collapsed the traditional boundaries between line and color and which would branch off, in the twentieth century, into myriad directions. It was Cézanne, after all, who said: '[d]rawing and painting are no longer different factors, as one paints, one draws: the more harmony there is in the colors the more precise the drawing becomes' (quoted in Rose 1982, 11). But this goes to show the stubbornness of a theoretical need to keep

6 For example, André Félibien, one of the *poussinists*, argued that painters who favor color 'prefer to satisfy the eye rather than the mind' (quoted in Lichtenstein 1990, 108).

color and line in generative opposition, even while artists were resisting any such distinction. Of course, with the discovery that painting and drawing were the same activity, modern art learned what was already the case in the unlicensed field of child drawing.

Hegel's Lectures and the Position of Drawing

Now I will focus on Hegel's *Lectures.* My aims are to explain briefly some aspects of his system for thinking about art and to suggest why Hegel is not interested in drawing, and then finally 'to redraw' certain lines of his thinking to suggest how we might tweak Hegelian aesthetics in such a way that makes child drawing visible. We will redraw Hegel through recourse to Walt Whitman. The intention here, especially with the idea of 'redrawing' or, frankly, *playing* with Hegel's ideas, is to provide some conceptual terms and loosen up some possibilities for the closer readings that come in later chapters.

First, for Hegel, art is the sensible presentation of the Idea. A successful piece of art is one that fully integrates its abstract content (that which is addressed to the mind) with its sensible, plastic form. The familiar content–form distinction (a mainstay of artistic and literary criticism, and toward which, as we will soon revisit, Heidegger is hostile) finds perhaps its loftiest expression in Hegel's system.[7]

Let's begin with a key passage from the *Introductory Lectures*, which prescribes the criterion according to which we can judge the 'excellency' of a work of art:

> [I]nasmuch as the task of art is to represent the idea to direct perception in sensuous shape, and not in the form of thought or of pure spirituality as such, and seeing that this work of representation has its value and dignity in the correspondence and the unity of the two sides, i.e. of the Idea and its plastic embodiment, it follows that the level and excellency of art in attaining a realization adequate to its idea must depend upon the grade of inwardness and unity with which Idea and Shape display themselves as fused into one. (ILA 78–79)

7 'Form and content are the most hackneyed concepts under which anything and everything may be subsumed' (PLT 27).

Art, here, is a dialectical form that historically and *developmentally* strives toward some eventual full expression: an ultimate unity of the sensuous with the spiritual. Art names a historical process, and a work of art is a well-wrought unity between a determinate Idea with a fixed Shape. Now, we can already see how a modern understanding of drawing as a preliminary conceptual form cannot be easily integrated into Hegel's dialectical drive towards some absolute. That is because, to channel Hegel's language, drawing is more intuitively conceived as a sensible form not of a realized or unified idea, but a sensible form of *ideating.* Drawing as such does not collaborate in the interface—the 'unity of the two sides'—between idea and plastic embodiment, but more reflexively at the level of practice, between art and artist.[8] Drawing *intervenes*, intricately, behind the scenes.[9]

Hegel, as we have already noted, was a colorist. '[I]t is colour, colouring', Hegel writes, 'which makes a painting a painting' (Hegel 1974, 838). *As* color, paint is the interface between art and viewer. On the other hand, as we have suggested, drawing is the interface between artist and medium. Hegel's suppression of drawing relates to a resistance to seeing the art object as specifically a *work*: as a product that has been worked on and worked out. Drawing is therefore flatly excluded from Hegel's taxonomy and becomes an ancillary element of visual representation with which the artist may begin to mold or shape a form without adding to it the depth and verisimilitude that enable the unity between the internal and external at the level of a shared visibility.

Hegel specifically sees drawing as dryly *quantitative.* It is the means of measuring out shapes and dimensions. It is, therefore, 'purely external': 'It is the drawing alone which provides the distance of objects from one another and also their individual shape [...] It is true that this is primarily related not to the expression of spirit but only to what appears externally' (Hegel 1974, 838).

8 In Hegel's narrative, art ultimately cedes its function to philosophy: '[A]rt ends by transcending itself, inasmuch as it abandons the medium of a harmonious embodiment of mind in sensuous form, and passes from the poetry of imagination into the prose of thought' (ILA, 96). Poetry marks the point at which art crosses over into the *conceptual* medium of the word.

9 I am thinking, here, of the anthropologist Michael Taussig's contention that 'drawing intervenes in the reckoning of reality in ways that writing and photography do not' (Taussig 2011, 13).

Hegel simply does not see in drawing any potential to convey inner intensiveness:

> [N]o matter with what richness of invention and wealth of imagination the inner spirit may directly emerge in sketches from the, as it were, more transparent and thinner veil of form, still painting must *paint* if it intends to portray its subjects in their living individuality and particular detail and not to stop, in its visible aspect, at present only an abstraction. (Hegel 1974, 838)

Here, drawing is figured as a transparent veil (we may recall, earlier, Derrida's remarks about writing as a kind of 'tunic'). While it may allow its subjects to be visible in their dimensions, it also covers or occludes them. As a preliminary element of pictorial representation, drawing must be concealed in turn by the arrival of another medium, which is here the application of paint or color—a secondary covering of the canvas that, paradoxically, uncovers the veil that drawing has introduced. The developmental metonym of child drawing is unavoidable here: drawing, like childhood, must be left behind or outgrown.[10]

Hegel does, however, concede that we ought still to confer 'significant value' upon the drawings of whom he calls 'great masters like Raphael and Albrecht Dürer' (Hegel 1974, 838).[11] But even here, drawing is patronized as a kind of childhood of art. There is a link between a philosophy like Hegel's that addresses itself to a condition of unsurpassable maturation—Spirit—and a seeming will to bracket states, both ontogenetic and creative, that privilege becoming and play. Indeed, there is a structural parallel between Hegel's instrumentalizing appreciation of graphic art and his attitude toward the child in the *Phenomenology* as a custodial object of the family. Hegel's colorism corresponds to the value that drawing is merely a private step towards the completed public work. Raphael, in particular, is an instructive case study. His drawings, as one contemporary exhibition catalog puts it, 'were not executed as independent artworks in their own right; they were part of the work of planning and preparing for the actual product' (Jacoby 2012, 13). Drawings are not 'actual products'. This is bound

10 The idea that drawing seems to require supercession by another medium will return in the next chapter, specifically through the myth of Butades.

11 We will come back to Heidegger's own appraisal of Dürer in 'The Origin of the Work of Art'.

not just by normative conventions of taste and aesthetics, but also by a respect for the biography of the artist that, in another paradox, removes the artist from the equation once the work of art is abstracted from the work that produced it.

Theory and Desire

In the *Lectures*, Hegel considers how we experience an artwork as a specific type of object. This is, we should note, a precursor to a question that Heidegger will consider in his essay, when he differentiates artistic spectatorship from the use of equipment and tools.

Hegel relies on a triumvirate set of what I will call object-dispositions, which allow him to position artistic appreciation differentially. The first of these object-dispositions, which is the 'lowest mode', is that of desire. This disposition, Hegel says, is an 'appetitive relation to the outer world', in which man 'has relations dictated by particular impulses and interests to the objects as themselves particulars' (ILA 41). This articulation of desire is essentially a drive towards the destruction or incorporation of the object that incites it. At the other end of the scale is what Hegel calls 'theoretical consideration by the scientific intelligence', which is interested in things not so that it can 'consume them as particulars', but so that it can become 'acquainted with them in their universality' (ILA 42).

The apprehension of art, for Hegel, is neither desirous nor scientific; it is a neither/nor disposition. Art inspires, instead, a kind of reverent beholding: we 'cherish', says Hegel, 'interest for the object as an individual existence' (ILA 43), not for what it represents or typifies. We behold a work of art as a singular or inviolate thing, not as a manifestation of a broader abstractable category or rubric. One of the important aspects of this triumvirate for Hegel is that these dispositions are *exclusive*. Desire is base and infantile (we could see it as a precursor the Freudian *id*); the theoretical intelligence is mature and sophisticated. Working within the logic of Hegel's system, we can suppose that the art of drawing—because for Hegel it is a means of measuring and quantifying—conforms too much to the abstraction of scientific apprehension, too much to the *higher* mode, to qualify as an object that can truly be appreciated as an example of art.

Now I will step outside of the logic of Hegel's system. It is a challenge to address this directly, because I am dealing with what Hegel's system excludes and leaves unsaid, but first, note that the strict division of apprehension into these three non-overlapping categories constructs a developmental hierarchy. The distribution of object appreciation into three exclusive modes, with art standing aloft from the baseness of desire and the abstract maturity of science or theory, is one of the mechanisms by which Hegel quarantines the kind of childhood that Lyotard speaks of in *The Inhuman* (the indeterminate, the unruly, the playful). But how might we redraw the lines here, in order to construct a theory that, in Lyotard's terms, is more attentive to the 'debt' to childhood?

Whereas aesthetic experience, for Hegel, is a neither/nor construction, I propose that we theorize the field of child drawing, by contrast, as a *collapse* of the hierarchy, and a *combination*, instead, of the dispositions of desire and theory. We can call this, for now, a *nondialectical union of theory and desire.* By this, I aim to mark out an area of expressive experience that abstracts objects by desiring them and that desires objects by abstracting them. This is a mode of expressive experience that wishes to incorporate the objects it selects, while also addressing itself to their universality. When I call it 'nondialectical', I simply wish to construct a model in which desire and theory are equally present and intermingled and are not synthesized into something else along a developmental trajectory.

In the poem 'There was a Child Went Forth', which was included in the 'Autumn Rivulets' section added to *Leaves of Grass* in its 1876 edition, Walt Whitman offers a radically different model of object-disposition, one that centers childhood as a site of poetic openness. I suggest that the model of child psychology that we find in 'There was a Child Went Forth' is equivalent to this idea of a nondialectical union of theory and desire. I read the poem as a fluent countermodel to the strict divisions of object experience that we find in Hegel's *Lectures.*

The poem begins: 'There was a child went forth every day, / And the first object he look'd upon, that object he became, / And that object became part of him for the day or a certain part of the day' (Whitman 2008, 282). So, the child beholds the objects that he sees, and he introjects them. He 'becomes' the objects he looks at, and they 'become' him. This is already a countermodel to the Hegelian system, because it is a nondialectical exchange. The child and the object become part of each other. And Whitman justifies the child's existence not by framing it in terms of an overarching life-journey, but in terms of its daily existence. The child does not go forth over decades as Hegelian *Bildung*; it goes forth *every day*, as a series. The poem then shifts into what, for Whitman, is a characteristically voluminous and partial list of all the objects that a child sees throughout this daily series: flowers, streets, animals, and so on. It develops into an overflowing catalog of things and their types: 'Vehicles, teams, the heavy-planked wharves, the huge crossing at the ferries' (Whitman 2008, 283). Contra Hegel, it suggests that the immediacy of desire for mutual incorporation and exchange has profound effects that long outlast the transient pangs of the 'appetitive'. The objects stay with the child 'for many years or stretching cycles of years' (Whitman 2008, 28). The child has gained a taxonomic understanding of the objects that he has seen and desired and is able to catalog and categorize them.

In Whitman's telling of the child's engagement with the world, in other words, theory and desire play equal formal roles. Of course, Whitman and Hegel were writing in different times, in different contexts. There are dramatic limitations to the comparison. And it is possible to develop a theory of literary experience based on a mutual presence of desirous and theoretical impulses *without* using childhood as a canvas for that theory. But nevertheless it is instructive how much Whitman's poem centralizes childhood, and how much Hegel's system casts it off entirely.

Heidegger and the Drawing of Art

Reading 'The Origin of the Work of Art', it is hard to overlook its dense rhetoric of drawing. It is full of linework. Despite Heidegger's forgetfulness of drawing as an art form (art forms enumerated throughout the essay: painting, architecture, carving, literature, music), a conceptually indispensable figurative language of lines and draughts aids Heidegger's delineation of what he calls the *truth* of the work of art. Heidegger's linework will be our primary focus in this section of the chapter.

Like Hegel, Heidegger aligns painting with *colore* at the expense and exclusion of *disegno*. Indeed, throughout the essay, in an inimitable and incantatory style, Heidegger, like Hegel, treats painting and color as synonymous. For example: 'There is something stony in a work of architecture, wooden in a carving, colored in a painting' (PLT 19). And, later: 'All this comes forth as the work sets itself back [...] into the lighting and darkening of color' (PLT 45). Drawing, it seems, is nowhere to be seen. For Heidegger, color is both the material and the essence of painting; it is part of the earthly stock of materials open to the physical manipulation of the artist. And drawing does not belong to the material of painting but, rather, to the immaterial origin of art itself, to the *prior conditions that are necessary for art to come into being*. It is worth noting, in passing, that in figuring this anteriority of drawing as the anteriority of form determining matter, Heidegger is closer to F.W.J. Schelling, Hegel's contemporary, than to Hegel. '[F]orm', Heidegger writes, echoing Schelling, 'determines the arrangement of the matter' (PLT 27).[12]

Whereas for Hegel, art is constituted between the unity of the two sides of the Idea and the Shape (in other words, content and form, a schema that Heidegger explicitly rejects), for Heidegger the whole question of the origin of the work of art begins, famously, with an instantiation of the hermeneutic circle. 'The artist is the origin of the work', Heidegger writes, '[t]he work is the origin of the artist. Neither is without the other. [...] In themselves and in their interrelations artist and work *are* each of them by virtue of a third thing [...] art' (PLT 18). In other words, art, in Heidegger's framing, emerges not between the unified sides of the Idea and Shape, but from the ever-mobile interplay between the maker and the made.

The graphic line becomes a necessary figure for the complex and tense drawing-together, in the object of the work of art, of what Heidegger calls, with deceptive simplicity, 'world' and 'earth'. We can begin by understanding 'world' and 'earth' as a phenomenological recasting of the nature/culture binary. 'World', that is, refers to the shared world of human endeavor and meaning: something proximate to a notion of culture. 'Earth' refers to the facticity (that is, it precedes our existence as ground) of the inherently meaningless materiality upon and with which world or worlds are instantiated and maintained. World corresponds to the temple; earth corresponds to the hill upon which the temple is constructed, and out of whose materials it is constructed. For Heidegger, to behold a work of art is to bear witness to the mutual interpenetration of the world and earth. The work of art is one of the ways in which that mutual enfoldment is starkly 'unconcealed' (Heidegger's word is *Unverborgenheit*, which corresponds to the Greek *aletheia*). A work of art shows the tense imbrication of shared meaning and dumb materiality. The *tension* of Heidegger's account of the truth of the work of art is that this un-concealment is always attended by an

12 Schelling writes that 'Form is [...] the primary element in all things whereby they also are adapted for art' (Schelling 1989, 128).

equal force of concealment. As much as the work of art reveals truth (as un-concealment), or makes it *happen*, it also covers it up (here, echoes of Hegel's characterization of the 'veil' of drawing): to behold what a work of art makes present is also to behold what it makes absent, the limits of what it reveals, and the limits of one's situated ability to behold or penetrate the imbrication of the world and earth which is, nevertheless, laid bare.

Heidegger calls this tense opposition (*Gegeneinander*) between world and earth a *struggle*, a *striving* (*ein Streit*) (GA 35). In one of his descriptions of this struggle, Heidegger writes:

> World and earth are essentially different from one another and yet are never separated. The world grounds itself on the earth, and earth juts through the world. [...] The world, in resting upon the earth, strives to surmount it. As self-opening it cannot endure anything closed. The earth, however, as sheltering and concealing, tends always to draw the world into itself and keep it there. (PLT 47)

The tug-of-war between world and earth, instantiated in the work of art and our experience of it, demands a linear figure. Sure enough, the constellation of linear and graphic figures that Heidegger deploys are constellated around the German *Riss* (GA, 35). Translated by Albert Hofstadter into either 'rift', or (rather more awkwardly, but necessarily) 'rift-design', *Riss* has a double valence, meaning rift, crack or fissure, but also drawing or draught, especially in the technical or architectural sense (Heidegger's graphic language is often deployed alongside his fondness for architectural metaphors and concepts of dwelling and habitation). The term *Zeichnung*, which translates specifically as architectural drawing, is deployed by Heidegger elsewhere to similar ends, especially throughout 'The Way to Language' in 1959, later collected in the *Basic Writings* (see Heidegger 2011, pp. 279–306).[13]

In 'The Origin of the Work of Art', this *Riss*, the line or rift between world and earth, is both fissiparous and generative, like a tectonic line: a tense boundary that is, at once, a *liminal* line of demarcation, which separates and connects, but also, at the same time, a *formal* line that

13 For a helpful gloss on *Zeichnung*, see Krzysztof Ziarek, *Language after Heidegger* (Bloomington: Indiana University Press 2013), pp. 54–56. For Ziarek, *Zeichnung* in 'The Way of Language' refers to 'the advent of signs' (2013, 56), emphasizing its originary graphic quality.

plots form and provides outlines. Heidegger's *Riss* suggests a forgotten immaterial and primordial form of drawing that unites and precedes all artistic media, a kind of ongoing, original drawing, which isn't a medium but perhaps a condition of mediality:

> The conflict is not a rift (*Riss*) as a mere cleft is ripped open; rather, it is the intimacy with which opponents belong to each other. [...] It is a basic design (*Grundriss*), an outline sketch (*Aufriss*), that draws the basic features of the rise of the lighting of beings. This rift does not let the opponents break apart; it brings the opposition of measure and boundary into their common outline (*Umriss*). (PLT 61 / GA 51)

At the stylistic level, this passage demonstrates how *Riss* operates as a constellating term in the essay. The *Riss* or rift, as a discrete concept, has garnered more attention, in critical analysis and commentary, than the cluster of three cognate terms that Heidegger goes on to use throughout the essay, whose specific meanings are lost in translation into English. They are: *Aufriss*, which refers to a sketch, but specifically to a *vertical* draught (in other words, an architect's drawing of the side of a building); *Grundriss*, which again means sketch, but especially a horizontal floor plan; and *Umriss*, which means outline.

By grouping *Grundriss*, *Aufriss* and *Umriss*, Heidegger figures the *Riss* not just as a breach or a tear, but as a generative schema—horizontal (*Grundriss*), vertical (*Aufriss*) and enclosing (*Umriss*). The *Riss* establishes a *Grundriss*—a floorplan—because it establishes or 'lights' the discrete arena or field in which it happens. It establishes, at the same time, an *Aufriss* because phenomena appear or 'stand', as if vertically, within the arena that has been established. And, finally, it establishes an *Umriss* because both the *Grundriss* and *Aufriss* are necessarily outlined as one form. With these cognate terms and the lines between them, Heidegger is quite methodically constructing, through linework, an abstract image of a notional work of art itself. It's not just a metaphor for composition, but for the ontological structure of truth as *world* and *earth*—a strife drawn out across a single, originary plane.

In architectural and artistic traditions, drawing is often seen as derivative, that is, a flat simplification of three-dimensional form. Heidegger inverts this hierarchy. For him, the plane of the *Riss* is *primary*. The work of truth in art—the way a being 'occupies the Open' (PLT 61)—is not a translation from depth into flatness, but a *setting-back* from the flat into the dense materiality of medium: into stone, wood and pigment ('the dark glow of colors' [PLT 61]). Drawing provides us with a language for *imagining* the primordial articulation where world and earth first confront one another. It is precisely in its minimalism and simplicity that drawing preserves the *Riss* in its most irreducible form. For Heidegger, drawing doesn't merely figure the world—it clears the space for world and earth to appear at all. This is, in other words, something ontological about drawing.

We can think further about this by turning to the passage where Heidegger cites Dürer, who was a draughtsman and engraver:

> Dürer [...] did after all make the well-known remark: 'For in truth, art lies hidden within nature; he who can wrest (*reissen*) it from her, has it'. 'Wrest' (*Reissen*) here means to draw out the rift and to draw and design with the drawing-pen on the drawing-board (*Reissen heisst hier Herausholen des Risses und den Riss reissen mit der Reissfeder auf dem Reissbret*). But we at once raise the counter-question: how can the rift-design be drawn out (*herausgerissen*) if it is not brought into the Open by the creative sketch (*schaffenden Entwurf*) as a rift, which is to say, brought out beforehand as a conflict of measure and unmeasured? True, there lies hidden in nature a rift-design (*Riss*), a measure and a boundary and, tied to it, a capacity for bringing forth—that is, art. But it is equally certain that this art hidden in nature becomes manifest only through the work, because it lies originally in the work. (PLT 68 / GA 58)

Heidegger's appeal to Dürer is not really about technical drawing, nor even representation. Again, it's about the originary condition that makes art possible. The metaphor turns on *reissen*, which means not only to rend or engrave, but to *wrest*, to snatch away. Heidegger layers this violent, extractive gesture with a technical specificity: the *Reissfeder* is a ruling pen, an instrument associated with architectural, cartographic and engineering drawing. Not freehand expression, but the measured delineation of a world-structure. (It is worth noting that, throughout, Heidegger's rhetoric *professionalizes* drawing.) What attracts Heidegger to Dürer's remark is not a mimesis of appearances but a deeper, structural mimesis: art imitates the unfolding of truth not by copying objects, but by replicating the form of its emergence.

The *Entwurf* does not resemble the *Riss*, but mimics it in kind: it projects. Note that projection is the mechanism of metaphor. With metaphor, one item is *projected* across one stratum into another. The projection in 'The Origin of the Work of Art' is not a tracing, but a *throwing*—a *Wurf. Entwurf* literally means both a sketch and a throw. The verb *werfen* (to throw) grounds Heidegger's concept of *Geworfenheit* (thrownness), the existential condition of being delivered into a world and time not of one's choosing. Here, Heidegger extends that logic: just as *Dasein* is thrown into the world, so too is the artwork thrown into the open, as a sketch of the rift that precedes it.

And here lies the strange paradox: projection, by nature, forgets the line that enables it. When an object is thrown, it follows a linear trajectory, but the line itself is not traced or preserved. There is no essential link or readable chain between a metaphor and that for which it substitutes. Heidegger seizes this to articulate the non-foundational, abyssal relation between *Riss* and *Entwurf.* Drawing, understood ontologically, is not about form-making, but about the forgetting of the primordial form that allows a discrete form to come forth.

This brings us to the crux of 'The Origin of the Work of Art', and the crux of my reading here. While, at the submerged and forgotten level of rhetoric, Heidegger establishes a certain ontological priority of drawing, at the level of *argument*, he famously concludes by asserting the priority of poetry (or *Dichtung*). This is an account of poetic language rooted in the graphic register of the *Riss* and the *Entwurf* that Heidegger established via his discussion of Dürer. Heidegger describes poetic language as a '[p]rojective saying':

> Projective saying is poetry (*Das entwerfende Sagen ist Dichtung*): the saying of world and earth, the saying of the arena of their conflict and thus of the place of all nearness and remoteness of the gods. Poetry is the saying of the unconcealedness of what is. Actual language at any given moment is the happening of this saying [...] Projective saying (*Das entwerfende Sagen*) is saying which, in preparing the sayable, simultaneously brings the unsayable as such into a world. (PLT 71/ GA 61)

Again, in the phrase, 'projective saying' ('*Das entwerfende Sagen*'), and specifically in the adjective *entwerfende*, we should hear both the familiar sense of thrownness and projection, but also the sense of drawing and designing. The important thing to note is that Heidegger's philosophy of the aesthetic function of language is attuned to a conception of the originary expressivity of drawing. It is a graphological conception of the poetic utterance.

For Heidegger, there are two orders of language: on one hand, *Dichtung* (poetry), defined as 'projective saying'—which we could further translate as drawing-saying—and on the other hand, 'actual language', or everyday saying. Heidegger's account of the latter, in sharp contrast to the likes of Saussure (who developed structural linguistics as a repudiation of nominative function of language), is based in an ontological account of 'naming'. 'Language', he writes, 'by naming beings for the first time [...] nominates beings *to* their being *from out of* their being' (PLT 71). Again, the action by which this naming takes place is projection, since it involves a displacement along a thrown line. The being is thrown into its place by dint of its being named, but as a consequence of that naming it also leaves something of itself behind in concealment. (Heidegger's account of language ought to be understood according to the graphic logic of the *Riss*.) Language-as-nomination does not just project the being into itself and out of itself, it also *draws* the being. A word, as a name, does not simply indicate or refer to an object. Language has a formal, outlining function: it traces the contours of that object by allowing it to be itself, as a discrete form, and in so doing it also absents the object from itself.

Everyday acts of naming take place at the unexamined ontic level of existence, whereas poetry is an *ontological practice* of language ('Poetry is the saying of the unconcealedness of what is', Heidegger writes, by which he means: truth *as such*). Heidegger describes poetry as the 'projection (*Entwurf*) of truth' (PLT 73/GA 63). So, poetry is the place where language draws and traces the contours of the rift-limits between meaning and matter. This is not merely figurative, but a literal expression of the unfolding of 'truth' such as the twofold movement of concealment and un-concealment. Finally, this explains the function of linework in Heidegger's essay. Heidegger does not describe 'The Origin of the Work of Art' as a poem, and it isn't a poem, but he does repeatedly align poetry with his thinking. He treats poetry as a privileged mode of revealing truth. If poetic language is a language of ontological outlines, that is, an artful practice that outlines beings out of their being, then it follows that a philosophical-poetic treatise on the nature of art like 'The Origin' must rely upon a figurative language of line-making.

In Chapter 6, we will turn to two of Heidegger's successors: Jacques Derrida and Jean-Luc Nancy. Both return to the figure of drawing, and both treat it as a form that is intimately and primordially bound to poetics. I signal this now so that we might perceive a wider 'graphic turn' in continental aesthetics: from Hegel's colorism, which rigorously distances itself from the discourse of drawing, through to Heidegger, whose argument prioritizes color but which is suffused by graphic flights and sketches at the level of rhetoric. Heidegger's writing clears the path for Derrida and Nancy, as we will see, to push further and to radicalize the graphic dimensions of phenomenological writing. For now, in Chapter 2, we will shift from a philosophical discourse in which child drawing is completely absent, to a discourse in which it is so often front and center: twentieth-century psychoanalytic writing.

CHAPTER TWO

Gifts and Strains: Psychoanalysis and Child Drawing

Prologue: Pins and Needles

In the Introduction we considered how Renee Gladman's *Calamities* articulates a position of 'not-drawing'. Not-drawing, we saw, is a form of writing. Not-drawing is writing that regards its emergence from drawing as an adult relates to an experience of childhood. We begin this chapter with another example of not-drawing. Midway through Rainer Maria Rilke's novel, *The Notebooks of Malte Laurids Brigge* (1910), Malte remembers a moment from his childhood when he was absorbed in making a drawing. After dropping a pencil under his desk, he must retrieve it:

> I really did need it urgently, and having to climb down after it was distinctly vexing. [...] [M]y legs seemed far too long, and I couldn't draw them out from under me: remaining too long in a kneeling position had numbed my limbs; I could not tell what was mine and what was the chair's. [...] I did make it to the floor, and found myself on an animal fell that extended under the table to the wall. [...] My eyes, accustomed to the brightness above and still wholly entranced by the colors on the white paper, were unable to make out anything at all below the table [...] I took my bearings from the table legs, and in particular made out my own outspread hand, moving all alone down below, a little like some aquatic animal exploring the seabed. (Rilke 2009, 60–61)

Malte breaks away from his drawing and this initiates a melodrama of post-natal ungainliness (not unlike Gregor Samsa's struggle to shift his new body from the bed in *The Metamorphosis*). The darkness of the under-desk is a hellish negative image of the sheet of paper. Malte must retrain his vision to accept a navigable space of three dimensions (not the two dimensionality of the paper that has just 'entranced' him). In rediscovering his body, he becomes aware of its strangeness; it is fragmented, out of proportion and animalized. For Lorna Martens, Rilke's novel explores how childhood memory is determined largely by its relation to 'things'. In *Malte*, things, Martens argues, 'are in control' (Martens 2011, 136); they exert an outsized influence on the affective life of the child. In this not-drawing passage, note how the retrieval of a pencil, the entrancing sheet of paper, and the fragmented thingification of Malte's own body take on the danger and drama of an expedition.

The scene is, ultimately, a detailed description of the sensation of pins and needles. Pins and needles (or, to give the medical term, paresthesia) occurs when the peripheral nerves are compressed in ways that impair their function. Like drawing, reading and writing are among the more physically inert creative activities. The focus involved in reading or writing—like drawing—typically involve prolonged sitting under a desk or work surface. When Walter Benjamin suggests that children's drawings, because they participate in a field of signs, ought to be read *horizontally* (Benjamin 1996, 82), perhaps it is because signs are better understood when seated.

Cognitive and phenomenological literary studies urge us to consider reading and writing as embodied experiences. Hans Ulrich Gumbrecht, for example, describes the 'presence effect' of literature (Gumbrecht 2006, 324), which refers to the ways in which literary experiences produce material encounters. But unlike, say, yoga, reading, writing and drawing often prompt us to forget and literally to neglect our bodies. We sit in awkward positions, forget our discomfort, go numb. The Uruguayan novelist Mario Levrero's *Empty Words* captures this: '[W]hen I spend a long time reading like I did last night, I don't notice the aches and cramps of prolonged bad posture until the moment I put the book down' (Levrero 2019, 72). Levrero is suggesting, like Rilke's child, that literary experience is a kind of negative embodiment: the body is everywhere but in (or at) the surface of the text.

Rilke's narrator links drawing to the experience of writing and reading as focused productions of meaning which require a channeling of the attention towards a manual surface of meaningful play. The sensation of pins and needles, as it does in *Malte* and in *Empty Words*, usually takes place as a somatic interruption of some intense psychical or mental reverie. Pins and needles belong to category of sensations in which the body comes back to *itself* after engaging with a drawing or a text. It is also a zone in which the body returns uncomfortably back to reality in all its sensorial strangeness.

I focus on this because it provides us with a counterpoint to some of the ideas we will encounter in this chapter. In psychoanalytic texts, the child analysand often draws to exert control over a proprietorial world of images and signs on the space of a sheet of paper. Drawing is a cordoned field of play in which the child may exert their omnipotence, in the psychoanalytic sense of the word. *Malte* shows us the flipside, exploring how imaginative realms of omnipotence must, if we are to live, be inhabited only temporarily. I preface this chapter by describing that zone because most of the texts I describe in this chapter direct towards the process of drawing and what it might tell us about the mental life of children and adults alike. As we will see, they think about the zone between the demarcated text of the drawing and the space of reality—the 'animal fell'—outside of that text.

Introduction

Twentieth-century psychoanalytic writing takes child drawing seriously, perhaps more than any other Anglo-European intellectual tradition. It constructs methods and theories for reading drawings by children and for exploring what they can tell us about fundamental psychical processes. Typically, as we will soon see, when a psychoanalyst develops an interpretation of a specific drawing or series of drawings, or extrapolates that interpretation into a theory of drawing, it will be a drawing that is produced by the analysand in a session, with the analyst present, interacting with the analysand as they draw. As Barbara Wittman argues, psychoanalysis tends to approach children's drawing as 'psychoanalytic instruments', the role of which is to produce 'objects of psychological research' (Wittmann 2010, 255). My approach in this chapter will be to engage with psychoanalytic texts and readings critically, while also organizing them thematically, as a resource for dislodging some of the more stubborn truisms about the imaginative productions of children, especially those ideas that emerge from romantic and post-romantic ideologies of the imagination.

The range of texts we encounter in this chapter argue for the specificity of child drawing. Here, child drawing is not simply a subcategory of comparable processes of symbolization or sublimation, nor an immature version of the artmaking that adults do, but a discrete order of expressive experience. I will treat psychoanalytic writing as theory, but also a genre of writing that itself is occasionally aware of its mimetic incapacity when presented with the formal possibilities of drawing, especially its diagrammatic possibilities (for example, the likes of Freud, Lacan, Winnicott are all markedly diagrammatic thinkers).[1]

The psychoanalyst Sophie Morgenstern, for example, sees child drawing as an exercise of the child's omnipotence. Marion Milner sees it, among other things, as a means of creating vital material. Melanie Klein sees it as a form of reparation as well as a fantasy of orientation. D.W. Winnicott, meanwhile, offers perhaps the most capacious and poetically flexible approach to child drawing. This is partly because, as is often observed of Winnicott, he has such a knack for inhabiting the child's psychical worldview.[2] Through these texts, we arrive at a flexible theory of child drawing as a means of testing and describing the boundaries between the self and the world. I will survey these various theories of child drawing with the aim of developing how, in psychoanalysis, child drawing is either—or simultaneously—a gift (an interpretable object that is given) and a strain (an expression of unconscious tension).

Freud and the Wolf-Man Drawings

Influential post-Freudians, especially in a British context, were much more specialized in the analysis of children than Freud himself, and children, as we have accepted, are much more inclined to draw than adults. But it is instructive to begin by considering a brief example of what Freud himself made of drawing, so that we can understand more fully the theoretical inheritance he left.

1 See, for example, Winnicott's diagrams in 'Psychoses and Child Care' (1952). He diagrams the relationship between the individual and their environment, the 'theoretical first feed', and the transitional object as it intervenes between infant and mother (Winnicott 1975, 223).

2 See, especially, Adam Phillips, *D.W. Winnicott* (London: Fontana 1988)

Freud is, of course, renowned for analyzing dreams, jokes, slips, and other parapraxes as primary material; drawings occupy a much more marginal role in his writings. There are notable exceptions, most notoriously the Wolf-Man's illustrations of his dream in Freud's 1918 paper 'From the History of an Infantile Neurosis'. Freud's case history, conforming with a conservative notion of what illustrations are supposed to do, regards the role of the drawing in his interpretation as providing *secondary confirmation* of the *primary material* of the verbal recollection of the dream. 'He (The Wolf-Man) added a drawing of the tree with the wolves', Freud writes, '*which confirmed his [verbal] description*' (Freud 1918b, 29; emphasis mine).

Freud's logophilia is legendary; he simply favored words over pictures. But in the Wolf-Man's drawing, the wolves are arranged in a tree. What leaps out immediately, to the viewer, is the way the wolves stare directly outward. To look at the drawing is to look at the wolves looking back at you. It turns the dream-content from a private recollection into an unmediated visual address. And for the Wolf-Man, the drawing itself is a means of accessing his childhood (the primal scene).

Freud, however, seems unmoved by that address, indeed as he is by anything else about the drawing's specific features.[3] 'Freud', Michael Taussig observes, 'ignores the drawingness of the drawing' (Taussig 2011, 13). Likewise Whitney Davis seeks to recover the drawing from Freud's logophilia, calling it a 'real artifact': '[the drawing] was an objective manifestation of the Wolf Man's subjectivity, and deliberately used by Freud to reconstruct its history. But it was also Freud's own subjective object' (Davis 1992, 72). Taussig and Davis are both suggesting that Freud misses something of crucial therapeutic and interpretive value. The drawing engenders a form of textuality by circulating between 'authors' and 'readers' and, to run with Davis' language, it takes on a fluid relationship between objectivity and subjectivity: it is a portable and readable object that is free to be received and orally interpreted.

The special status of drawing, in other ways, owes to its textual qualities. Morgenstern, Klein, Winnicott and Milner are much more

3 There is a wealth of literature on this topic. In addition to Taussig and Davis, see, especially, Stefanie Teitelbaum's 2016 article 'Do I have to Draw you a Picture? Sigmund Freud, Imagery, and the Wolf-Man's Drawing'. Teitelbaum says of the drawing, and by implication all such drawings, '[t]he drawing has a quality of a photo-negative of the preconscious, the psychical apparatus for the creation of art' (Teitelbaum 2016, 635).

inclined than Freud to heed and read the drawing-ness of drawings, to treat them as textual artifacts. The rest of this chapter will be organized first conceptually around omnipotence, currency, orientation, and then typologically around squiggles and outlines.

Omnipotence (and Large- and Small-Scale Violence)

The turn towards children's drawings as psychoanalytic instruments in the 1930s and 1940s took place against the darkening backdrop on several converging fronts of political violence, virulent nationalism and the shadow of war. In a study of Marian Milner and Virginia Woolf's writings in the 1930s, Helen Tyson shows how 'the historical vicissitudes of fascism traversed the terrains of psychic, cultural, and political life, unsettling any easy distinction between the inside and outside of the mind' (Tyson 2020, 3). Those same 'vicissitudes' find themselves etched across a whole field of private visual production in the same period.

In Chapter 3, we will begin with a history of the *colonias infantiles* of the Spanish Civil War and the reams of violent drawings that they produced. But I turn briefly now to Aldous Huxley's 1938 catalog essay on *colonias infantiles* drawings. In the essay, Huxley adduces children's wartime drawings in the articulation of a stark anti-war message. He calls for a 'general solution to the problem of large-scale violence and [...] to succour those who, like the child artists of this exhibition, have been made the victims of the world's collective crime and madness' (Huxley 1938, 8). This is emblematic. In the twentieth century children's drawings offered poignant and politically powerful visual testimony of the damage done by 'large-scale violence'. In the 1930s and 1940s, intellectuals and artists like Huxley, with no small influence from the atmosphere of psychoanalysis, were aware of both the sophistication and creativity of children as they were of the realities of violence, whether imminent or unfolding. Huxley's implicit argument is that if we learn to appreciate and therefore value child art and therefore the rich mental lives of children more, we may be inclined to consider more the violence that war inflicts upon the minds of children.

But drawings also register the interactions and transfers between (political, international) large-scale violence and (domestic, phantasmatic) small-scale violence. Melanie Klein's *Narrative of a Child Analysis* documents her 1941 sessions with a young patient called 'Richard',

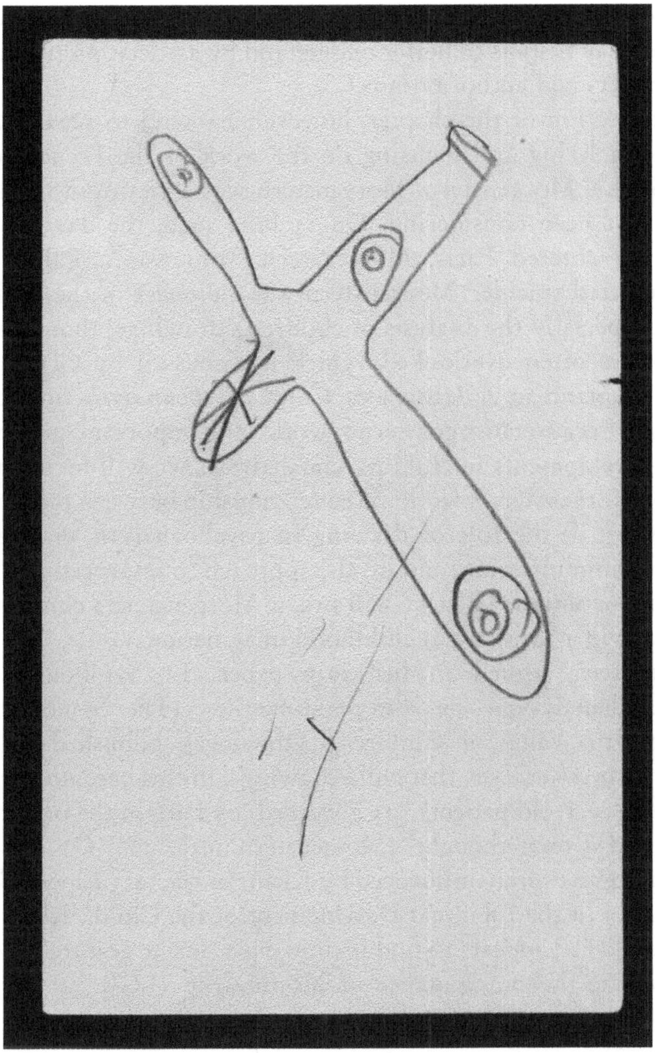

Figure 1. Drawing of a Spitfire by 'Richard', from Melanie Klein's notes. ('Richard 1941', held at the Melanie Klein Archive at the Wellcome Collection, reference PP/KLE/B.46). Included by permission of the Melanie Klein Trust.

whose anxieties about war and imperial conquest were laid bare in a series of drawings that came to be known as the 'Empire' drawings, but also dozens of drawings that depict tanks, battles and especially warplanes. One drawing shows a Spitfire (Figure 1). Klein's wartime work suggests that understanding the psychical positions and drives of childhood may help us to better understand by association the impulses of war-makers and authoritarians.[4]

In this section of the chapter, however, I intend to set out a space for contextualizing and focusing on the work of the French psychoanalyst Sophie Morgenstern. Morgenstern was a victim of the horrors we have just been considering. On 13 June 1940, the day before the Nazi forces entered Paris, Morgenstern, who was a Polish-French Jew, committed suicide.[5] Morgenstern was a pioneer of the analysis of children, especially the analysis of children's drawings, though she and her work are often overlooked, which is discussed by Claudine and Pierre Geissmann in *A History of Child Psychoanalysis* (1998).[6] I say overlooked because Morgenstern's work laid important groundwork for later developments in child psychoanalysis. We will focus on three aspects of Morgenstern's work: i) the relationship between omnipotence and drawing, ii) the role of drawing in psychoanalytic practice, as a means of communication, and iii) the approach to interpreting drawing as a gesture or action. Then we will situate Morgenstern's conclusions in relation to wider ideas about childhood imagination.

Morgenstern argued in her 1939 paper 'Le Symbolisme et la valeur psychanalytique des dessins infantiles' (The Symbolism and Psychoanalytic Value of Children's Drawings), published in *Revue française de psychanalyse*, that child drawings, in this case, the drawings of two nine-year-old patients, are governed 'by faith in the omnipotence of [the child's] own thought' (Morgenstern 1939, 48).[7] On this point, Morgenstern was surely influenced by Klein. In her 1923 paper 'The Role of the School in the Libidinal Development of the Child', Klein argued that 'the child [...] appears to find in drawing a "magic gesture", by which he can realize the omnipotence of his thought' (LGR 72). Drawings

4 More speculatively, the interest in child drawing in the early and mid-twentieth century may be seen to register a futile and retrogressive wish to get back to the life of a child, seated benignly at a drawing table, making simple pictures.

5 Her work would be notably revisited in postwar Paris, with the lectures on child psychology delivered by Maurice Merleau-Ponty at the Sorbonne between 1949 and 1952. We will come back to this in Chapter 4.

6 '[S]trangely for psychoanalysts', they write, on the subject of Morgenstern's work being neglected by French psychoanalysts in the 1940s and 1950s, 'they were to forget their collective past' (Geissmann 1998, 157).

7 All translations of Morgenstern are mine.

therefore offer an insight into the child's faith in their own psychical mastery over the world around them, which is *their* world, prior to any adaptation to what Freud called the reality principle. The child treats the drawing as a space in which they can conjure before themselves the objects of desires and drives. '[D]rawings', Morgenstern writes, clearly showing the influence the primitivist turn in Freud's 1913 *Totem and Taboo*, 'allow us to find a relationship between the thought and the art of the child and that of the neurotic and the primitive, coming from the same emotional and intellectual orientation' (Morgenstern 1939, 48).

Readers of psychoanalysis will be familiar with this equivalence, and with the role played in psychoanalytic theory of stabilizing and primitivizing parallels with roots and geneses, and so-called 'less developed' human cultures and states. For the Freudian psychoanalyst, cultural development is clutter, and if we can learn about universal unconscious tendencies by studying the supposedly *less* culturally cluttered societies of 'primitives', so too can we learn from the drawing habits of children. Of course, the very gesture of categorizing children or entire societies as 'primitive' to mine them for insights into a presumed universal psyche carries with it a deeply problematic set of developmental and hierarchal assumptions.

Morgenstern argues that children's drawings must be taken as primary material, and that they illustrate unconscious dynamics and drives in a direct, interpretable and original way. For example, she describes the anxieties of one of her young patients in relation to the paternal phallus. This boy's drawings, Morgenstern writes, 'are teeming with phallic symbols in the shape of sticks, pipes [...] and swollen tongues hanging from the mouths of baroque animals, snakes, hedgehogs, and other fantastic animals' (Morgenstern 1939, 46). I hesitate to pick this example because it is almost exactly what one would expect a parody of psychoanalytic interpretation to be. But it is also intuitive. Morgenstern suggests that the primal scene is resistant to narrative description, but that the child can draw it in an easy manner that is functionally abreactive, that has not been conceptually translated into words, and which does not require entering into a dynamic of verbal communication and therefore entering into the possibility of being addressed by the analyst (drawing becomes a means of self-displacement, of addressing without making oneself addressable).[8] This is with the

8 Mary Jacobus calls this the 'the drawing cure' (Jacobus 2005, 120).

caveat that the child may venture an oral interpretation of the drawing themselves, but on and in their own terms.

Morgenstern first elaborated the importance of drawing to her practice in the 1927 paper 'Un cas de mutisme psychogène' ('A Case of Psychogenic Mutism'), in which the process of drawing in the analytic session provides a means for the analyst to communicate with her selectively mute nine-year-old patient 'petit Jacques' (Morgenstern 1927, 493) (note how this mutism is an analytic constraint that forces drawings to take on therapeutic significance). In the case history, Morgenstern describes how Jacques is drawn out of his mutism by his own drawing, venturing to offer his own oral interpretations of them. Morgenstern observes that Jacques much prefers answering 'complicated questions' (Morgenstern 1927, 501) with drawings rather than words. Again, the function of his drawings is to provide interpretable referents to be taken up in talking.

Let us move onto another aspect of child drawing in Morgenstern's view: its physicality and gesture of drawing. For Morgenstern, it is not just what children draw that has analytic value, but *how* they draw. First, we should situate this in the context of the nineteenth-century practice of graphology, the study of handwriting as a reflection of character. In 1909, the graphologist (and phrenologist; there was often, apparently, an overlap) George Beauchamp argued that reading handwriting opens to the graphologist a window into the 'human soul' (Beauchamp 1909, 11). This suggests a structural kinship with psychoanalysis because it supposes that outer effects are traceably tethered to inner causes.[9] While the largest claims of un-falsifiability of doctrinaire graphology are consigned to scientific history, there is clear empirical merit to its core premise. If one writes angrily or hastily, one's anger or haste are likely to be discernible. But at times in her work Morgenstern borders on recouping the blunt causal logic of graphology, whereby different traits are systematically indexable to character. 'We even suppose', she writes, 'a correlation between the drawing technique and the neurotic symptom' (Morgenstern 1939, 48). A stiff drawing technique, for example, bespeaks a 'rigid attitude'; a child whose neurotic fixations are mobile and adaptable demonstrates a technique that is 'supple and light' (Morgenstern 1939, 48). Through the ambivalent lens of graphology, what distinguishes drawing from writing is that it provides

9 Indeed, Max Pulver, a noted twentieth-century graphologist, was profoundly influenced by Freud.

a much wider and freer field of gestures and techniques, less subject to convention and constraint.

Owing to these three qualities—its suggestions of 'faith' in omnipotence, its advantages over verbal recollection, and its gestural character—Morgenstern argues that 'drawing proves to be *the most varied and appropriate expression of the conflicts of the infantile psyche* [...] [T]he study of their symbolism enables us to reach [...] *the origin of the child's estrangement from reality*' (Morgenstern 1939, 48; emphasis mine). It is worth emphasizing the point that here drawing stands above other symptoms and expressions as a point of entry into analysis and interpretation. It can, if studied carefully enough, lead the analyst, like a line of string, right to the root cause of a neurotic symptom. What I really want to linger on, however, is the subtle challenge that Morgenstern issues to the romantic notion of drawing as an exercise of the child's sovereign imagination, what Jeanette Sky calls 'the myth [...] of the primacy of the childhood imagination' (Sky 2002, 375).

Let us situate this before we unpack it. Contrary to popular belief, children do not have more active imaginations than adults. Writing in the same period as Morgenstern, the influential Soviet psychologist Lev Vygotsky dealt a blow to this widely held belief by arguing instead that children are *less* imaginative than adults: 'the child imagines less than the adult but trusts the products of it more and has less control over them' (cited in Ayman-Nolley 1992, 79). Contemporary psychological research supports this claim, as much as analyses like Morgenstern's demonstrate it (see, for example, Harris 2022). Morgenstern is operating in a very different register to Vygotsky, but her contention, similarly, is that children are more likely to go along with, *to trust*, the urges and caprices of their expressive flights than adults, not that they are simply better at imagining. Psychoanalytic approaches like Morgenstern's still have value in the work they can do to cut against the still largely prevailing idea that children are inherently better imaginers.[10]

As will become more relevant when we turn to consider the trio of

10 It's not quite contemporary, but an illustrative example: '[w]e will do well', writes Clarence Whaite in 1961, 'to listen and respond to the innocent delight of children in the things of everyday life, to exercise our gifts of imagination, not let them become atrophied' (Whaite 1961, 2). This is from the introduction to the exhibition catalog for the 1961 International Exhibition of Children's Art, that was held at the South London Gallery in Camberwell. Whaite was the Director of Art at the Institute of Education, University of London.

Klein, Milner and Winnicott, there is a broad trend in psychoanalytic theory to mistrust ideologies of the imagination.[11] Morgenstern's claim that drawing can show us the 'origin of the child's estrangement from reality', reverting to the Freudian reality principle, aids us here. Ideologies of the imagination tend to be constructed in a binary relationship with a stably opposed 'reality', in which reality is inevitably the marked term, and almost always freighted with psychologically naive values of creative sovereignty and degrees of giftedness.[12] Instead, psychoanalytic 'reality', as Morgenstern shows, conventionally refers to a principle of adaptation. It is simply the factual world beyond the ego's control to which it must accommodate itself as it lives and grows. What children's drawings, in Morgenstern's account, show us, is the extent to which infant egos are originally 'estranged' from the principle. Furthermore, in the omnipotent graphic play of Morgenstern's patients, there is an overlap between value and form, since the shape that the drawing takes is guided by the psychical values attached to the picture, and the psychical values attached to the picture are also guided by the child's mastery of their motor skills in the manipulation of its form.

To stop drawing is therefore to be refamiliarized with the factual world—not easily dominated by either valuation or formalization—outside the drawing, indeed like the young Malte, orienting himself on the 'animal fell' under his desk.

Currency (and Counter-Abjection)

Like Morgenstern, Melanie Klein and Marion Milner are interested in the activity and the form of the graphic productions of children, and also in the proposition that these productions can reveal original withdrawals from reality. But Klein and Milner are more invested than Morgenstern in the ways of the social function of drawing: its actual, intersubjective existence. That is, they alike approach drawing as the generation of meaningful and valued material that has a variety of associated

11 Winnicott, for example, prefers the gerund term 'fantasying'; Melanie Klein uses the capacious concept of *phantasy*.

12 Wallace Stevens' reality and imagination schema provides an example of this, although Stevens himself was always busy tinkering with and troubling the logic and stability of the binary, for example, in his *Adagia*, 'The imagination is the liberty of the mind and hence the liberty of reality' (Stevens 1957, 44).

functions. Klein, for her part, deployed drawing in her analytic practice as part of her wider 'play technique'. With this technique, the analytic session becomes a dynamic and varied exploration in which the analyst interprets not just a patient's words but their 'free play' interactions with toys and drawings (see Klein 1955, 23–27).

In this section, I will explore how a psychoanalytic framing of children's drawings as literal currency and as figurative compensation, that is, modes of textual production arrogated transactional value and which can therefore compensate a perceived deficit or prior wrong. This corresponds to what Klein calls 'reparation', the process by which the child (or, indeed, adult) seeks to make amends for unconscious fantasies of extreme violence inflicted upon the body of the mother. Klein argues for example in her 1929 paper 'Infantile Anxiety Situations Reflected in a Work of Art and the Creative Impulse' that children draw as a means 'to make good the injury psychologically done to the mother' and 'to restore people' (LGR 218).

As other critics have noted, graphic expression is a particularly apt and direct medium for reparation; channeling Klein, Juliet Fleming argues that the fact that graphic mark-making 'can be reparative goes without saying, but that one of its modes of reparation is to fill space is worth underlining' (Fleming 2016, 125). It is not just that a white space is filled out—it is that that filled-out space can be subsequently gifted and exchanged. With drawing, the space of play—the sheet of paper—can be fluently transferred into a space of real social exchange.

The most notable set of drawings in Klein's analytic history is the set of geometric wartime drawings produced by her patient Richard, which we have already touched upon. Klein discusses these in the 1945 paper 'The Oedipus Complex in the Light of the Early Anxieties', in addition to the *Narrative of Child Analysis*. These drawings, as a whole, have come to be known as the 'Empire' drawings (see Figure 2), since most of them depict top-down diagrams comprising different partitioned and colored zones with, as Klein puts it, 'the different sections standing for different countries' (LGR 373).

The child's use of what Klein reads as such a minimal, cartographical form affords a genre for articulating a total integrity of relations among internal objects on a level plane. In relation to cartography, Klein elsewhere relates the capacity for drawing to an inhibition of what she calls 'orientation' (we will come back to focus on this concept in the next section). The Empire drawings allow Richard to, as Klein puts it, 'express [...] the internalization of his objects [...] When Richard

Figure 2. Empire drawing by 'Richard', from Melanie Klein's notes. ('Richard 1941', held at the Melanie Klein Archive at the Wellcome Collection, reference PP/KLE/B.46). Included by permission of the Melanie Klein Trust.

finished [one of his] pattern drawing[s], he made a line round it and filled in the background with red. I found that this represented his "inside", containing his father, mother, brother and himself in relation to each other' (LGR 390). So, drawings (or perhaps, more specifically, diagrams) allow the child to externalize, simplify and outline a complex tangle of phantasmatic relations that, if left unconscious or unspoken, are exhaustingly inscrutable. Strictly speaking, this is not 'reparation' as Klein would call it, but it is still a form of compensation, since the page provides a means of 'making up' for a felt deficit, in this case an incapacity of the imagination, without paper, to picture synoptically the web of relations in which it lives and labors.

Where these compensatory functions relate to the drawing at the level of representation, its functions as currency relate to the drawing's features of portability and materiality. In *Narrative of a Child Analysis*, the same analysand, Richard, presents the drawing to Klein as a 'present'. '[H]e understood', Klein writes, 'that these drawings had some value for me' (NCA 17). In part because children are so affectively invested in their drawings, they assign those drawings proportionate transferable value. The drawing is magically produced capital and a means of bartering. Later still, in the course of analysis, when Richard gifts Klein (or 'Mrs. K') another drawing, he appears to feel guilt. He wants to make an identical copy of the drawing for his mother: 'Mrs. K interpreted that Richard's wish to make an exact copy to give to his mother also express his feeling that he ought not to prefer Mrs. K to Mummy' (NCA 62). The wish to produce a kind of personal paper currency is bound up in a need to reserve a fungible object that one can produce to ward off reprisals.

We find related ideas in Milner's work. Of the British school, Milner is perhaps the analyst who most consistently and widely embraces drawing, in its infantile and adult manifestations. Like Klein, Milner theorizes drawing as graphic production motivated by a drive to attain and maintain a sense of economic balance. Milner's play technique, though, is self-reflexive, and her writing style is best described as a practice of self-psychoanalysis. Emilia Halton-Hernandez accurately calls it an autobiographical cure (Halton-Hernandez 2021). The material that furnishes her self-psychoanalysis is characteristically what Milner calls her 'free drawings'—essentially a private practice of automatic drawing, which takes Klein's principle of the play technique and turns it into an autobiographical practice. Milner explores her practice of free drawing most thoroughly in her 1950 book *On Not Being Able to Paint*. Rye Dag Holmboe calls Milner's free drawings 'meta-drawings'—a 'means to reflect upon the process of making' (Holmboe 2021, 54).

Milner's last book, *Bothered by Alligators*, published posthumously in 2012, takes up the analysis of a 'story book', a hybrid graphic work of drawings and stories, written by her son when he was seven years old. Before we discuss an extract from this book, we should note that Milner, especially in comparison to the likes of Klein, is resistant to a technical psychoanalytic language, and indeed resistant to systematized psychoanalytic frameworks in general (instead preferring a form of spontaneous analytic writing that is akin to a conceptually rigorous form of automatism). One must therefore exercise caution when it comes to extracting theories from her work. Nevertheless, in *Bothered by Alligators*, Milner makes the following observation, in relation to her young son's 'shock there could be on first discovering that what drops out of one's body is not alive, but just dead stuff to be thrown away':

> However, I also thought that J. must have managed to deal creatively with this shock through the gradual discovery that he could learn to make meaningful marks on paper, marks which in the end had become the story book, something live enough to make a bridge of communication both with other people and with hidden parts of himself. (Milner 2012, 157)

Drawing, like excrement, is a product of the body.[13] But Milner suggests that the child's drawing represents a defensive counter-response on behalf of the ego to the production of useless or 'dead' waste (what we might, after Julia Kristeva, call the abject: anything that troubles the boundary between the inside and the outside, between life and death [see Kristeva 1982]). In other words, J.'s drawing is a kind of counter-abjection. Milner calls them *free* drawings not just because they are freely done, but because *they let something free*: they express a life drive and create images of value that might be received by others. These images of value can move and live beyond the child. To be precise, in Milner's conception of drawing, the drawings are not, themselves, communicative, but conduce to communication, as a 'bridge'. The metaphor—'something live enough to make a bridge'—is perhaps a peculiar one. Bridges don't live. It is quite important that they don't. But the point is that drawing is a dynamic act that encapsulates traces of

13 Elsewhere, Klein, too, writes about the fecal or anal associations of drawing, especially in relation to the sudden untrammeled production of scribbles. In 'The Role of the School in the Libidinal Development of the Child', drawing is the 'procreation and production in the unconscious of the object represented': '[a]t the anal stage of organization it signifies the sublimated production of the faecal mass' (LGR 72).

movement and so endures dynamically in the mind of the child, and can be imagined, consciously or unconsciously, to live on, to wander off, to go somewhere else and be received by someone else.

A stubborn tradition—the tradition to which Rilke's *Malte* belongs—depicts child drawing as something that the child does privately. In *Malte*, a solitary man reflects on the solitariness of drawing, and on the even more solitary experience of stepping away from his drawing to find his lost pencil. But Morgenstern, Klein and Milner all counter this image by staging ways in which graphic production is implicated in intersubjective economies of exchange, compensation and repair. Rather than a retreat into the imagination, child drawing emerges as a crucial modality through which psychic conflict, social attachment and imaginative play converge. In this view, drawing is more than just expressive, it is constitutive of the child's evolving relation to others, to value, and to a sense of orientation in the world. Next, we will turn to focus on this sense of orientation.

Orientation and Gender

What is orientation? It will enrich our discussion of psychoanalytic approaches to orientation if we first turn, briefly, to a philosophical exposition of this same question. We will come straight back to Klein and to Milner.

In the 1786 essay 'What Does It Mean to Orient Oneself in Thinking', Kant argues that orientation is a process by which one coordinates an inner intuition with a given external object or point of reference (for example, the Pole Star): 'I orient myself *geographically* only through a *subjective* ground of differentiation' [Kant 2018, 5]). The example Kant gives when describing this 'subjective ground of differentiation' is the case of the left and right hands. For Kant, one's inner feeling of the difference between the left and right hand can aid one's bearings in dimensional space.

I won't get into the ins and outs of Kant's argument; this idea is enough for us to get going with. Instead, let us focus on the motif of the hands. Contemporary theory tends to approach the hands in terms of what they can do and what they can hold or connect us to.[14] But when

14 Through our hands, we become technical; for example, in a 'Hand Manifesto' that prefaces a whole volume on the intersections between 'the manual and

we consider also that the hands help us to orient our sense of where our bodies are in relation to inner and outer coordinates (Kant's idea of inner and outer coordinates takes on new significance when we consider the expanded field of internal coordinates to which psychoanalysis gives us access), we are reminded too that simply having hands—having the *potential* to grip, to point, to gesture and to draw—plays a fundamental role in our spatial or proprioceptive bearing.

Through our hands we orient ourselves: we know where left is and where right is. But if the capacity for orientation privileges the hands—not just their tactile and prehensile capacities, but in their proprioceptive potentiality—then we should consider the extent to which orientation is bound up with the conceptual and formal processes of graphic expression. But how exactly are orientation and drawing related?

Before we turn our attention back to Klein and psychoanalysis, Kant's treatment of objects as orientational anchors—exemplified by the constancy of the Pole Star—should not be conflated with the psychoanalytic theory of object relations. Whereas Kantian objects serve as stable reference points for spatial and cognitive orientation, psychoanalytic objects are affectively and structurally complex. They may be unconscious, partial, split or internalized, and function within a dynamic field of desire and identification. For Klein, orientation and expression are tightly interlinked. Klein is deeply invested in the notion of orientation, not least in the way her thinking often resembles a form of conceptual mapping, tracing the lines of the crisscrosses and conflicting trajectories of introjective and projective identifications, and the partitioning and splitting of objects that takes place in the unconscious. She is helped along, too, with an expanding corpus of drawings by her child patients that resembled maps (again, like the Empire drawings).[15]

the mental', Jesse J. Prinz compiles a list of all the functions of the hands: 'they speak, sculpt, spar, and shape our world. They are both input systems and output systems. They allow us to survive as individuals, and they link us together socially' (Prinz 2013, xvii).

15 I add, too, that these drawings still generate new readings; Carolyn Laubender, for example, has more recently read Richard's drawings as an unconscious 'nuanced critique of European empire-building' (Laubender 2021, 324). They do indeed *look* like parodies of empire building, with their profuse and arbitrary annexations of adjacent space. Perhaps Richard's maps, too, demonstrate that children often have a knack, in their rehearsing of grown-up follies, to be uncannily satirical.

Klein describes at length what she calls the 'faculty of orientation' in her 1923 paper 'Early Analysis', in relation to her five-year-old patient Fritz. The faculty of orientation, she writes, is 'determined by the desire to penetrate the mother's body and to investigate it inside, with the passages leading in and out and the processes of impregnation and birth' (LGR 93). If, as we have supposed, orientation always names an object relation, for Klein it begins from the primary object of the mother, the whole mother, in her impenetrable mystery.

We see this same idea since developed elsewhere in psychoanalytic theory. In a 1994 paper in a special issue of *Yale French Studies* on the relationships between writing and drawing, the French psychoanalyst Serge Tisseron articulates something very similar to Klein's account of drawing as maternal orientation. 'The child's earliest graphic activity', Tisseron writes, 'constitutes a place where the processes of the early mother–child relation are reproduced and stabilized. It represents a first containing structure for the child' (Tisseron 1994, 35). Again, *graphic* orientation is a means by which the child can materialize external relations that otherwise remain threateningly un-represented. Tisseron's contention is that this is a dialogic relationship: 'the page answers back as his mother would, and even better than she since it does so in a religiously exact manner (*au doigt et à l'œeil*)' (Tisseron 1994, 35).[16] More recent studies have expanded this principle—that drawings offer a uniquely powerful means for children to orient themselves within family structures—away from traditional Oedipal models. One study of drawings by children from LGBTQ+ families argues that drawings allow children to trace and bear witness to 'experiences of kinship that words cannot represent' (Dyer et al. 2020, 539).

The advantage of a sheet of paper, as a space of play or 'play frame'

16 At the same time, Tisseron's article serves as a cautionary example for the broader argument of the present study, for the way in which he universalizes the connection between child drawing and literary experience. That is, he argues that the 'inscriptive process' (Tisseron 1994, 41), which encapsulates the whole generic panoply of poems, novels and essays, develops out of the surrogate-mother relationship that each child forms through drawing. I find this assertion so all-encompassing—it encompasses all children and all genres—that it loses its critical purchase. There is not a single link, but a constellation of links between child drawing and literary experience. Instead, I want to register how psychoanalytic hermeneuts like Klein and Tisseron themselves offer discrete examples of the power that child drawing exerts on the critical imagination.

(the term from Bateson that I broached in the Introduction) is that it collapses space into manageable proportions. It therefore provides a foundation (or a 'containing structure'—Tisseron's term) for a fantasy of orientation. For Klein, the desire to orient oneself is primary, and libidinally determined. And because it is libidinally determined, it is a perversion that needs to be repressed. This repression finds subterranean routes of expression in a variety of sublimations. '[I]nterest in geography' (99), for example, is one of these sublimations, and so too, of course, is 'the capacity for drawing' (LGR 99). This conclusion appears to stem from Klein's interpretation of Fritz's drawings which, like Richard's drawings, are cartographic in form, and tend to represent 'railway-lines with stations and towns' (LGR 99).

One of the pleasures of reading Klein is that she admits pluralities and over-determinations. There are many overlapping causes and interpretations for graphic production. It can, as we have seen, be both a sublimation of a penetrative quest for knowledge as well as an act of reparation, although these two explanations are not as contradictory as they might initially seem (to know the body of the mother, inside and out, is to know how it might be restored or healed). This brings us to another connection between manual orientation and graphic expression. The hands have the power to grab; they are instruments of possession. The drawing of a map is an acquisitive gesture, and cartography is linked, by formal analogy, to colonialism. In his typology of lines, Tim Ingold says that cartographical lines signify as 'appropriation of the space surrounding the points that the lines connect' (Ingold 2016, 87). Perhaps 'orientation' almost always hints at a projective trajectory of conquest, right down to the word's eastwards-looking etymology. Of course, though the word 'orientation' is entirely unrelated to the term Orientalism, Edward Said himself reminds us that to seek to know—and orientation manifests a pursuit of knowledge—is so often prelude to more violent acts of incorporation.

In psychoanalysis, the acquisitive streak (to which orientation is linked) is equated with the masculine libido. The faculty of maternally directed orientation that we find in the likes of Klein and Tisseron, and the acquisitive libido that structures it, is structured around Oedipal gender determinations. The act of making a mark with a pencil, pen or crayon is coded as male, and the material support is coded as female. Freudian psychoanalysis obsessively associates masculinity with activity and femininity with passivity. Indeed, in *The Problem of Anxiety*, Freud himself writes that writing 'has acquired the symbolic meaning of coitus' (Freud 1936, 15). But the association extends far beyond psychoanalysis and participates in a much wider gender discourse that positions the graphic act as, at worst, a hideous fantasy of sexual domination. In *Gramophone, Film, Typewriter*, the media theorist Friedrich Kittler speaks of an 'omnipresent metaphor' that 'equated women with the white sheet of nature or virginity onto which a very male stylus could then inscribe the glory of its authorship' (Kittler 1999, 186). Susan Gubar, within a literary-critical context, writes of the same tradition (she calls it 'pen-penis writing'), and makes the point that it 'excludes woman from the creation of culture, even as it reifies her as an artifact within culture' (Gubar 1981, 247).[17]

As countless critics have argued, especially since the 1970s and 1980s, psychoanalytic theory provides a scaffold for a male-centered normative discourse.[18] An almost equal number of critics have argued that psychoanalytic theory furnishes a robust and flexible array of methods and concepts that may be deployed not just in the internal critique of psychoanalysis but in the critique of other systems of power.[19] Nevertheless, for the psychoanalytic imagination, the drawing child is almost always a *boy*, he is a Richard or a Fritz. He is Rilke's Malte, groping for his pencil under the desk. With this discourse in mind, to argue that child drawing informs literary experience is by extension to risk organizing wildly diverse orders of literary experience around the kernel of a default male sexuality.

I suggest first that a critical archaeology of the reception and representation of child drawing (the advantage of psychoanalysis is

17 To give one more example, in his 1914 journal, the artist Paul Klee wrote: 'In the beginning, insertion of energy, sperm. [...] My drawing belongs to the masculine sphere' (quoted in Lyotard 2011, 223).

18 For critiques of the male-centered orientation of psychoanalytic theory, see Juliet Mitchell, *Psychoanalysis and Feminism* (New York: Pantheon Books 1974); Nancy Chodorow, *The Reproduction of Mothering* (Berkeley: University of California Press 1978); Luce Irigaray, *Speculum of the Other Woman* (Ithaca: Cornell University Press 1985); and Jane Gallop, *Reading Lacan* (Ithaca: Cornell University Press 1985).

19 For arguments emphasizing the critical utility of psychoanalytic theory, see Jacqueline Rose, *Sexuality in the Field of Vision* (London: Verso 1986); Slavoj Žižek, *Looking Awry: An Introduction to Jacques Lacan through Popular Culture* (Cambridge: MIT Press 1991) and Judith Butler, *Gender Trouble* (London: Routledge 1990), especially the chapter 'Freud and the Melancholia of Gender'.

that it does both) can play a key part in understanding how dominant cultural and conceptual modes perpetuate androcentric norms from infancy. Furthermore, the fact that child drawing is so often male-coded is not a new discovery.[20] Many writers who valorize or mourn or write about child drawing are dealing directly or indirectly with the contested history of these gendered dynamics. As we will see in the next chapter, when the poet Marianne Moore identifies with the drawing of a 'schoolboy from Spain' in her poem 'Tom Fool at Jamaica' she is, in this respect, participating in what other critics have identified as her poetry's subversion of reified gender relations.[21] And as I will explore in depth in the final chapter of this book, Anne Carson's exploration of drawing generally proceeds as a feminist reclamation of a male-marked field.

Each of the psychoanalysts we have considered so far in this chapter are invested in approaching and interpreting child drawing as a prototypical form of literary experience. It is a counterintuitive notion because we tend to think of literary experience as necessarily involving the presence of words and, more importantly than words, the presence of sentences or syntax. But literary experience is not reducible to or strictly coextensive with literacy. It is a category of aesthetic experience that involves the material presence of a text and an immaterial imperative to read and reckon with the text ('to read' here means both to interpret and to bring into discourse).

In the first part of this chapter, I have explored what I regard to be the three most valuable concepts in the psychoanalytic approach to drawing: *omnipotence*—the way child drawing allows the subject to navigate the tension between the factual world of 'reality' and the interior world of 'imagination' by conjuring a field of magical production in which stories and images are granted life and presence. We have considered *currency*—how drawings become textual insofar as they are conceived as fungible and portable cultural material that can be traded with and given to others as well as a means of correcting the strain of an imbalance (such as the balance between dead material and vital material). A text is an object assigned value as a *gift*, not in the sentimental sense that the reader has been literally gifted the text directly, but that the text is an artifact

20 We ought to note the superficial exception of Pliny the Elder's myth of the origin of drawing, the myth of Butades, although that is a tale of an adolescent girl's drawing being effaced by the father. We will come to this in Chapter 6.

21 See, in particular, Jeanne Heuving, *Omissions Are Not Accidents: Gender in the Art of Marianne Moore* (Detroit: Wayne State University Press 1992).

conferred with the aesthetic aura and economic demand of a gift. And we have considered the even wider category of *orientation*, in which the subject uses drawing to gain knowledge of that which is withdrawn from them, starting (and perhaps ending) with the body of the mother. This is a pursuit of knowledge that is tied to a need to find containment and safety in unwanted independence. Each of these capacities is related to the formal potential of the elementary line—the line that gives shape, the line which can be drawn between the giver and the recipient, and the cartographic line that connects places and people. In the next sections of the chapter, our discussion will be guided by D.W. Winnicott, for whom all three of these categories remain relevant, but whose work demands a less conceptual, and a much more formal, organizing principle, precisely around the expressive and psychical functions of two different types of line: squiggles and outlines.

Squiggles (and String)

The categories of experience encapsulated by Winnicott's famous terms 'transitional object' and 'transitional phenomena' amount to a theory of orientation. Compared to the likes of Klein, Winnicottian orientation is not so rigidly determined by gender dispositions, nor is it so structurally inflexible. Nor does Winnicott's work situate drawing as an aggressive or omnipotent incursion from a sovereign ego over a field of conquest, but as an activity that is much more tentative and liminal, or to use one of Winnicott's favored terms, 'intermediate', as in 'intermediate area of experience' (PR 19).

Before we elaborate on this, I will situate Winnicott's writings in relation to the analytic trends we have so far considered, and then plot his critical reception among literary scholars. Of the analysts we have discussed, Winnicott is closest to Milner—both biographically (Winnicott was, as is often noted, Milner's analyst) and in terms of their playful and exploratory approaches to the pliability and provisionality of concepts and interpretive structures. 'Both', as Nina Farhi puts it, 'more perhaps than any others, freed us from the inhibitions of dogma' (Farhi 2001, 65). It is not a coincidence that both Milner and Winnicott were obsessed with the interpretive and expressive potential of the wandering line, and that they similarly regarded drawing as a model and tool with which to think. Both, suggests Rye Dag Holmboe, 'used drawing to facilitate an exploration of the interplay of edges [...]

encouraging the experience of merging and oneness' (Holmboe 2021, 63). We might even go further than this. Both regarded drawing as in various ways a primary form of expression of psychical relatedness.

Winnicott's work received a belated (but enthusiastic) induction into the canon of literary theory and criticism, especially compared to the likes of his French counterparts. The 1994 collection of essays, *Transitional Objects and Potential Spaces: Literary Uses of D.W. Winnicott*, is emblematic of this reception. In the introduction to that book, Peter L. Rudnytsky writes that 'Winnicott's ideas remain comparatively unknown among those in the universities [...] who are drawn to psychoanalysis and employ it in their own work' (Rudnytsky 1993, xi). Winnicott-inflected approaches to literary scholarship have since tended to take up two related tasks. The first is conceptual. Critics seize on Winnicott's provocatively open-ended proposal in *Playing and Reality* that all cultural experience, including of course literature, originates in the child's need for play and for finding necessary comfort in an area of experience that is between complete interiority and external reality. The second is thematic and literary-historical. Critics identify in Winnicott a set of thematic preoccupations—among which, obviously, is childhood—that align Winnicott within an intellectual and literary lineage. Wordsworth is frequently cited as a key interlocutor.[22]

I am going to take a different approach. I aim to show more specifically how Winnicott's sustained interest in drawing and its analogues (for example, playing with string) outlines a prototype of textual practice. But before we consider the squiggle and the piece of string, let's rehearse one of the central arguments of *Playing and Reality.*

Consider the following passage: '[N]o human being is free from the strain of relating inner and outer reality, and [...] relief from this strain is provided by an intermediate area of experience which is not challenged (arts, religion, etc.). This intermediate area is in direct continuity with the play area of the small child who is "lost" in play' (PR, 18). At the level of style, I note first that this passage features a characteristic example of how Winnicott relies upon gerunds and processes (like 'relating', not

22 See, for example, John Turner, 'Wordsworth and Winnicott in the Area of Play', in *Transitional Objects and Potential Spaces: Literary Uses of D.W. Winnicott*, edited by Peter L. Rydnytsky (New York: Columbia University Press 1993), pp. 161–188, and the chapter 'Communicating and Not Communicating: *Wordsworth and Winnicott*', in Mary Jacobus, *The Poetics of Psychonalysis in the Wake of Klein* (Oxford University Press 2005), pp. 148–172.

relation) over rounded-off concepts. Human life itself, for Winnicott, is defined as a 'strain of relating', a state of interminable tension. In 'Living Creatively' from 1970, Winnicott calls this the 'paradox that must never be solved' (Winnicott 1990, 266). I think there is already something inherently literary about this idea. In the introductory chapter, we considered Peter Brook's idea that 'plot starts' when a 'life' is stimulated 'into a state of narratability, into a tension' (Brooks 1977, 291). For Winnicott, the *need* for plots, for plotlines, for lines as such, responds to the fact that life is always already stimulated into a state of tension, into a tense line between one element of a paradox (the inner world) and its other element (outer reality).

Further, this idea of the 'strain' is, in some ways, faithful to the economic (and biological) theory of 'tension' (*Spannung*) that we find throughout Freud's work, and especially in *Beyond the Pleasure Principle.* Both the life and death drives, as Brian O'Connor rightly points out, 'share an urge for tensionlessness' (2016, 440). *Pleasure Principle* is, at bottom, not a study of pleasure or pain but of the *state of tension with which life is coterminous.* Winnicott is making a very similar point, but crucially exploring that state of tension as a *relational* quality rather than a biological quality, which is what Freud supposes. '[T]he ruling tendency of psychic life', Freud writes, 'perhaps of nerve life altogether, is the struggle for reduction, keeping at a constant level, or removal of the *inner stimulus tension* (Freud 1922, 71; emphasis mine).

Crucially, one never outgrows the need for, or reliance upon, transitional phenomena. They simply shift into more rarefied or culturally acceptable forms of psychical reliance, such as religion and appreciation of the arts (or, as we have just supposed, literary experience). Winnicott's own term for this is cultural experience. The role of what Winnicott refers to as the 'good enough' mother is to ease and guide the infant's adaptation to a reality that does not bend to their needs or verify their omnipotence. '[T]he mother's main task', Winnicott writes, 'is disillusionment' (PR 17).

Transitional phenomena require the demarcating and setting aside of a privileged zone of play that provides relief from this strain. We might again recall Rilke, and the jarring feelings of stress and strangeness experienced by Malte when he steps away from the zone of his drawing. The sheet of paper is a readymade, intermediate zone of play. As we have seen, drawing is a form of expression and representation, but also a way of magically creating a proprietorial object (a 'not me', as Winnicott calls it [PR 2]). The child draws to picture something or to tell a story, but also to generate something that they own and hold and which they might give to someone else.

Winnicott is a formalist insofar as he is concerned with plotting and marking out orientations and configurations of space. I mention this so that I can point out how his work chimes—in underacknowledged ways—with recent thinking around form and the so-called new formalism (indeed, I am convinced that there is much more work to do on what Winnicott can teach us about formalism). In *Forms*, Caroline Levine refers to the 'affordances of form', which articulates how particular formal structures—be they literary, visual or spatial—enable or constrain certain modes of experience, feeling or attention. 'Each shape or pattern', Levine writes, 'lays claim to a limited range of potentialities. Enclosures afford containment and security, inclusion as well as exclusion' (Levine 2015, 6). While Levine says nothing about Winnicott, their respective projects share a strikingly similar vocabulary: both attend to how shapes and spatial arrangements organize cultural experience. Levine approaches this via literary form; Winnicott, through the drawings, play and speech of children.

Drawing, playing and talking go hand-in-hand in Winnicott's practice. It is here that we come to the squiggle. Like Morgenstern and Klein, Winnicott used child drawing as a tool or 'instrument' for entering into therapeutic communication with children. With the squiggle game, Winnicott writes, he devised a 'simple method of making contact with a child patient' (Winnicott 2016, 415). The game is straightforward and flexible. The analyst casually picks up a piece of paper and proposes a game. The analyst then executes a squiggle (without thinking about it) on the sheet of the paper, and then asks the child if the line 'looks like anything', as Winnicott puts it (Winnicott 2016, 416). The child is then encouraged to add to the squiggle so that it looks more like the thing that they think it is or should be. The squiggle that initiates the game is, in fact, exactly the same kind of line as that valorized in the opening sentence of Paul Klee's *Pedagogical Sketchbook*: 'An active line, moving freely, without goal. A walk for a walk's sake' (Klee 1953, 16). The game continues, with the child passing the squiggle back to the analyst. They continue doing this.

The squiggle game is a simple exercise in play that elicits collaboration and taps into the inherently communicative and interpretive properties of graphic play. The squiggle, in the exchange, becomes a collective image-text, endowed with a contested meaning and a nascent legibility. Participants read the drawing and subject it to their reading, and this creative work—which is shared—creates the value of the drawing as a text.

Because we are going to go on to distinguish squiggles from outlines, let's say that a squiggle is a line that has a certain formal independence ('moving freely, without goal'). In his 1960 paper 'String: A Technique of Communication', Winnicott describes playing the squiggle game with a seven-year-old patient at Paddington Green Children's Hospital. The child's engagement with the game is either lazy or literal. He interprets all of Winnicott's line drawings as variations on string: 'lasso, whip, crop / a yo-yo string, / a string in a knot, / another crop, / another whip' (Winnicott 1965, 154). It turns out, through the case history, that the boy is very, very interested in string. He spends a lot of time playing around with it, joining items of furniture and other objects together: 'They might find a cushion, for instance, with a string joining it to the fireplace' (Winnicott 1965, 154). As in Freud's fort/da game, in which the reel and string enact a dramatization of presence and absence, the child's use of string compensates for separations that cannot yet be symbolized.

Winnicott's interpretation of the boy's string-mania is that 'this boy was dealing with fear of separation, attempting to deny separation by his use of string, as one would deny separation from a friend by using the telephone' (Winnicott 1965, 154). String, here, becomes a squiggle that exists externally in three dimensions. In both cases—in drawing and in the child's string play—the line is a means of coordinating and, again, orienting objects in relation to one another.

Winnicott sees in string two interrelated functions: '[s]tring', he writes, 'joins just as it also helps in the wrapping up of objects and in the holding of unintegrated material' (Winnicott 1965, 156). It binds, like the string tied around a birthday present, invoking the aesthetic of wrapping and gifting (again, drawing as gift). It also ties disparate elements together. String becomes powerfully symbolic as both a container and a conduit.

This argument becomes more interesting when Winnicott says that he regards his patient's use of string as '*an extension of all other techniques of communication* [...] In this respect string has a symbolic meaning for everyone' (Winnicott 1965, 156; emphasis mine). The term 'extension' needs our attention. 'Extension' doesn't just imply that communication has been outstretched materially into space, but also that activity and 'techniques' required for communication have overflown dangerously from their normal rules and circumstances. There is something immediately threatening about this. Think, for example, of one of the oldest tropes in horror fiction: the 'extension' of communication into the uncanny (the ghostly voice on the other end of the telephone, for example, or the entity communicating via a medium or satanic possession). Indeed, the extendedness of string becomes frightening for Winnicott's patient. Winnicott claims that since the boy has been using string to deny separation, this develops into a problem with pathological potential: '[a]s a denial of separation string becomes a thing in itself, something which has dangerous properties and has to be mastered' (Winnicott 1965, 156).

String, as we will see, is the opposite of an outline. It is a kind of line that is beheld as being too actual. We might therefore think of drawing and squiggling as a means by which the ego attempts to 'master' and to claim for itself the twofold capacities of the line both to delineate and to link. The squiggle game is empowering for this reason—it demonstrates that the line can be conquered, played with, and spoken about casually. It also offers an outlet for a fantasy that tension—and the line is always a figure for tension, for tug-of-war—can be mastered. Let us tease out some of the implications of this and bring it closer to a theory of literary experience, with the help of a return to Tim Ingold (who is, after all, the master taxonomizer of lines). To recall, Ingold calls writing, as 'linearization', the 'death of the line' (Ingold 2016, 155). That is because, for Ingold, in simple formal terms when we learn to write we learn to tame our squiggles. When we write, our lines cease to wander and instead they make letters. If writing is the death of drawing—as the death of the line—then the child no longer has direct or unmediated recourse to the ability to neutralize and master its unnerving formal potential. Nevertheless, that same formal potential is there, latent, submerged, suppressed, ever present and carried on in the practice of writing and the production of literary texts. To mourn drawing in writing is therefore, perhaps, to mourn the anxious mastery over the frightening symbolic potential of the line.

Outlines

Outlines are the enemy of squiggles. Squiggles are independent, material elements that wrap things up and join them together. Outlines are immaterial: they literally do not exist. Winnicott's 'intermediate area of experience', the play frame of transitional phenomena, is bounded by a nonexistent outline *par excellence.*

That outlines are fictional, formal constructs imposed upon the world by the viewer, as opposed to natural phenomena, is an axiom that extends at least as far back as the Renaissance. In his *Natural History*, Pliny the Elder attributes the invention of drawing to a spontaneous (and perhaps what Freudian analysis would later call hysterical) gesture of a lovesick daughter who draws, in outline, the shadow of her departing beloved, so that the lingering presence of the outline represents the absence of the object (we will focus on this episode in Chapter 6). The Renaissance art theorist Ludovico Dolce said that: 'nothing offends the gaze such as contour lines, which should be avoided (since nature does not produce them)' (Roskill 1968, 155). The literal nonexistence of outlines is an especially popular assertion among Romantic thinkers, since the foundational roles of the outline in our most basic and seemingly instinctual mode of pictorial representation—drawing—immediately underscores the generative powers of the human imagination. John Ruskin cautions against outlines in his *The Elements of Drawing* (1857): 'There are no outlines in Nature, and the ordinary student is sure to draw them falsely if he draws them at all' (Ruskin 1971, 33). William Blake writes it in his notebooks: 'Nature has no outline, but Imagination has' (cited in Carson 2023a, 77). Delacroix writes in a journal entry in 1857 that 'Contour and touch are equally absent in nature' (Delacroix 1995, 357). More recently, the novelist Rachel Cusk's whole *Outline* trilogy riffs, in its central metaphor, on the material nonexistence of outlines as an analog for the absence of fixed personality.

In his landmark 1972 collection *Steps to an Ecology of Mind*, Gregory Bateson transcribes a dialogue (what he calls a 'metalogue') with his young daughter on the very topic of things having outlines. 'Why do things have outlines?' his daughter asks. This is a wonderful example of the kind of rug-sweeping philosophical questioning that Gareth Matthews writes about in his *The Philosophy of Childhood*). 'Father: "Do they? I don't know. What sort of things do you mean?" D: "I mean when I draw things, why do they have outlines?"' (Bateson 2000, 27). I am obsessed with this question. Bateson's answer to his daughter is unequivocal: 'I think it matters. Perhaps in a way, it is *the* thing that matters. And other things only matter because they are part of this' (Bateson 2000, 29).[23] For Bateson, it matters because the ability to abstract regions of knowledge (of any kind, presumably) requires

23 Similarly, in *A Step-Latter to Painting*, which we were about to consider in the

at its very foundation an ability to disentangle those objects from one another, to understand their distinctness and what makes them distinct, but also how they abut and relate to one another. But there is also an irony in Bateson's language. Outlines do not 'matter' in the literal sense; they are, as we have said, immaterial. But they represent something like the immaterial basis of our ability to apprehend materiality itself.

In a psychoanalytic context, the material nonexistence of the outline is a threat. We've already seen how, in Winnicott's thinking, the twofold function of the formal line is threatening to the ego's sense of separateness, but also threatening to the ego's orientation of its relations with others, since ultimately neither individuation nor orientation can be successfully contained by the ego's omnipotence. More broadly, Winnicott's theory of transitional phenomena is a theory of the outline; the entire concept is formed in the in-between, a third area that is neither purely subjective nor entirely external, but one that marks and tracks—however faintly—the squiggly edge between what is 'me' and what is 'not-me'.

It is Marion Milner's *On Not Being Able To Paint* (1950) that perhaps gets to the nub of the peculiar threat to the integrity of the ego posed by the drawing of an outline. Milner's personal experience of learning to draw involves revisiting and harnessing a childhood practice of drawing while learning to accept the nonexistence of outlines. Milner cites her friend, the English printmaker Jan Gordon's 1934 manual *A Step-Ladder to Painting*, in which Gordon writes: '[t]he outline is [...] the first and plainest statement of tangible reality' (Gordon 1934, 19). But Milner knows from experience that this is not the case. She describes it as a kind of shattering revelation. She describes, in detail, the act of looking at two jugs on a table: '[w]hen really looked at in relation to each other their outlines were not clear and compact, as I had always supposed them to be [...] [H]ow was it possible to have remained unaware of this fact for so long? [W]hy was such a great mental effort necessary in order to see the edge of objects as they actually show themselves [?]' (Milner 2010, 18).

Milner's speculation is that perhaps we have repressed the actual nonexistence of outlines, and that a 'great mental effort' is required to see things how they really are (blurrily interrelated and interpenetrated)

context of Marion Milner's *On Not Being Able to Paint*, Jan Gordon writes that 'The outline is of great importance in every kind of life' (Gordon 1934, 20).

because this fact has profoundly deleterious consequences for our sense of psychical wellbeing. The outline becomes an anxiously constructed buffer against disintegration. One can hear the resonance of Winnicott when Milner writes: '[s]o I could only suppose that, in one part of the mind, there really could be a fear of losing all sense of separating boundaries; particularly the boundaries between the tangible realities of the external world and the imaginative realities of the inner world of feeling and idea; in fact a fear of being mad' (Milner 2010, 19). This is yet another big claim on behalf of the practice of drawing. Drawing offers recourse to the 'mind' that is fearful of all-encompassing disintegration. To draw is to ward off madness by practicing formal integration (recall, again, the scene of disintegration that occurs in *Malte*, when he *stops* drawing). But Milner is too processual to embrace this as a conclusion. For her, to draw is to experience an ebb and flow of the apprehension of integration and the possibility of disintegration. It is more the *promise* of drawing, the idea of it, as opposed to its practice, that offers a fortification of a sense of the boundedness of things. Outlines are the thing that matter most.

For Milner, in the actual practice of drawing, one finds the interconnectedness of things affirmed by the process:

> [b]efore beginning one could spiritually envelop the object and feel inspired, transcending space and separateness. But once begun it was necessary to face the fact of being a body that does not transcend space as the spirit can. *At the moment of having to realise the limits of the body, when beginning to make marks on the paper, all the anxieties about separation and losing what one loved could come flooding in.* (Milner 2010, 68; emphasis mine)

What Milner gives us here is an exquisite description of an act of drawing in and through time. For her, first one 'spiritually envelops' an object—that is, selects it or ideates it. There is something about that object that stands out in perception and appears at least worthy of being sketched or outlined (we might recall Walt Whitman's model of child psychology from Chapter 1). At this stage one's sense of individual orientation among discrete objects is affirmed, since to 'spiritually envelop' an object is to identify that object as an external node to which one stands in some kind of relation. But 'once begun' the drawing represents, at its greatest extension, a kind of breakdown.

We will come back to the theory, and history, of the outline when we read A.R. Ammons in Chapter 5. We will find that Ammons, like Milner, regards the creativity of mark-making as a means of regulating and exploring the existence and nonexistence of outlines. For now, let us return to Winnicott's conception of life as an unresolvable 'strain of relating' and how this strain finds expression, if not relief, in the practice of drawing. What we find in Milner's work is the suggestion that the ego's compulsive quest for bounded and intermediate experience inevitably encounters error and rebuff. Drawing may represent, in theory, a zone of outlined experience *par excellence*, but its practice may bring along with it a profound apprehension of the erosion of those boundaries.

My aim in this chapter has been to demonstrate the rich array of ways in which a practice of psychoanalytic formalism (that is, directing psychoanalytic hermeneutics toward the study of form) constructs a discourse of child drawing as a primary field of expression. This is because the child patient, as we have seen, is assumed to be relatively disinhibited, to trust more in their imagination than an adult might, and to have less command and confidence in language and therefore more of a need for pictures. And drawing, complementarily, is assumed to be the easiest and most available medium, and the medium that therefore offers the path of least resistance to the expression of forms. Furthermore, we have seen how psychoanalysis reads child drawing as *symptom* (for example, a sublimated aggression towards the mother's body), as *cure* (for example, abreacting a child's trauma at witnessing the primal scene,) and as *communicative supplement* (for example, the squiggle game). As a symptom, and as a cure, and as a means of unblocking and aiding communication, child drawing becomes a sort of psychoanalytic Swiss army knife.

We have surveyed multiple ways in which psychoanalytic discourse conceptualizes child drawing—not simply as an expressive activity, but as a model for relational, symbolic and formal engagement with the world. In doing so, it begins to trace how drawing might function as both a foundation for and a metaphor of literary experience: an affectively charged, materially grounded and formally dynamic mode of meaning-making. The next chapter will radically recalibrate in focus to pursue this analogy more concretely, by following a single, actual drawing by an actual child into its literary afterlife.

Finally, at the start of this chapter, we considered how war and violence are made visible in children's drawings, and it bears repeating that the discourse of child drawing must always be historicized. We have been dealing very much with a construction of an early to mid-twentieth-century discourse of child drawing, and we ought to view this dialectically. Children like Klein's patient Richard draw warplanes when they live under the threat of being bombed. But psychoanalysts do not stand above children as being somehow historically transcendent, and their theories too, just like children's drawings, are equally liable to register and be shaped by the pressures of their individual realities. The discourse of child drawing, itself, is constructed in the trembling outlines of the intermediate area between adult and child, analyst and analysand.

The drawing we will look at in the next chapter is one that is produced in wartime, specifically in the Spanish Civil War. We will consider how the cultural diffusion of psychoanalysis, and wartime and postwar attitudes towards the figure of the child, are equally important influences on a mid-century conception of child drawing.

CHAPTER THREE

Snails and Whales: Marianne Moore and the Case of the *Colonias Infantiles*

Introduction

We start this short chapter with the observation that ideas and ideologies of childhood are historically and culturally contingent. In *Centuries of Childhood: A Social History of Family Life* (1962), Philippe Ariès argued that childhood, in fact, was an invention of the seventeenth century: 'in medieval society', Ariès wrote, 'the idea of childhood did not exist' (Ariès 1962, 125). Although there is no single twentieth-century 'idea' of childhood, the advent of psychoanalysis, with its construction of the polymorphously perverse child, contributed hugely towards dispelling dominant Enlightenment paradigms of childhood as innocence or *tabula rasa*, while challenging the very idea of a stable, linear distinction between childhood and adulthood. Jacqueline Rose calls this the 'problem of the relationship between adult and child' (Rose 1998, 61). 'After World War II,' writes the art historian Jonathan Fineberg, 'the assimilation of psychoanalysis into the mainstream [...] gave way to a more abstract *feeling* of childhood as the context for the appropriation of the mind or the memory of the child' (Fineberg 1997, 208).

Fineberg is writing specifically about visual art, and even more specifically about artists like Jean Dubuffet and his conception of Art Brut, but he is setting out the same historical and cultural context that will inform our discussion in this chapter. As I noted in the Introduction to this book, my claim is that the influence of child art upon literary modernism was comparable to its influence on modern visual art. That the likes of Picasso and Klee derived inspiration from children's art is well known. The English painter Roger Fry wrote in a 1917 article 'Children's Drawings' in *The Burlington Magazine* that 'the visual life of almost all grown-up people' could learn from children's drawings and their 'habit of attributing strong emotional values to all objects surrounding them' (Fry 1917, 226), sounding not a little like the Whitman of 'There Was a Child Went Forth'. But, while much has been made of the elevation and emulation of child drawing in twentieth-century art, there is yet to be an extensive or systematic study of comparable effects in poetry or narrative writing. Gertrude Stein is a notable example, whose later style, with the likes of *Ida: A Novel* (1941) and the wonderful, hilarious children's book *The World is Round* (1939) sought precisely to discover a stylistic and syntactic 'feeling' of childhood.[1]

The historical context for this chapter (and, indeed, the following chapter) is the mid-century. As Fineberg argues, mid-century modernism was, compared to earlier twentieth-century literary and artistic movements, more inclined to *abstract* childhood than works that came before. I do not attribute this solely to the 'assimilation' of psychoanalysis, though its ambience is a significant factor, and I hope that some of the psychoanalytic conceptions of child drawing that we charted in the previous chapter will resonate as we discuss specific texts, not just in this chapter but throughout the rest of the book. Another factor, which we discussed in Chapter 2, is closely intertwined with the rise of psychoanalysis itself: the widespread cultural consciousness—and accompanying guilt—not only of the psychological harms that mechanized war and violence inflict upon children, but also of the figure of the psychological child as a cultural canary whose symptoms, including drawings, could be read for signs of societal illness or dysfunction. Finally, through the 1940s, trends in mainstream clinical psychology, drawing on psychoanalytic precepts, elevated drawing as a means of assessing character and personality with, as Cathy Malchiodi points out, the 'emergence of projective drawing tests' such as Karen Machover's Machover Draw-A-Person (DAP) test, developed in 1949 (see Malchiodi 1998, 5). For the sake of the current study, I am simply

1 I note that both *Ida: A Novel* and *The World is Round* have been the subject of a resurgence of interest in recent years. See, for example, Logan Esdale, 'Gertrude Stein's Twin'. In *Textual Practice*, 25.11 (2011), pp. 989–1014, and the seventy-fifth anniversary edition of *The World is Round* published by Harper Design in 2013.

wary of replicating the abstraction of child drawing by speaking in equally abstracted and sweeping terms of whole cultural and historical environments. It is for this reason that, in this chapter, we turn to a specific drawing and a specific poem, and set them within their historical and cultural contexts.

The Spanish Civil War and a Child's Drawing of a Horse Rider and a Snail

Much academic research has been undertaken on children's drawings produced during times of war.[2] What makes the Spanish Civil War exceptional is that it produced a set of material circumstances that caused an astonishing flourishing of child art. After the uprising that sparked the war in 1936, a wave of refugees fled Madrid and surrounding areas for Republican-controlled eastern Spain. Among them were an estimated 100,000 children, many of whose parents had been killed (see Viñao 2015, 405–417). Faced with an influx of young refugees to the east, the Republican government established what became known as the *colonias infantiles*, institutions that were dedicated to the education and care of displaced children (see Braster and del Pozo Andrés 2015, 455–477). Given both the educational mission of the colonies and their limited resources, drawing became a central, daily activity. As one historian observes: 'one of the most remarkable things to emerge from these remarkable institutions were thousands of drawings done by the children' (Geist and Carroll 2002, 22). Before long, Republican officials and international sympathizers alike recognized the political power of the drawings, and therefore their potential to generate empathy, as well as charitable donations. Many drawings were shipped to the US and to the UK in a series of fundraising campaigns.[3]

The American Friends Service Committee organized an exhibit of

2 See, for example, Manon Pignont, *La guerre des crayons: quend les petits Parisiens dessinaient la Grande Guerre* (Paris: Parigramme 2004). The title translates as 'The Way of Crayons: When Young Parisians drew the Great War'.

3 There are contemporary parallels. On 21 March 2024, the United Nations Relief and Works Agency (UNRWA) published the web article 'Lasting Trauma: Drawings from Three Palestine Refugee Siblings in Gaza'. The drawings by Khayri, Mena and Mira are devastatingly similar to those in the

colonias drawings, 'Children's Drawings and the Spanish Civil War', at the Lord and Taylor department store on Fifth Avenue in New York in 1938. The exhibit was shown again at the Institute of Modern Art in Boston in 1939, and again at the Worcester Art Museum the same year (see Turner 1988, 44–59). Aldous Huxley, by then living in the US, contributed a catalog essay to the initial exhibition under the astonished title *They Still Draw Pictures!*, which was published by the Spanish Child Welfare Association of America (we briefly discussed this catalog essay in the previous chapter). Many of the drawings selected to feature in the catalog were those that depicted the machinery and devastation of the conflict, with a notable predominance of warplanes (exactly as we saw in the drawings of Melanie Klein's patient Richard). '[T]he plane', as Huxley writes, 'with its bombs and machine guns, is the thing that, in the world we live in and helped to make, is significant and important above all others' (Huxley 1938, 7). For Huxley, the plane represents the devastating ease with which mass violence can be exported and inflicted upon others. But I wish to focus on a drawing that was included in the original Lord and Taylor show, but was not included in *They Still Draw Pictures!* catalog, presumably because it did not show warplanes or bomb sites, but of a horse rider and a snail (Figure 3). It is by a six-year-old boy from the *colonias infantiles* apparently called Julio Gomez.

Marianne Moore and the Drawing

The drawing by Julio Gomez eventually ended up in the possession of Marianne Moore, who refers to it in her poem 'Tom Fool at Jamaica', which was published in the 13 June 1953 issue of *The New Yorker*, long after Republican Spain had lost the Civil War in 1939. The poem begins, 'Look at Jonah embarking from Joppa, deterred by / the whale'. Two lines later, it contrasts Jonah with Julio: 'Be infallible at your peril, for your system will fail, / and select as a model the schoolboy in Spain / who, at the age of six, portrayed a mule and a jockey / who had pulled up for a snail' (Moore 1987, 162). We will discuss these lines at length. But, first, some context.

'Tom Fool' was Moore's first poem to be published in *The New Yorker*, coming two years after a December 1951 edition of *Newsweek*

They Still Draw Pictures! catalog. In one drawing by the six-year-old Menna, a child sleeps in bed while rockets fall from the sky (see UNRWA 2025).

Figure 3. Drawing of a jockey, horse and snail by 'Julio, *6 años*'. Sold at the Lord and Taylor exhibition of *colonias infantiles* children's drawings, reproduced in *The Complete Poems of Marianne Moore*. Included by permission of Faber and Faber and by Viking Books, an imprint of Penguin Random House.

dubbed Moore the 'Best Living Poet'. I mention these facts to highlight that 'Tom Fool' was published at a moment when Moore's profile was high indeed, after what many critics regard as a post-1951 turn in Moore's work from an allusive high modernism to a more accessible and playful mid-century output.[4] As Moore writes in the explanatory notes that were later added to the poem (and which included a reproduction

4 Moore's 'post-1951' work is the subject of critical reappraisal in Elizabeth Gregory's *Apparition of Splendor: Marianne Moore Performing Democracy through Celebrity, 1952–1970* (Newark: University of Delaware Press 2021). Gregory's argument, supported through some very insightful close readings, is that this later work, less celebrated than her earlier, high modernist poems,

of the drawing): 'A mule and a jockey, by "Giulio [sic] Gomez 6 años" from a collection of drawings by Spanish school children. *Solicited on behalf of a fund-raising committee for Republican Spain, sold by Lord and Taylor; given to me by Miss Louise Crane*' (Moore 1987, 284; emphasis mine). I doubt that Moore was fully aware of Julio's circumstances. After all, her note suggests that it was not she who attended the *They Still Draw Pictures!* exhibit at Lord and Taylor, but her friend and patron, the philanthropist Louise Crane, and it is not quite accurate to say that it was drawn by a schoolchild, but by a child who was under the care of an improvised wartime institution.

The subject of 'Tom Fool' is whimsical and as distant from topics of war as one can conceivably imagine. It is principally a celebration of a champion racehorse, Tom Fool, whom Moore was jolted to write about after reading the words of the jockey in the 3 March 1952 edition of *The New York Times*, in a column that 'took [her] fancy' (Moore 1987, 285). The idea of writing a poem about an object of curiosity that takes one's fancy already has something of child drawing about it. John Ruskin begins his *The Elements of Drawing* by describing the quintessential child drawer, a figure that tends to draw 'the things it can see and likes' (Ruskin 1971, 10).

After setting up the opposition between Jonah and the schoolboy from Spain, 'Tom Fool' swiftly moves on through a racehorse-paced conveyor belt of allusions and items—Victor Hugo, Tom Fool, Fats Waller, as if they are assembled in the stands. With all this contextual knowledge, that 'Spain', in the first stanza, is rhymed with 'detain' ('hard going for a statesman whom nothing could / detain') reads as an ironic echo of Julio's status in eastern Spain, not in detention but in sanctuary, and his Spanishness is mentioned not for the sake of contextual accuracy, but because it adds to his curiosity in a poem that collects curiosities.

At the start of the chapter, we considered Jonathan Fineberg's description of a trend in mid-century art, in the wake principally of psychoanalysis, to conjure an 'abstract feeling of childhood'. By turning Julio into a 'model', Moore is indeed interested in an abstract, generalizable feeling of childhood. She *projects* (and 'selects') a conception of child drawing that might be held up as an example to be emulated by the poet who—in looking playfully, selectively and capriciously at a

'extends the anti-hierarchal ethics that animated her work from the state, in daring and innovative ways' (Gregory 2021, 5).

world of materials (including the *New York Times* column that initially sparked her fancy)—already evinces an affinity with a notional drawing child. In this case, that projection occurs as a kind of commodification of the drawing that forgets the perilous historical circumstances of its making. The mention of Julio's drawing is the story of a minor document of a settled war, unwittingly taken up into the bric-a-brac fabric of a high-profile poem, published in a period of peacetime prosperity by a poet who was refining her own deeply aestheticized celebrity image. Indeed, Moore gets his name wrong.

In the poem, the reference to the drawing takes its place among a characteristically eclectic collage of quotations and allusions (here, for example, to the Biblical Jonah). As Linda Anderson argues, Moore's collagistic poetry 'relied on selection [...] dismantling hierarchies and valuing multiplicity' (Anderson 2015, 15). This capricious and mischievous selectiveness distinguishes Moore's citational style from contemporaries like Pound and Eliot.[5] Bonnie Costello—who is always astute on the connections between modern American poetry and the visual arts—explains the 'collage' elements of Moore's poetry this way: '[t]hough poetry's medium is uniform (letters), it can produce a more various surface than painting. Moore's poems [...] take advantage of the diverse relations among words; grammatical, imagistic, aural, visual, semantic, stylistic, contextual, to create powerful incongruities and bidirectional signals' (Costello 1981, 212). For Costello, this corresponds to a definition of collage.

My claim is that there is a selective disposition towards the poetic surface that can be aligned instead with child drawing. A collage is a picture that is comprised of pasted together elements (collage comes from the French word *coller*, to paste/glue). The difference is precisely that whereas collage makes use of different found materials, as Costello herself points out, poetry—like drawing—is comprised of only one medium—letters. The aim of Moore's poetry is to do as much with the simple medium of the shape of letters as is possible on the surface of her page. Her selection is a *psychological* investment in objects that converts them into a uniform medium, not a collage-like investment that directly assembles those selected elements. We will focus, at length, on the idea

5 In addition to Anderson, see Chapter 3, 'Scrapping Modernism: Marianne Moore and the Making of the Modern Collage Poem'. In Bartholomew Brinkman, *Poetic Modernism in the Culture of Mass Print* (Baltimore: Johns Hopkins University Press 2017), pp. 105–140.

of child drawing as a distinctive mode of selection in the following chapter.

Hence the incongruousness, in 'Tom Fool', of a Biblical allusion alongside a drawing by a child. The effect of the provenance that Moore gives as a footnote is to plug the individual history of one of her poem's constituent parts and thereby underscore the aggregate historical nature of her lyric. Every allusion, quotation or ekphrastic description has its own history, so that a poem like 'Tom Fool' might come to be seen itself as a kind of drawing, as a formal gathering of intersecting lines. At the same time, the footnoted provenance of six-year-old Julio's drawing serves to situate the poem 'Tom Fool' as itself a constituent part of, and another episode in, the drawing's actual history as a peculiarly prized object.

Let's focus on the distinction Moore is making between Jonah and the Spanish schoolboy, or more specifically between the whale and the snail, the governing rhyme in the poem's first stanza. As narrative images (for they are both narratives contained in images), they offer contrasting encounters with symbolic animals (like Julio, Moore made animals her subjects). First, the Biblical story of Jonah, swallowed by a whale as he seeks to shirk his God's commandment to deliver a message of repentance to the city of Nineveh. The story of Jonah and the whale belongs to a cultural repertoire of stories absorbed by children in societies like Moore's mid-century America (the 1940 Disney film *Pinocchio*, which spectacularly mediates an episode of Jonah-esque whale-gulping, looms in the cultural imagination). This is the generational reception and social reproduction of tradition, of guidebooks, storybooks, schemata, cinematic spectacle and narrative tropes, and ultimately of a whole repertoire of signs and schema as a shared bank, a 'system'. Like whales, these systems loom up from the past and snatch us up their jaws. There is no life outside. We began this chapter by noting the contingency of 'childhood' itself, but one could predicate childhood, in part, on the experience of being taken up in such jaws, and the effort to accommodate oneself to them.

The second mode of reception or encounter is that of Moore's reception of the schoolboy's drawing. This is the lived, material reception of a humble yet auratic artifact which arrests one, which asserts itself into one's path, like the snail arresting the path of the jockey. In other words, the delight of the Spanish schoolboy's drawing is that it acts as a visual metaphor of itself. The way Moore quite deliberately traces the many-staged trajectory of the drawing is connected to one of the traits that most children would associate with snails: their slime trails. We can therefore contrast the whale—the sublime aggregate social force (remembering Hobbes' chosen metaphor for society) that moves inscrutably beneath the surface, with the snail—a small, marginal, slime-drawing external agent. To rehearse this in the diction of Moore's poem, language and cultural 'systems' of meaning-making and narrative repetition, considered in the round, are not 'infallible'. They *fail;* they are not airtight or complete. One of the reasons for this failure owes to the pinball-like circulation of objects and ephemera and attention-grabbing matter that 'detain', arrest and interrupt us. The blurring of names and faces experienced by the champion jockey is simply an exaggeration in miniature of what the passage of life is like. The minutiae, the individual and singular elements, for which we have names, but names which seem not entirely adequate, or which only have life and purchase in the immediacies of conversation.

In developmental psychology, as we discussed in the Introduction, child drawing is attended by the function of testing and stretching the nominative and narrative capacities of the systems of speech and communication in which the drawing makes incursions. It is a way of stepping towards, but also creatively skirting, systems and conventions of writing and language. Note how Moore sides with, and selects, 'school' boy and snail over Jonah and whale. The poem instructs us, or itself, in an imperative mood, to '*select as a model the schoolboy in Spain*'. The poem selects, as from an array of available models and tangible artifacts, the child drawing as its model. In the spirit of the reflexivity of that drawing—the way the snail can be read as an emblem of the drawing itself—Moore's imperative is to *select selection* itself; to foreground the role played by selections, as opposed to *ex nihilo* creation, in the act of making.

Moore, herself, drew avidly, although, as others have noted, she chose not to publish her own drawings.[6] Child drawing constitutes a formative but enduring arena for the practice of playful, imaginative and selective combination and organization into ephemeral and expressive formal wholes. Again, it is not selection in the manner of a collage; it is a process through which the maker invests themselves in their object and expresses it playfully with lines. Julio's drawing is one example. It is an imaginative drawing that draws from a mental stock of familiar and

6 'Drawing was a habit with her', writes Bonnie Costello, 'second only to that of writing' (Costello 1981, 187).

known images: a snail, a horse, a rider. It draws on the light surrealism of fairy-tale convention, through a simple arraying of those stock choices on the paper. Its economy of lines nevertheless invests the picture with small details, like the bow on the jockey's cap, the horse's eyebrow and the snail's rounded antennae.

I defer to Elizabeth Gregory's masterful reading of the poem as a playful 'high/low game': '[b]y commenting on unfolding events, and thus joining the wider cultural occasion around Tom Fool's growing success, the poem crosses into the realms of both sports journalism and a [...] game exploring the connection of celebrity to democracy, which Moore herself is playing' (Gregory 2021, 57). Moore is, also, mischievously identifying herself with Tom Fool—an elite poet identifying with a peerless racehorse. We might, again, be tempted to draw an analogy between the local pleasure Moore takes in unexpected or heterodoxic combinations and analogies with the same pleasure taken by the child in combining isolated pictorial elements as incongruous as a jockey and a snail. It deals with events by celebrating levity and invention with seriousness.

Julio's drawing is, in a variety of ways, far from being a typical drawing by a child. It is precociously well observed, witty and precise. It is far better than many of us would expect a six-year old's drawing to be (and presumably, we can count Moore among this group, hence the hint of wonder in her noting 'at the age of 6'). Without wishing to labor an uncharitable comparison, we might simply note the contrast between this drawing and the Empire drawings of Melanie Klein's patient Richard, who was ten. I am reminded that children's drawing, like poetry, is so often subject of a discourse of naturalized genius and giftedness. A good child's drawing is something to marvel at. It is something that some special people do well, and we appreciate it as audiences in large part because it offers textual testimony of specialness. A 2000 paper on giftedness in the journal *American Psychologist*, for example, describes drawing ability or graphicacy (but not writing), alongside arithmetic and music as one of the 'domains' of the child savant (Winner 2000, 160). The gift of graphicacy (drawing competence) offers Moore a means of naturalizing by analogy an ironic aura of poetic genius and celebrity. This analogy serves somewhat to puncture the auratic quality of poetic genius by linking it to the supposed naivetes of child drawing. But it is also saying that perhaps poetry is for adults what drawing is for children: a field in which the gifted are at liberty to flex their gifts.

Readers will no doubt have registered a tension in my own reading of 'Tom Fool'—between an unambivalent appreciation of its formal inventiveness, its 'rich surface', and the playful whimsy with which it unknowingly ranks a war refugee's drawing alongside the achievements of a champion racehorse. I do not intend to impeach Moore for this, and I have tried to negotiate the tensions with sensitivity. It would be a stretch to read 'Tom Fool' as a poem of a postwar post-trauma, in which the poet is reduced to a kind of child, picking among and collecting objects that impress with their skill, speed and intensity of feeling. And yet I do read in 'Tom Fool' a kind of retreat that demonstrates not just the political shortcomings, and the willful naivety, of the notion of 'selecting' as a 'model' the idealized position of a child, but an implicit sense of historical anxiety and vulnerability underlying its fastidiously assembled allusions.

CHAPTER FOUR

Georges-Henri Luquet, Maurice Merleau-Ponty and Francis Ponge: *Graphic Infancy*

Now we will develop further one of the themes of the previous chapter: the particular mode of selection that is characteristic of child drawing, in distinction to other more established modes of selective expression that we would associate with, above all, collage. We remain in the mid-century: at the center of my focus in this chapter will be the philosopher Maurice Merleau-Ponty, whose critical engagements (on the subject of children's drawings) with the earlier philosopher Georges-Henri Luquet (1876–1965) and the poet Francis Ponge lend this essay its overarching structure. Through a discussion of Luquet, Merleau-Ponty and, finally, Ponge, I will elaborate a phenomenology of selection. This refers to a process whereby child drawing—and, beyond that, modes of expression that exploit the routes of perception that child drawing makes available—emerges from a primary 'choice situation' (a term I take from E.H. Gombrich) based on material circumstances that are brought to bear upon the sheet of paper as a field of action or transitional experience. Here, selection emerges as a third term from a theoretical spectrum comprising the poles of attention and expression. Ponge is exemplary for the way in which he both viewed poetic expression as a material engagement with the world, but also in his complementary critical fascination with modern drawing. I will argue, through Ponge, that this selective phenomenology is markedly poetic, since it informs and undergirds a linguistic attitude that treats language as a material reservoir of possibilities negotiated on the page.

Eventually, I will tie this phenomenology to the word at the conceptual heart of this chapter: *dilection*. This is a term used by Ponge to describe the drawings of Pablo Picasso's Blue Period. Obsolete in English, dilection comes from the Latin *diligo*, which means both 'to love' and 'to select'. Emphasizing this double value, I use dilection to name a co-determination of affect and selection (whereby to love is to select and to select is to love). I wish to develop a poetic concept of dilection as a name for visual and verbal instances of affective expression that do not transcend the choice situation of which they are permutations, that therefore do not subtract the object from its surroundings and contexts, but which are constituted and sustained by their derivation from those choice situations. This intervening co-determination of affect and choice oscillates between attention and expression, and is, I will argue, a principle of graphic infancy.

Before I move on, I will give a brief outline of what I have referred to as the spectrum of attention and expression, the spectrum that the related terms of selection and dilection are deployed to resist. To a significant degree, the history and theory of drawing plays out upon this spectrum. On one end is the academic model of mimetic attention, stretching back to the Renaissance ideal of *disegno*, through to the Romantic rhetoric of what John Ruskin calls the '*innocence of the eye*' (Ruskin 1971, 27)—which constrained drawing to the rectitude of resemblance at the cost of expressive freedom. 'It is not required of your drawing that it should be free', Ruskin finger-wags in his 1857 manual *The Elements of Drawing*, 'but that it should be right' (Ruskin 1971, 33). Ruskin's innocent eye—which stands for a perception that is direct, unmediated, formally autonomous—therefore aspires to a condition of infancy, what Ruskin calls a 'sort of childish perception' (Ruskin 1991, 18). With this in mind, I will refer back to Ruskin's concept later in the essay. On the other end of the spectrum is the ideal of drawing as a kind of pure expression, which probably hit its apex in the Surrealist practice of automatism. For André Breton in 1941, what he called 'the essential discovery' of Surrealism is that 'without preconceived intention, the pen that flows in order to write and the pencil that runs in order to draw spin an infinitely precious substance' (Breton 1972, 68). The Surrealists divorced drawing from the will to trace the contours of the external world and allied it to the subject instead of the object, and also to writing or *écriture* more than painting.

Merleau-Ponty Contra Luquet

At the risk of conceptual over-determination, I want to overlay the attention/expression spectrum with the classical pairing of mimesis and poeisis. For Luquet, as an activity of attention, child drawing aspires to direct mimesis. For Merleau-Ponty, on the other hand, child drawing is an *expression* that corresponds to poeisis. I intend this in the sense that Martin Heidegger, an important forebear in Merleau-Ponty's thought, invests in poeisis as a 'bringing-forth' (Heidegger 2011, 230), but also a sense of crafting and bricolage: bringing forth by bringing together available elements. Through Luquet and Merleau-Ponty, I underscore the selective compositional energies that inform graphic expression. My aim is to conceptualize further a phenomenology of expressive selection that finds, here, its purest articulation in the drawing of children, but which also, given its withdrawal into a judicious subject position of picking and choosing, lends itself to an intermedial perspective.

An unprecedented longitudinal analysis of child drawing, Luquet's 1927 *Le Dessin enfantin* (*Children's Drawings*) exerted a deep and enduring influence in the field of developmental psychology, from Jean Piaget's early adoption through to more recent scholarship in the field.[1] In the lectures given by Merleau-Ponty while Chair of Child Psychology and Pedagogy at the Sorbonne from 1949 to 1952, Luquet appears as one of the philosopher's key references and, on occasions, theoretical punchbags (though Merleau-Ponty accepts, and builds upon, many of Luquet's observations). Luquet and Merleau-Ponty share the premise that what is especially interesting about child drawing, and what merits theoretical investigation, is its innocence—exactly the kind of quality that Ruskin suggested all drawing should emulate. As this convergence suggests, the history and theory of art, though seldom drawn to children's drawings as objects of study in themselves, is conversant with the discipline of child drawing insofar as it posits childhood as a mimetic (or indeed expressive) ideal. Particularly instructive for my argument is E.H. Gombrich's refusal, against Ruskin, of a 'sharp division' (Gombrich 1977, 310) between mimetic and expressive acts. Gombrich argues that neither representational nor expressive art is innocent: 'In our response to expression no less than in our reading of representation', he writes, 'our expectations of possibilities and probabilities must come into play' (Gombrich 1977, 316). The meaning

1 See, for example Jolley 2010, Cox 2013 and Freeman 1980.

and affective force of both figurative and expressive art—and our ability to recognize them as such—require our knowledge or intuition of the available conventions ('we cannot judge expression without an awareness of the choice situation, without a knowledge of the organon') (Gombrich 1977, 319). Art history, in Gombrich's hands, becomes the discourse and repository of those choices and relations.

To return to the corresponding distinction between representation and expression in the drawing of children, one must contend, precisely, with the ignorance of what Gombrich calls the 'organon': the established conventions of formalized drawing. The choice situation for the child drawer is not one of an established system or code—it is more material than it is structural, more grounded in the immediate phenomenal situation of the act of drawing (the choices among crayon colors and visible or known objects and their constituent elements). In their accounts, Luquet and Merleau-Ponty alike are not interested in the child's acquisition of learned and constructed methods of pictorial representation, though Luquet makes brief remarks about the child's later 'development in technical skill' that is 'acquired in a specialised culture' (CD 142). I therefore want to remain sensitive to the implicit theories of innocence—in both its sensory and experiential modalities—in both Luquet and Merleau-Ponty's approaches.

I will start with Luquet. As I discussed in relation to Bishop's poem 'Sestina', for Luquet, children draw from an 'internal model' (CD 47): a secondary mental image of a perceived object, as opposed to a direct attempt at visual representation (which, according to Luquet, is how adults draw).[2] In contrast with the contemporaneous flourishing of psychoanalytic interest in child drawing as sublimation, Luquet's approach to drawing is undergirded by a philosophy of perceptual realism. Luquet sought to demonstrate how the child's graphic development reflects an increasingly refined awareness of objective realities, culminating in an ability to observe and represent things as they really are (it is, therefore, a journey from one form of innocence to another: from the innocence of undeveloped ability to the innocent eye of unclouded representation). The course of this development is guided by two factors: firstly, it is concomitant with the child's increasing

2 Luquet's concept of the 'internal model' is comparable to Lev Vygotsky's more influential concept of the 'spontaneous concept': for Vygotsky, children's drawings are an expression of a 'spontaneous concept'—i.e. a mental object derived from direct lived experience (see Vygotsky 1987, 39–285).

capacity to be attentive to things—to attune their attention to the world, and, secondly, it is constrained by the expanding range of their graphic aptitude and ability. Individual expression and aesthetic sensibility play next to no role.

Luquet's model is split into stages. The first is 'fortuitous realism', with which Luquet beholds the scrawling and scribbling play of toddlers ('mere lines with no figurative intent') and focuses on the way in which drawings of this kind sometimes bear 'accidental resemblances' to objects (CD 87–88). The second stage is 'failed realism', where a will-to-represent succeeds the non-figurative play of the first stage. 'Children want to be realists' (CD 93), Luquet argues, a will derived from a need to know, adapt to and master their environment. But, at this stage, their ambition outstrips their ability, owing, primarily, to the 'limited and discontinuous character of [their] attention' (CD 93). Drawings of the failed realism stage are hamstrung by what Luquet calls a 'synthetic incapacity', that is, a failure to co-ordinate elements of a given object into a coherent, recognizable whole (CD 98). The third and most important stage is 'intellectual realism', where the child starts to draw from the abstracted image of the internal model, and thus the stage that for Luquet is most characteristic of child psychology. As if overcompensating for their previous synthetic incapacity, the intellectual realist tries to synthesize a composite ideal of a given object—'to present the greatest number, if not all, of the essential elements of the represented object' (CD 105). There is a characteristic lack of linear perspective. A good example of an intellectual realist drawing is a potato field drawn by a seven-year-old Dutch boy (see Figure 4), executed as a plan, and comprised of two elements that are invisible in an actual field of potatoes: the squared boundary and the subterranean rows of tubers, arranged horizontally (incidentally resembling the planar linearity of writing).

Finally, like hermit crabs, children 'abandon' the final provisional stage of intellectual realism for the straightforward 'visual realism' that, for Luquet, is characteristic of adulthood (CD 123). In short, Luquet takes child drawing and subjects it to the rigid order of a single, straight line: from mind to eye, a direct trajectory from early scribbling to the ultimate telos of mature mastery, the aesthetics of exquisite resemblance that is epitomized by something like Leonardo's *Study of a Woman's Hands*.

Broadly considered, there are obvious shortcomings to such a narrow and narrativized approach, least of all, as Norman Freeman points out,

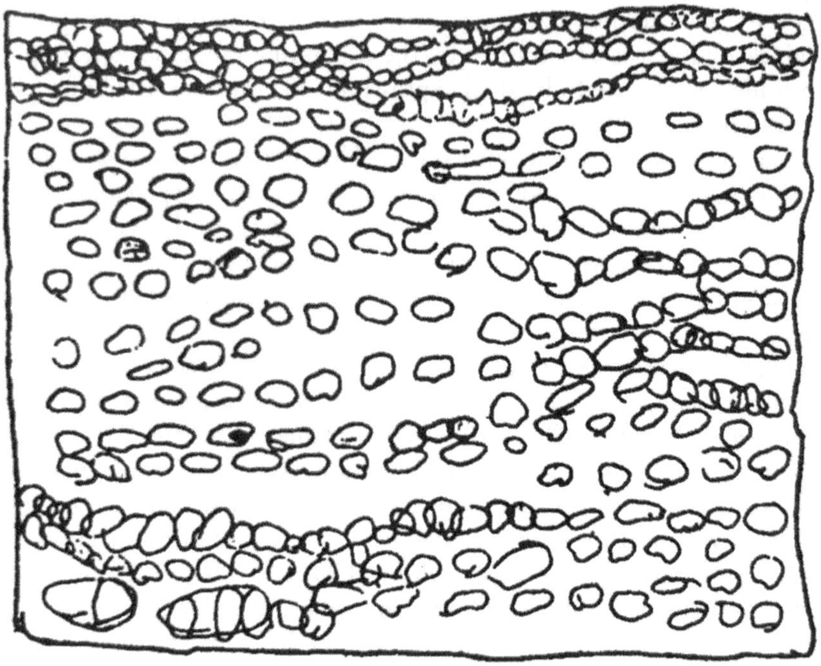

Figure 4. 'Dutch boy, 7 years [...] Field of potatoes' (Luquet 2001, 104). Identified by Luquet as example of 'intellectual realism'. Included by permission of Alan Costall.

the peculiar inflexibility of the stage model, a model that Luquet insists is universal (Freeman 1980, 141). Luquet's account clearly conforms to a structure of innocence, in that it takes place as a series of irreversible progressive transitions. As Christopher Green puts it, 'Luquet leaves the unmistakable inference that the ways a child and an adult see cannot mesh in any sense' (Green 1998, 221).[3] Like all narratives of innocence, it foregrounds the internal journey of the subject—even when the child becomes an adept drawer, this occurs as the fruition of an innate

3 Such criticism of *Le Dessin enfantin* tends to overlook Luquet's own internal reservations about his model. The final chapter of *Le Dessin enfantin* sets out a number of qualifications—not least the admission that the stages are 'less clear in practice' (CD 142). Luquet also concedes that some adult drawing conforms to intellectual realism, although this is framed in terms of a developmental impairment.

potential sooner than it is informed by external influences and examples. With his focus on the mere chance operations of resemblance in the 'fortuitous realism' stage, Luquet relegates the expressive, exploratory and affective forces of infant drawing to secondary status. Similarly, his approach to 'intellectual realism' takes one of the most distinctive and multivalent aspects of drawing as a medium—its capacity to visualize conceptual intensities and links, its interaction with *thinking*, in addition to seeing—and reduces it to an auxiliary process of formative mimesis. And with his chronology of stages, there is little place for the anterior role of infant drawing in the development of other faculties (notably writing), nor for the way in which aspects of Luquet's earlier stages overlap and persist into adulthood—with, for example, practices of doodling and 'non-figurative' drawing that are, surely, more widely practiced than works of studied draughtsmanship.

Luquet is one of two figures that dominate in Merleau-Ponty's lecture notes on children's drawings; the other is Sophie Morgenstern, whom we encountered in Chapter 2.[4] While Merleau-Ponty accepts Luquet's work as 'consistently accurate' (CPP 165), for him the greatest flaw of *Le Dessin enfantin* is Luquet's reliance upon a normative discourse of attention. As I have already suggested, whereas for Luquet drawing relates to attention and thus the negation of expression, for Merleau-Ponty this formulation is reversed. '[D]rawings of children', he writes, 'can never be seen as a copy of the world which offers itself to them, but rather as an attempt at expression' (CPP 165). Indeed, 'attention', for Merleau-Ponty, is a kind of conceptual anathema, which stands for a loose agglomeration of what he regards as faulty assumptions on both sides of the realist/idealist coin. It is instructive to return to Merleau-Ponty's remarks on the history of attention early on in his 1945 book *Phenomenology of Perception.* With one of his characteristic metaphors, Merleau-Ponty pictures attention as a 'searchlight' (PP 26), which illuminates something that has always been there, and which, by

4 In his notes, Merleau-Ponty summarizes Morgenstern's work on children's drawings, especially *Psychanalyse infantile: Symbolisme et valeur Clinique des creations imaginatives chez l'enfant*. Merleau-Ponty's reading of Morgenstern is that 'if children's drawings have any cathartic virtue, even though they do not verbalize their conflicts, it is because these conflicts are not locked up in some unconscious space' (CPP 176). I am not sure this does Morgenstern justice, but for Merleau-Ponty's full exegesis of her work on children's drawings, see CPP, 173–176.

corollary, will activate the same inherent sensations in all who direct their attention towards it. The spectator of the searchlight is passive. 'The history of the concept of attention' presupposes the 'priority of the objective world' (PP 24), Merleau-Ponty writes. Such a presupposition is made at the expense of what Merleau-Ponty conceives as the primary role of perception.

I suggest that Merleau-Ponty resists a generalized concept of attention in part because theories of attention so often elevate quantitative activity over the qualitative domain of phenomenology. To give another example, a more contemporary historian of attention, Jonathan Crary, defines attention as a subtractive process: 'a disengagement from a broader field of attraction, whether visual or auditory, for the sake of isolating or focusing on a *reduced number of stimuli*' (Crary 1999, 1; emphasis mine). Behind this, we can discern the influence of Henri Bergson's similarly subtractive account, in 1896, of what he refers to as the 'necessary poverty' of perception (Bergson 1911, 31). I also point back to the terms of Luquet's intellectual realism, with its over-compensatory overwhelming of the 'greatest number' of details in a representation of a given object, as a kind of additive countermovement of the subtractive force of the child's attention. For Merleau-Ponty, the quantitative activity implied by such concepts of attention misses the point: 'Consciousness is no less intimately linked with objects of which it is unheeding than with those which interest it' (PP 28). Merleau-Ponty's thinking here is inflected by the Gestalt principle that figure cannot be separated from background; consciousness—and, by extension, the untutored drawing of children—does not divide up the world *partes extra partes*, nor really engage in the kind of counting and subtracting that the discourse of attention imposes upon it.[5]

In the notes from his Sorbonne lectures on child psychology and pedagogy, Merleau-Ponty critiques Luquet's *Le Dessin enfantin* on the basis that it is geared around an 'adult-centric' norm of attention (CPP 168). The discourse of attention is always normative, always making judgments as to what is an adequate or inadequate exercise of attentiveness. For Merleau-Ponty, it is not at all that the child drawing

5 For two useful articles on Merleau-Ponty's complex relationship with Gestaltism, see Benjamin Sherados, 'Merleau-Ponty's Immanent Critique of Gestalt Theory'. In *Human Studies* 40 (2017), and Lester Embree, 'Merleau-Ponty's Examination of Gestalt Psychology'. In *Research in Phenomenology* 10.1 (2022).

is the product of what Luquet calls a 'limited and discontinuous' attention, but that:

> The objects to which one 'does not pay attention' are not actually present in the configuration of the actual field. For example, when the child constantly draws things as separate, it is because this is the way they correspond to his actual mental experience [...] it is necessary to understand that the drawing corresponds to the loose structure of the child's perceptual field. (CPP 168–169)

The actual correspondence between graphism and perception *is* the foundation, rather than secondary evidence of a prior ground and, as this foundation, graphism and perception feed into each other in a cyclical way, mediated by what Merleau-Ponty calls here 'mental experience'.

Luquet generally only allows for experience in the narrow sense of *practice.* Whereas for Luquet the exigency of drawing derives from the fact that all children, as dutiful copyists, are possessed by a mimetic urge, for Merleau-Ponty it is motivated by an active, fundamentally expressive process. In this context, expression does not mean the sovereign, reflexive capacity of a subject to express an interiority of its own, but, instead, a dialectical and continuous co-determination of subject and object, which Merleau-Ponty refers to as a 'junction': 'a drawing is an expression of the world for the child and never a simple imitation [...] we must take "expression" in its full sense, as the junction between that which perceives and that which is perceived' (CPP 170). Expression, as Gombrich reminds us, cannot but draw selectively from a repertoire of given possibilities: but here, the expression of the child's drawing, as poeisis, draws directly from the world (and thereby, in a twofold movement, *brings the world forth*, to make good on my promise of a Heideggerian register). Though it is not explicit in his lecture notes, what fascinates Merleau-Ponty about child drawing—and, indeed, one of the things that attracts him later to the impressionism of Cézanne, in 'Eye and Mind'—is that it is free from the mediating conventions of academic drawing. Drawing, for Merleau-Ponty, ought to be *immediate.*

On the topographic dimensions of their arguments, contrast Merleau-Ponty's junction—a mobile point of convergence—with Luquet's narrative linearity. Whereas Luquet's narrow aesthetic telos is graphic mastery, Merleau-Ponty's account moves in a more intermedial direction, and against the unidirectional structure of innocence-to-experience.

The comportment of child drawing, of selecting and expressing the world, remains ever available to perception. That is not to say that Merleau-Ponty rehabilitates Ruskin's innocent eye, since he reverses the traditional structure that *subjects* the eye to the external world. The eye of the drawing child is not innocent, because it always, from the very beginning, brings its experience to bear on the world it perceives and expresses. Furthermore, drawing cuts or juts materially across sensory modalities—it is significant as both a visual beholding and a manual holding. 'The child's drawing is a *contact* with the visible world' (CPP 419) Merleau-Ponty writes, in direct contrast with Luquet's internal model.

Merleau-Ponty's resistance to Luquet under the sign of attention downplays Luquet's own internal reservations about his model. Specifically, Luquet is closest to Merleau-Ponty in the reflective and speculative final chapter of his book, where he sets out his own resistance to what he refers to, not unlike Merleau-Ponty, as 'the general empiricist thesis of the passivity of mind' (CD 145). This is important for my argument since, against empiricism, Luquet alights at the importance of selection:

> a selection guided by the importance children give to the elements [of the object they are drawing], and the interest they take in them. Thus, at the very outset of childhood, the mind is very far from purely receptive, but is, instead, active in a fundamental way in elaborating what is presented to it. (CD 145)

Luquet thus sets up an internal tension between the mimetic drive and an attendant, affective relation to the object that is not reducible to straightforward representation. Selection becomes the hinge between attention and expression.

Merleau-Ponty leans on this hinge to the extent that he refutes one of the axiomatic distinctions between writing and drawing. Opposed to imitation, drawing, in Merleau-Ponty's account, becomes an *indexical notation of a perceptual experience*: 'marking down on paper our symbol of coexistence with the thing' (CPP 418). It is precisely because of this notational quality that Merleau-Ponty connects drawing to writing: 'drawing is, in some ways, a particular case of writing [...] it is no more necessary to think of the drawing as the projection of the thing on paper than it is necessary to assume that the child's "A" must just look like the letter "A"' (CPP 418). Correspondence to a standard model is less significant than expressive content. The sheet of paper, as the flattened field of expression upon which the child makes their exploratory contacts with the world, plays an important role in Merleau-Ponty's thinking: 'Since the drawing represents an attempt to transpose onto a single plane what we see in depth, we use expression more than imitation' (CPP 164). The plane is to drawing as grammar is to writing—a conditional constraint that makes the subjective expression of the phenomenal world possible.

It is through this broader theorization of expressiveness that Merleau-Ponty identifies an analog between child drawing and the poetry of Francis Ponge. Merleau-Ponty suggests that Ponge's poems (as well as Cézanne's paintings) evince the 'same tendency' as child drawing, since, as Merleau-Ponty puts it, 'each object is a *complex*' (CPP 172). By 'complex', Merleau-Ponty is referring to the way that any object before our perception is a site of overlapping relations, aggregated discrete elements and linguistic determinants (Luquet makes the point that the title assigned by the child to the drawing is *part* of the drawing). Faced with an awareness of these pluralities, the drawer—like the poet—must commit to a series of selections that best express how the object affects them—and what those selections exclude are equally significant in the constitution of the expression. Elsewhere in the lectures, referring to Ponge's famous poem 'Le Galet' ('The Pebble') from his 1942 collection *Le Parti pris des choses*, Merleau-Ponty resumes the analogy between the poet and child drawer: 'Ponge observes things in the impact they have on him and not as exterior to him. The pebble he analyses is the pebble of the child' (CPP 421). This account of Ponge's poetics corresponds to what Jane Bennett refers to as 'writing up', by which she refers to a mode of writing attuned to the continuities and permeations between the material world and the embodied consciousness of the writing subject (and which thus complement's Merleau-Ponty's dialectical account of expression). Bennett, who herself makes the direct analogy between writing up and doodling, provides a sharp theoretical lens through which to frame the modes of expression I am discussing (Bennett 2020, ix–xxv). Ponge 'writes up' the pebble as the child draws an object—that is, the expression of the object proceeds from a mode of selection that can never isolate the object from the unlimited spatiotemporal networks and relations that constitute it and support it before perception. For Ponge, the pebble is contiguous with the whole sea: 'il laisse à travers lui passer toute la mer, qui se perd en sa profondeur sans pouvoir en aucune façon faire avec lui de la boue'/ 'it lets the whole sea filter through, which disappears into its depths without in any way being able to make mud out of it' (OC I 56 / VT 76). Merleau-Ponty's references to Ponge in his lectures are brief and illustrative, *en passant*; my aim, in the next section of the essay, is to take seriously the equivalence that he suggests, and try to flesh it out from within the terms of Ponge's own aesthetic project.

Taking Sides, Drawing Lines: Francis Ponge at Work

That Francis Ponge loved the art of drawing and felt a deep affinity with modern *dessinateurs* is amply demonstrated by his spellbound essays on the drawings of Braque, Picasso and the lesser-known modernist Jean Hélion.[6] 'Ponge, to be sure', writes Craig Dworkin, 'had a graphic imagination' (Dworkin 2020, 159). Much like Luquet and Merleau-Ponty, Ponge believed in the primacy and persistence of drawing; for him, the drawings of masters like Leonardo and Rembrandt were more enduring than their paintings, which were, in contrast, subject to the generational vagaries of taste: 'Nous pouvons l'être éternellement de leurs dessins'/ '[W]e can be eternally sure of their drawings' (OC II 585) /VT 161). This enthusiasm for drawing—particularly artists, like Picasso, who regarded child drawing as a model—accords with Ponge's own poetic quest for a particularly childish mode of seeing. In his diary-like 'My Creative Method', he outlines the ideal of a 'naïve classification puerile des choses' ('a naive childlike classification of things'), which would 'rénové le monde des objets' ('renew the world of objects'), and thereby provide a level means of relating impressions of the world to 'sensibilités contemporains ou futurs' ('sensibilities of today and the future') (OC I 521 / VT 88). In the drawings of the masters, and in his own childish method, he perceived a similar futurity, a similar amenability to universal resonance.

This is, of course, redolent of Ruskin's conception of childishness and the 'innocence of the eye' (Ruskin 1971, 27), but even more indebted to Charles Baudelaire's updated definition of creative genius in 'The Painter of Modern Life' (1863) as 'childhood recaptured at will' (Baudelaire 2010, 11).[7] Like Luquet and Merleau-Ponty, both of whom emphasize

6 I retain the French *dessinateur* here in the absence of a serviceable equivalent in the English language ('drawer' being too denotative of furniture and 'draughtsperson' too awkward, inflexible and technical).

7 'The Painter of Modern Life', as I have mentioned, is arguably more concerned

the selective comportment of graphic infancy, an ethic of selection is central to Ponge's conceptualization of his method: 'les qualités de tel ou tel objet choisies pour être explicitées seront de préférence celles qui ont été passées sous silence jusqu'à présent' / 'the characteristics of the object selected for explanation will be preferably those neglected until now' (OC I 521 / VT 88). Poetic expression proceeds from an attitude of affective selection, here based upon a principle of novelty, but derived from the selective affinities originally cultivated in child drawing.

My entry point into Ponge's poetry will be the most literal, thematic example of drawing from *Le Parti pris des choses*, in the poem 'La Fin de L'Automne'. My focus will be on Ponge as a poet of the selective phenomenology characteristic of child drawing—an expression of the world made through an embodied disposition towards a choice of available, differential objects, both the visible objects that one draws and the tangible objects with which one draws. I want to focus, in particular, on two minor and complementary objects that figure in 'La Fin de L'Automne', which are equally objects of draughtsmanship: the ruler (as instrument) and the desk (as work surface, as ground, and as a field of selection). Like 'Le Galet', 'La Fin de L'Automne' concerns itself in part with the generative difficulty of expressing an object in transition (what Merleau-Ponty calls a 'complex') and thus distinguishing it from the anterior and posterior states that constitute it but which are themselves, of course, equally transitional. The poem is not about winter, but the period spanning the marginal overlaps from the end of autumn to the beginning of spring. With the approach of spring and its 'petits bourgeons' (OC I 16), or little buds, the poem cuts off, and does so through a first-person incursion of the actual moment of writing—the graphic event of the writer drawing away, quite literally, from the act of description: 'Mais là commence une autre histoire, qui dépend peut-être mais n'a pas l'odeur de la règle noire qui va me servir à tirer mon trait sous-celle-ci' (OC I 17) / 'But here begins another story, which depends on perhaps but does not smell like the black ruler that will aid me in drawing my line under this one' (my translation). On the face of it, this is Ponge concluding with the commonplace metaphor, in both English and French, of 'drawing a line' beneath a subject as a way of leaving it behind. However, the otherwise superfluous details of the color and,

with drawing than it is with painting; Constantin Guys is the consummate *dessinateur* of modernity, with his 'on-the-spot drawings from life' (Baudelaire 2011, 9).

almost parodically, the smell of the ruler, serve to root this moment in the sensory experience of the graphic act. Note the similarities with Matthew Battles' essay on the 'sensuous and immediate' pleasures that are peculiar to the act of doodling: 'the pliant bouquet of crayons and the stink of coloring markers' (Battles 2004, 108). This kind of sensuous immediacy ensures that Ponge's line is in fact perhaps the *least* figurative moment in the poem.

It is a critical commonplace that Ponge's poetry is a written poetry sooner than it is a spoken poetry.[8] But, with the drawing of the *trait*, Ponge's writing is foregrounded as a manual, graphic process—though mediated and supplanted by typography (one of the visual effects of Ponge's blocks of prose is that they foreground a kind of alienated textuality). Drawing relates to writing as one season relates to another. The black ruler figures in the poem as a minor, transitional object (in the Winnicottian sense of an object that mediates between the interiorized subject and the exteriorized world), a spatial analog of temporal seasonality. It aids the shift from the poetic subject, half-present at the end of the poem, to the 'things' in the world that Ponge will go on to address, describe and define in a sequence of discrete performances. The '*histoire*'—the writing—of spring 'depends', in both senses of the word: intransitively, in the sense of being suspended and left unfinished, and transitively, in the sense of depending *on* ('*depend [...] de*') the technical objects that furnish the graphic, linearized act of writing.

Given not just the conceptual kinship, but also the obvious similarities of diction, Ponge's dependable black ruler is a French cousin of William Carlos Williams' red wheelbarrow.[9] The rule, like the barrow, is a manipulable, manmade object whose utility as a tool is elided in favor of its thingly interconnectedness. In this respect, Ponge (like Williams) subscribes to an ontology that things, like words, are differential. Ponge himself, in 'My Creative Method', underlines the importance of the 'differential quality' afforded by analogies (the main remit, for Ponge, of poetry): 'Nommer la qualité différentielle de la noix, voilà le but, le progrès' / 'To name the differential quality of the walnut, that is purpose, that is progress' (OC I 537/VT 107). The function of the

8 Robert W. Greene, for an earlier example, describes Ponge as the '*scripteur* par excellence' (Greene 1979, 61).

9 Andrew Epstein notes a kinship between Ponge and American poetry and thought, especially the Objectivist strain inaugurated by William Carlos Williams (see Epstein 2012, 48).

ruler is that it facilitates the differential movement of Ponge's *trait.*[10] That *trait*, as a passage of withdrawal executed via a transitional object, is also, equally, a *retrait*. The end of 'La Fin de L'Automne', with its possessive 'mon trait', is notably one of few instances of first-person interpellation in a collection famous for its assays in suspending the self. 'La Fin de l'Automne' is the second poem in *Le Parti pris des choses*, after the inaugural poem 'Pluie', whose descriptions of rain—which anticipate the waterlogged motif of 'La Fin de l'Automne'—occur as the observations of a situated viewer. That viewer is subject to the possibility of physical and linguistic dissolution among illimitable taxonomies of rain, since such a transitory, vigorous plenitude threatens to overwhelm the selective affection of the subject. The drawing of the line in the subsequent poem, 'La Fin de l'Automne', serves to announce the actual dissolution of that situated viewer. Ponge sides with things via ruler and line.

Emily McLaughlin explores how, throughout *Le Parti pris des choses*, Ponge develops the analogy between plant growth and writing (see McLaughlin 2020, 242). 'La Fin de L'Automne', in contrast, is concerned not with growth but with the decline of vegetal life, the 'dépouillement' (OC I, 16) or stripping that precedes renewal. As such, Ponge's analogic focus is on a stripping back of the scene of writing to its bare materials: a quest for the genesis of writing. A personified Nature 'déchire ses manuscrits, démolit sa bibliothèque, gaule rageusement ses dernier fruits' / 'rips up her manuscripts, demolishes her library, angrily thrashes her last fruits from the trees' (OC I 16 / VT 33). Like graphism, both written and drawn, 'La Nature' as the subject of Ponge's poem is understood as a site of potential action coterminous with a loose aggregation of materials. The end of autumn, a time of dearth and death ('Habillé comme nu'/'Dressed in nakedness' [OC I 16 / VT 32]), becomes difficult to define and pin down, precisely because its aggregation of materials is characterized by a relative lack of dynamic and therefore distinguishing features. Selection, and thus

10 Note, also, the amount of verbal qualification—broaching the sensory body of the *scripteur*—inserted by Ponge between '*depend*' and its corresponding preposition '*de*', and how this functions comparably with the enjambment that separates the same verb from its preposition in Williams' 'so much depends / upon'—that is, inflecting a felt reticence into a poem that otherwise claims to do away with a subjective locus in favor of an unadorned, philosophically realist presentation.

expression, becomes a task. Ponge's figure for this breakdown is water: an 'amphibiguité salubre'/'salubrious amphibiguity' [OC I 16 / VT 32]), where the stuttering portmanteau 'amphibiguité' performs lexically the collapse of differentiating features that it describes.

Maintaining, again, an equivalence between the ecological and the graphological, Ponge writes that Nature ('La Nature'), at the start of winter, 'se lève brusquement de sa table de travail' ('abruptly gets up from her desk' [OC I 16 / VT 32]). Nature becomes defined by its own *désœuvrement*, or worklessness. The 'table de travail'—the desk, the work-table—stands for a phenomenal field of potential expressive action, which has been *cleared*; by this potential, recalling Merleau-Ponty's dialectic, I refer both to the expressive possibilities of nature (where nature is understood precisely as a field of expressibility), and the expressive potential of the subject. The desk is not merely the support for the work of writing or drawing: it is, at the same time, the field upon and from which the subject organizes the combinatory elements—notations of experience—with which the work will be crafted.

The work-table or desk, the material surface upon which equally material elements are selected and manipulated in an activity of poeisis, is a recurrent motif in Ponge's writing. It belongs to a cluster of terms related to the space of composition, notably the 'atelier' (workshop or studio)—the subject of one of Ponge's later prose poems—and the 'établi' or workbench. These latter two terms feature prominently in Ponge's essay on the drawings of Georges Braque (published as *Braque-Dessins* in 1950), to which I will now turn. An ekphrastic impulse animates Ponge's evocation of Braque's 'atelier', since it implicitly takes its cue from the artist's own *Atelier* series of paintings. Commenced in 1939 with the painting *Atelier I*, these works depict vibrant interiors enlivened by accumulated domestic objects; they depict the scene of painting, painting painting itself. Focusing on Ponge's evocations of Braque's workspaces, I tease out some of the internal connections between poetry and drawing in Ponge's aesthetics. For Ponge, the workbench of drawing is where the artist retreats from the easel to find solutions, to think, to combine elements and ideas: 'L'on voit alors notre artisan quitter sa forge [...] et s'approcher de son établi, don't il débarrasse un coin. Il prend bout de crayon sur son oreille, il prend un bout de papier, et il y pose son problème, et il y trace son dessin, il y trouve sa solution' / 'We see our artisan leave his forge [...] and go over to his workbench where he clears a space. He takes the pencil stub from behind his ear, takes a scrap of paper, puts his problem on it, sketches his drawing, finds his solution there' (OC II 588 / VT 164).[11] Braque clears his workbench as La Nature clears her desk in 'La Fin de l'Automne': expression literally takes the place of the object, that is, it is conditional upon an act of clearing. This act of clearing, combined with an effort of thought, is of the same order as the evacuation that occurs with Luquet's 'internal model', whereby the drawn object is not present, but is both reconstituted and revealed on the page. Here we can discern the affinity between Luquet's account of child drawing—as a non-perspectival 'co-ordination' of discrete elements—and Braque's cubist drawing. Braque's drawings, for Ponge, are not merely preliminary studies, the workings-out before the work, but the location of a more immediate contact with the world—where the world is discovered and uncovered 'à chaque instant' / 'at every moment' (OC II 588/VT 165). Drawing, for the *dessinateur*, is a means of expressive *reconstruction* of the world, 'le monde par fragments, comme il leur vient'/ 'the world in fragments, as it comes to them' (OC II 586 / VT 163). The world arrives, but arrives in disarray: the passivity of this arrival cedes immediately to the imperative of work, the necessary labor of expression. Ponge compares the modern *dessinateur* to the 'small-town mechanic' who puts automobiles back into order 'avec les moyens du bord, souvent réduits'/ 'with the means available, often very limited' (OC II 586 / VT 163). This is poeisis as bricolage, as the assembly of raw parts into expressive wholes.

For Ponge, words and things, in their manipulability, are materially equivalent. As Gerald Bruns puts it, in Ponge's ontology, 'words cease to be instruments of the spirit and become instead components of the thingworld' (Bruns 2001, 205). The 'thingworld' is thus at the expressive disposal of the poet. Ponge himself sums up his method with the equation: 'PARTIS PRIS DES CHOSES *égale* COMPTE TENU DES MOTS' / 'TAKING THE SIDE OF THINGS *equals* TAKING ACCOUNT OF WORDS' (OC I 522 / VT 89). In the world, words and things alike are characterized by a diachronic mutability, fraying and disseminating across space and time. As graphic notations, writing and drawing mark words and things as moments of sense in otherwise fluxional continua. Always aware of the etymological journeys of words, when Ponge writes in his essay on Braque: 'Dessein, dessin, design… Ce

11 Note the resonance between Braque quitting his forge and Ponge drawing away from the poem in 'La Fin de l'Automne'. The physical act of withdrawing is always a *part* of the work; drawing, where each line marks a duration, makes this withdrawal manifest in a way other arts do not.

sont trois forms du *même mot*, jadis unique' / Dessein, dessin, design... Three forms of the same word, once unified' (OC II 588 / VT 164)—he is not just highlighting the semantic and etymological proximity between *dessin* and *design*; he is, more importantly, *demonstrating* how the attitude of designing—that is, assembling, graphically, available related elements—informs his own attitude towards language.

Ponge is affected by each individual word, affected in and by his selection of each word, in the same way that the child affectively selects each element that comprises the drawing. He describes this affect in 'My Creative Method' with a painterly register, collapsing the distinction between visual and verbal expressiveness: 'No word is used which is not immediately considered an individual; whose inner light is utilized, and shadow too' (VT 100). Ponge's attitude toward the affective presence of individual words, and the role played in processes of expression by the poet's *responses* to those affective presences, bears the influence of Surrealist poetry. André Breton calls this the word's 'aspect': 'the expression of an idea depends as much on a word's aspect as on its meaning' (Breton 1996, 101). To return to Ponge's words, the individuation only occurs with the isolating act or *consideration* of the affective choice of the artist. Ponge evokes the *dessinateur*'s technique of chiaroscuro to encapsulate both linguistic difference—the metaphoric play of light and shadow that constitutes differential meaning-making—but also the literal satisfactions of graphism in the poet's manual reckoning with the 'aspect' of the word.

This brings me, finally, to the notion of *dilection*—the coextension of choice and love, selection and affection. By this, I mean the way in which expression takes place as a series of affective investments in chosen elements. In his essay on Picasso's drawings, Ponge distinguishes between the artist's Blue and Rose periods with the respective words *dilection* and *delectation*. For Ponge, these terms are distinct but related, referring to complementary modes of drawing. *Dilection*, for Ponge, relates to the choice of the *dessinateur* (and choice's interplay, in the execution of the drawing, with chance). Consulting the dictionary, Ponge writes that 'la racine de la dilection est le choix'/ 'the root of dilection is choice' (OC I 102 / VT 167). *Delectation* relates, on the other hand, to the transient proprietorial pleasure proper to drawing. The root of delectation, Ponge notes, is *lacire*: 'faire tomber dans un lacs, c'est-à-dire une sort de piège fait d'un assemblage de cordons, ce qui convient généralement aux dessins et surtout à ceux du genre qui nous occupe: simple et déroutants, comme des tours de ficelle'; 'to catch in a trap of laced string, which generally applies to drawings, and particularly to drawings of the type we are talking about: simple yet perplexing, like windings of string' (OC II 641 / VT 169).[12] We should also take this as a description of what it means, for Ponge, to inscribe a word that one likes. To inscribe a word that one likes in a poem is literally to catch (not to kill, or halt) its sense among the linear marks that make it up, and to trace that meaning through description. Writing, for Ponge, is like playing with string (and we should note the resonances with the role of string play in Winnicott's thinking about child experience): winding and unwinding, outlining, tying together.

The trace, the signifying graphic mark, becomes the thread, the line of continuity, to be followed but not unwound. Ponge's description here could equally apply to writing—the transient 'capture' of inscribing fixed but delicate moments of sense within a durational graphic trace. Delectation is conjoined with *dilection*; affection is conjoined with choice: an originary co-determination that sustains the practices of poetry and drawing alike. Both Ponge and Picasso seek the *dilection* of the dilettante (to indulge, like Ponge, in the pleasure of etymological associations): the amateur, who comes to both words and things with an attitude of innocence. Innocence is defined here precisely by an openness to the co-determination of affect and choice in the development of expression. The art of the dilettante sustains graphic infancy into adulthood.

12 Note, here, the resonances with Winnicott: the drawing as string; string as drawing.

CHAPTER FIVE

A.R. Ammons: *The Nature of the Line*

This chapter and the next focus on the relationship between poetic lines and graphic lines. In this chapter, I focus on the poet A.R. Ammons, particularly his work of the 1960s. Throughout his whole career, Ammons' poems have an obsessively graphical and line-oriented formal imagination: he is a real poet of linework. Sometimes the poems are generatively aware that they aren't drawings, as in the case of 'Corsons Inlet', which we will focus on at length further along in the chapter. Sometimes they thematize the literal act of drawing, like in 'Buttermilk Falls' ('I sit down, draw a clear line' [Ammons 2017b, 95]), and, even more literally, in the poem 'Line Drawing' ('to clear / a place off for whatever we have to say' [Ammons 2017b, 342]), both from 1996's *Brink Road*.

Often, Ammon's poems run breathlessly after a moment of descriptive lucidity, and achieve lucidity in the process, something which Ammons repeatedly connects to graphic line-making.[1] We see this tendency most directly in the early poem 'Lines', which is the closest Ammons comes to a straight ekphrasis of linework: 'Lines flying in, out: logarithmic / curves coiling / toward an infinitely inward center' (Ammons 2017a, 96). This is a crucial example because Ammons' dynamic descriptions of lines encounter the crosscurrent of heavy enjambments that draw attention to the brittle fixity of the poem as an artifact of lineated language. 'Coiling' is but one of many present participles that accumulate throughout 'Lines': 'exploring', 'intersecting', 'paralleling', 'twisting', 'noding', 'deranging', 'clustering'. These are participles that alternate between verbs of relation or correlation like 'paralleling' and verbs of

1 For an insightful, early critical account of Ammons' 'linear modes', see the chapter of that name in Alan Holder, *A.R. Ammons* (Boston: Twayne 1978), pp. 111–159.

mutation or corruption like 'twisting' and 'deranging'. To draw (or describe) a line, it seems, is both to relate and to warp.

Rather like the Baudelaire of 'The Painter of Modern Life', drawing is posited as a benchmark for an idealized mimesis attentive to external mutability. Baudelaire writes that the drawings of Constantin Guys realize a 'struggle between the determination to see everything, to forget nothing, and the faculty of memory, which has acquired the habit of registering in a flash the general tones and shape, the outline pattern' (Baudelaire 2010, 22). One way of reformulating this is that memory in *practice*, that is, in memorialization, cannot keep up with the affect or mood from which the will to memorialization emerges. The *dessinateur* of Baudelaire's essay wants to remember more than they can. Ammons' drawing poems operate in this lineage, and Ammons values drawing for what might be called, after Baudelaire, its 'childhood recaptured at will' (Baudelaire 2010, 11): a cleansing of the lyric observer of its acculturations, and a return back to its whims and drives. Ammons, as we will see, frequently gestures towards a space of transitional play in which the subject of the poem is restored to an implied infancy.[2]

Let's focus first on the 1965 art poetica poem, 'Poetics', which, indeed, articulates its approach to poetry through recourse to an extended metaphor (is it a metaphor?) of free and playful drawing: 'Not the shape on paper—though / that, too—but the / uninterfering means on paper' (Ammons 2017a, 465). The poem's significance lies not in its conceptual anchors—terms like 'shape' and 'paper'—but in the passage of its syntax as it connects and navigates those anchors. In other words, it calls attention to its own textual linearity, its threadlike movement. Nevertheless: let us suppose that the 'shape' is a specific actualization of form, a product (say, a sketch of a tree), whereas the 'uninterfering means on paper' is the means of achieving such a shape (say, the movement of a pencil): the processual time of creation in which the poet contacts and expresses the forms that they are making. In 'Poetics', something about

2 Ammons also sees life itself as a kind of tense passage, exactly a vital (or vitalistic) tension from point to point. The poem 'Possibility Along a Line of Difference', for example, conceives of the imagination as 'crazed / by that difference' (Ammons 2017a, 424) which is instantiated inevitably by the passage it makes through life. That lines instantiate difference will become a different kind of preoccupation in the next chapter, when we turn to Derrida.

this process of making—which of course requires the active interference of the maker—is paradoxically 'uninterfering'.

The paradox of creation without interference becomes clearer in the closing stanza of the poem: 'being available [...] to any shape that may be / summoning itself / through me / from the self not mine but ours' (Ammons 2017a, 465). Note how, even more than in the previous excerpt, abstract content is threaded by three compactly linked prepositions ('to', 'through' and 'from'). Again, Ammons' concepts gain purchase only in movement. The interaction between abstract content and an abundance of prepositions again underscores the linework of Ammons' syntax as it tracks across line breaks. The linework here is made even more complex as, on two occasions in this short passage, the poem subverts reflexive structures by turning them outwards and setting them into a kind of play. Reflexive constructions, in general, highlight the ability of the grammatical subject to perform actions upon themselves as both the agent and the object of their own action. But for Ammons reflexivity is seldom grammatically or relationally self-contained; here, the shape's 'summoning [of] itself' is immediately folded into the 'through me' that follows it, and the subsequent line constellates outwards even further by clarifying that this 'me' is, it turns out, a plural 'ours'.

What does it mean to be available to a shape that is summoning itself from a shared self? We might be tempted to read this as a version of automatic drawing. But the way in which Ammons' *ars poetica* here appears to be endorsing automatism is counterintuitive, since Ammons is consistently a poet of attention. Automatism is, meanwhile, an art of inattention. But the 'shape' that comes does not bubble up from below (from an unconscious or primordial state), as we find in Surrealist automatism, nor does it come about from a deliberate suspension of the drawer's attention.

Numerous critics have singled out Ammons as a poet of attention *par excellence*. Andrew Epstein, for example, argues that '[f]or Ammons, trying to pay careful attention to the minutiae of daily life [...] amounts to an ethical stance' (Epstein 2016, 111). In 'Poetics', Ammons describes a way of getting in touch with and becoming 'available' to a shared self and this self is synonymous with a certain form of attention. To be 'available', in this context, is to be discriminatingly attentive. It is rather more submerged, but 'Poetics' engages too in the metonymic association between drawing and childhood by valorizing a state of being stripped back to an unadorned 'availability' to what one sees—and to expressing that availability (to channel the terms we explored in the previous chapter).[3]

The Gesture of Art

In a 1962 letter to the poet Denise Levertov, Ammons summarizes almost everything I have been claiming for his poetry and poetics so far, while also dimly echoing, in the primacy of drawing that it implies, Heidegger's conception of the work of art as a linear *rift-design*:

> The moment the line has been drawn, fidelity to nature is impossible, because it has no lines, but only the massive events of transition [...] Art has to draw a line. My question is, what is the nature of the line to be? Is it to be texture, organic realization? Is it to be numbers of feet, lines, syllables? Or what? And how artful and arbitrary? (Ammons 2013, 203)

Let us first link this to the wider category of what Renée Riese Hubert calls the 'postmodern page'. 'Ever since Mallarmé', Hubert writes, '[...] visual and verbal productions have focused in many ways on the specific problem of the surface, page, or canvas, whether in a state of emptiness or plenitude' (Hubert 1988, 132). For Ammons, the 'impossibility' of 'fidelity to nature' is not a lament, but an opportunity for formal experimentation. 'Art has to draw a line': what happens when one attempts to make art *about* nature is that this gesture cuts itself off and generates its own formal questions. I use the word 'gesture' deliberately because one of the affordances of a language of graphism, for Ammons, is that it betokens a light and nonviolent physical gesture. Giorgio Agamben writes that '[w]hat characterizes gesture is that nothing is being produced or acted, but rather something is being endured or supported' (Agamben 2000, 57). But perhaps we might repurpose that term from Ammons' 'Poetics'—'uninterfering means'—to rethink what gesture means. A gesture is a means of bodily movement that does not interfere. A gesture that connects with another body or object ceases to be a gesture at the moment of connection. Drawing, akin to the paradox

3 Indeed, Ammons inherits this directly from the Whitmanian model of child psychology that we considered briefly in Chapter 1.

of the 'uninterfering means', is a kind of point of contact between the gestural and the tactile.

The formal questions that are engendered by Ammons' line of art are rich insofar as posing them and considering their answers creates a field of imaginative exploration and play. We can, with reason, call it a transitional zone. The advantage of doing so is that it highlights the virtual nature of this space. It is not that Ammons is subscribing to a hard-and-fast ontological division between nature and culture, but that the poem acts as an outlining of transitional space (the transitional space as an outline) that resists binaries and instead sets thinking into motion and flow. The move of Ammons' thinking here—and a significant underpinning logic of what we might call Ammons' 'ecopoetics'—can be tracked in the simple displacement of the word 'nature' in his letter to Levertov. Nature 'has no lines', Ammons writes, but the line itself has a kind of nature ('the nature of the line').

When Ammons writes that nature itself 'has no lines' (as he puts it elsewhere in 'Corsons Inlet', 'in nature there are few sharp lines' [Ammons 2017a, 92]), he aligns himself—of course—with the centuries-spanning axiom that, as John Ruskin put it, 'There are no outlines in Nature' (Ruskin 1971, 33) (we considered this in Chapter 2 when we discussed the history of the outline). But Ammons, here, goes further. Like Tim Ingold, he questions if culture is nothing more than a vast system of lines. Indeed, the letter to Levertov is strikingly redolent of another anthropologist, Edmund Leach, who wrote that '[v]isible, wild Nature is a jumble of random curves [...] But the tamed, manmade world of Culture is full of straight lines, rectangles, triangles, circles and so on' (Leach 1976, 51).

If all art 'has to draw a line', then poetry has a particular advantage over all other media, because poems involve at least three different types of line, and are capable at the same time of describing linear forms verbally. First, letters, and the graphic marks that make them; second, sentences, and the lines of thought that they construct; and, finally, poetic lineation. Ammons engages this typology of lines and the *nature* of them (taking 'nature' to refer simply to a complex system of typological variety). His poems are ecologies insofar as they instantiate and play with various tensions between, and interdependencies of, one type of line and another. There is something about the transitional zone of art *in general* that allows us to play with the basic formal elements, the girding and bounding lines, that comprise the lives that have been constructed for us. This is the central tension in Ammons' poems, between the squiggling and swirling that is always going on in the infinitely dynamic lines of the ecological field ('the massive events of transition') and the humble and strictly located lines that one can trace on the page.

Ammons Not-Drawing

Now we will focus on one of Ammons' best-known poems, 'Corsons Inlet', first collected in his 1965 volume of the same name. We will read 'Corsons Inlet' as an example of not-drawing, a text that constructs itself in opposition to graphic play.

In addition to being a not-drawing, 'Corsons Inlet' is a walk poem, whose speaker tracks along the narrow inlet that gives the poem its title. Indeed, 'Corsons Inlet' inscribes itself in the metonymy between walking and drawing as activities of free line-making, again rather like the active line on a walk that begins Paul Klee's *Pedagogical Sketchbook* (in Chapter 1 we considered how Winnicott's squiggle also corresponded to this type of line). The relationship between walking and drawing is a much more central dynamic in 'Corsons Inlet' than has been previously acknowledged, to the point that the poem is as much about what it means to trace marks and movements on a sheet of paper as it is about an actual walk through an actual place.

Early in the poem, the mobile 'I', walking along the jagged New Jersey shoreline, describes being 'released from forms, / from the perpendiculars, / straight lines, blocks, boxes, binds / of thought' (Ammons 2017a, 91). But is this not, in fact, a more apt description of *free drawing*—and *free verse*—than of walking? To draw a squiggle is precisely to be released, thoughtlessly or playfully, from the tyranny of straight lines. The same is true of free verse: to disregard metrical and typographic constraints is to break the poem loose from the 'perpendicular' discipline of conventional lineation (and a sonnet stanza is, after all, a kind of block or box of thought). This passage also reprises a theme from Ammons' 1962 letter: the distinction between nature and culture, where culture is composed of rigid, linear forms and nature is not.

Yet it's a curious way to describe the experience of walking in nature. The speaker lingers on the alliterative chain of banal shapes—'blocks, boxes, binds'—as if seduced more by the internal play of language than by the landscape itself (which, to be fair, the poem does reach in exquisite detail). What we see here is a kind of lateral or linear pleasure akin to that of walking or drawing, following a trail of associations simply for the pleasure of movement. At the same time, the heavy enjambment that carries these lines forward ironically reminds us that Ammons' rejection of formal constraint is itself *enacted* in straight lines of verse, an arrangement that still obeys the basic architecture of the page.

'Corsons Inlet' reconciles gradually the premise that the shifting world that is beheld along its walk is completely resistant to description: 'The sum of these events / I cannot draw' (Ammons 2017a, 92). The process of the walk itself—and the lineated description of the walk—stands in for the drawing that cannot hope to be made. As I started off this chapter by saying, Ammons is generatively aware that his poems aren't drawings. 'Corsons Inlet', repeatedly, *negatively* predicates itself in relation to drawing. Ammons writes: 'I have / drawn no lines:/as/ manifold events of sand / change the dune's shape' (Ammons 2017a, 92). In these lines, characteristically, the thematization of an absent drawing—graphic, line-based mimesis—sits in a tense relationship with Ammons' scattered lineation. Not-drawing becomes a basis from which to proceed for the particular kind of ecological melancholy Ammons is after, because it defines writing as what is it *not*, a representative incapacity. Of course, Ammons is a poet and lines are his material—or, more specifically, lines that are themselves comprised of graphic marks that have been codified into notational units. It becomes his task to see what he can do from the confines of the straight line: to break it, extend it, and take it apart. Ammons' line breaks, as in 'Poetics', respond to a need to recalibrate and recenter a line of thinking that is extending out from a point of departure, to resist the singular linearization of thought even as it imposes itself at the level of the sentence. Note how the conjunction 'as', the fragile, solitary keystone on which the poem teeters, is given a line of its own, to draw attention to the hinge between linearized syntactic order and the jumbled lines of a fantasy of mimetic fidelity that resists such order.

What does 'Corsons Inlet' have to do with child drawing as we have been discussing it throughout this book? The self of Ammons' poem seems to be a hardy coast walker and a learned namer of birds and shrubs. He is, in other words, certainly not a child, nor even childlike. The poem is about what cannot be drawn rather than what can.

But, at the same time, all child drawing is almost always concerned exactly with what cannot be drawn. By this I mean that, as we have seen, psychoanalysis finds in the material of child drawing a means of reading the imagination and the unconscious, precisely because these materials swerve away from or resist strict eye-to-hand mimesis. Similarly, the whole point of a study like Georges-Henri Luquet's is to theorize the mimetic incapacities of child drawing and what these incapacities can tell us about the developing mind (and body) of the child. The study of child drawing is never the study of accomplished graphic work, and even when a child is regarded as a graphical genius it is not usually because their drawings display any remarkable verisimilitude, but more likely because they show intricacy, compositional novelty or eccentricity.

'Corsons Inlet' follows eddies and flows of feeling as it catches momentum and finds new objects to describe and add to its composition. It does not attempt to represent those objects, but instead it contents itself with recalling and describing vivid and yet inadequate ciphers of observed phenomena—let's call them, after Luquet, 'internal models'—and, again, adding them to the rushing flow of its composition. As I have argued, 'Corsons Inlet' is *as much* about the act of committing a walk to (and on) paper as it is about a recollection of a walk in nature—creating lively textual material that can be shared, repeated and added to. The poem ends with the open-ended 'tomorrow a new walk is a new walk' (Ammons 2017a, 95). The effect of this closing line is to suggest that 'Corsons Inlet', as a text, is one among many spontaneous tracings, part of a daily possible activity, not an exceptional or epiphanic literary object. The poem disavows the lines it cannot draw even while comporting itself in remarkable ways with the postures of child drawing.

Children's drawings are notoriously flat. Think of the Empire drawings in *Narrative of a Child Analysis*, the drawing of a horse by the Spanish refugee in Marianne Moore's 'Tom Fool', or the cross-sectional drawing of a field of potatoes included in Luquet's *Le Dessin enfantin*. Illustratively, none of these drawings features any semblance of shade or perspective. They flatten the world, whether they turn it into a topography, or a screen, or a kind of x-ray scan. Poems too, tend to be strictly two-dimensional surfaces. Like a children's drawing, a poem like 'Corsons Inlet' achieves a distinctness of vision *because* of its material flatness as a surface.

Most familiarly, at least perhaps for Western readers, a child's drawing might do this by marking out the sky as a line or layer of blue at the very top of a sheet of paper. There are whole studies of this phenomenon.[4] A blue sky-line does not represent the sky through resemblance, it symbolizes it as an 'internal model', and (to recall Merleau-Ponty) it *expresses* the child's sense of unfolding orientation in space, as well as in language (that the sky is a limit, 'up there'). We might categorize a whole visual tradition of children's drawings that mark the top of the page with a horizontal line of blue, and the bottom of the page with a horizontal line of brown or green to mark out the ground. Somewhere between the sky-line and the ground-line will be the central subject of the drawing: a house, perhaps, or a couple of stick figures.

These drawings are vertically organized expressions of an orientation of space: we may focus our attention on the subject (the house or the stick figures) in the center of the page, and we might make a comment on it, but our eyes will register that the top of the sheet is marked as the top and the bottom of the sheet is marked as the bottom. A very similar experience of framed looking is, I think, being activated when one reads a poem like 'Corsons Inlet'. As one focuses on the moving 'subject' of one's visual attention—the line of poetry that one is reading at a given moment—one is also aware that the sheet of paper is a vertically organized frame and that, in this case, the top of the poem represents what is past, the passage along which one has recently traveled, and the bottom of the page represents a point toward which one is moving, if not some kind of horizon or a destination. The lines of 'Corsons Inlet', like the child's sky-line, mark out the parameters of a shareable world by means of flattening. A sky-line marks out the sheet of paper as a site where distinctions between top and bottom, ground and air, are formally inscribed but not spatially realized. A poem like 'Corsons Inlet' unfolds across a two-dimensional surface that conveys depth (emotional, conceptual, ecological) through adherence to its flatness.

Conclusion

By way of a brief conclusion, I turn to another American poet writing in the same period. In his 1965 essay on abstract expressionist painter Frank Stella, 'Frank Stella: A Way to Go', Robert Creeley describes a formal possibility that has long fascinated him: he fantasizes about

4 For example: Vicky Lewis, 'Young Children's Painting of the Sky and the Ground'. In *International Journal of Behavioural Development* 13.1 (1990), pp. 49–65.

'moving the center white line, on a road, so that it goes off the road, and all the cars smash up in the ditch' (Creeley 1970, 353). On face value, it is the complete opposite of Ammons' notion of 'uninterfering'. But if all lines are cultural, then the 'center white line' of an American highway is perhaps a paradigmatic example, or perhaps even the line of culture par excellence, at least in this cultural context. Creeley is, for all sorts of reasons, a very different poet to Ammons. Nevertheless, Ammons, like Creeley, associates straight lines with the imposition of cultural constructions and systems of order. He uses poetic lineation precisely to interrupt and stutter habitual linear ways of reading.

Creeley's mischievous image evokes a desire to tamper with the lines and the tracks that are laid out by culture, not to destroy them wholesale, but to ruffle their authority and to reveal how they guide and constrain the movements of their subjects. (This impulse is mirrored in Creeley's own poetry, where enjambment unsettles the reader's experience of meaning, redirecting the flow and cadence of thought and its habits.) Creeley's fantasy of rerouting traffic—vandalizing the normative line—starts to look less like acting out and more like a theory of poetic form: a theory that the line, that *all* lines, can be bent, broken or re-routed to guide out a new kind of experiencing. Ammons does something similar in 'Corsons Inlet', where his scattered and meandering lines draw our attention to the lines that frame and guide our reading.

We can experience poems like we experience roads or paths: we follow along a track that has been laid for us, and which has necessarily been traversed before. What poets like Ammons do is manipulate with and play with the lines of the tracks, so that we as readers become more reflexively aware of the action of following.

CHAPTER SIX

Jacques Derrida and Jean-Luc Nancy: *Rhetoric and Rhythm*

Prologue: The Myth of Butades

According to Pliny the Elder, the world's first drawing was an expression of love. It is the myth, writes Pliny,

> of Butades, a potter of Sicyon, at Corinth. [...] [H]is daughter, who was in love with a young man, drew in outline on the wall the shadow of his face thrown by a lamp. Her father pressed clay on this and made a relief, which he hardened by exposure to fire with the rest of his pottery. (Pliny 1952, 372–373)

Although it has been institutionalized as the origin of drawing, note how many media are tangled together in this short narrative. The daughter makes a drawing. The father makes a sculpture. There are more: the projection of the shadow anticipates the basic mechanism of cinema. And then there is the myth itself, which is a literary narrative, weaving all of these media—in their concrete and spectral manifestations—together.

The myth of Butades has been commented upon countless times; it is a touchstone for a significant proportion of scholarly, philosophical and literary accounts of the history and theory of drawing. Derrida, as we will soon see, is among such studies. Indeed, the fact that an origin myth has endured in the discourse of drawing (there is no equivalent myth, with equivalent impact, for the 'origin' of writing or painting) suggests an historical investiture in the mythical or originary properties of drawing, and the linking of drawing to a narrative of adolescent development.

Despite this, there are many aspects of it that, to my mind, have not been sufficiently addressed. For example, the fact that drawing is invented by a young woman, not by a boy (as we will have seen, representations of child drawing tend to focalize male experience). She is an adolescent, not a child, but a *daughter*, defined, narratively, by the father who is caring for her and who redeems her drawing. In the myth, the outline registers a melancholic female desire, while the father's clay model asserts proportion, likeness and control. His sculptural intervention both supersedes the daughter's drawing and (we assume) placates her melancholy. The Plinian origin story thus allegorizes the suppression of child drawing *and* the suppression of the daughter: the likeness molded by Butades—preserved, we're told, until the destruction of Corinth—outlasts and overwrites the daughter's fleeting gesture.

For Jean Fisher, Butades' daughter's 'act is not memory as Proustian recollection, but [...] a gift to memory where the act of making is simultaneously an act of memorizing. This is the event of the work, and its character is immediacy' (Fisher 2003, 219). The drawing, Fisher says, is a material 'gift' to the memory, a kind of reflexive externalizing. The contrast with Proust is worth lingering on. Proustian involuntary memory involves a kind of dual temporality, which we might visualize in the terms of the line and the point. The narrative line of memory, of the *Recherche*, shoots spontaneously from the eventual point of the prompt (the dipping of madeleines in tea). Butades's memory-making, in contrast, has no linearity; it is *all point*. That is, memory and 'event' occur together, punctually.

'In Pliny's tale', Deborah Tarn Steiner argues, 'the beloved and his image do not so much resemble one another as exist in a relation of metonymy. [...] The part assumed by the shadow in the episode confirms that contiguity, not similarity, plays the leading role' (Tarn Steiner 2001, 3). I'm not so sure. Butades' daughter doesn't trace the outline of her lover's body, but his shadow—a projected, displaced likeness. A shadow is not contiguous with the object that casts it; it depends on a gap, an angle, a removal. Like metaphor, it operates not through proximity but substitution: one form standing in for another across a field of difference. The drawing on the wall is an image and it is a metaphor: an image-metaphor. It is an image because it is a secondary visual representation of an original object. At the same time, it is a metaphor, because it has displaced the original object into something else entirely. (Outlines, as we encountered in Chapter 2, tend toward metaphor, insofar as they posit an integral form to compensate for a fantasy of objectual presence.) By image-metaphor, I mean that an original nonverbal intensity, desire or moving impulse—we could call it, after Rousseau, a passion—is projected into a rudimentary image, an outline, and that rudimentary image serves as an expressive foundation—and an entry point into semantic *and* syntactic signification. When Butades' daughter traces an outline line on the wall, it is an image insofar as it is a visual trace of a specific event, and a metaphor insofar as it takes place as, and is taken up into, a linear and grammatical structure of displacements and transpositions (the whole scene is an overlay of displacements, from daughter to father, from the beloved to his outline, from drawing to sculpture).

Introduction

One of the ideas in this book has been that drawing, the kind of drawing we do as children, elicits speech in strange ways. In this chapter, we are going to approach that function of drawing as a kind of *rhetorical force*. This rhetorical force is one of the factors that distinguishes what I have been calling 'child drawing' from more traditional, art-historical conceptions of drawing. As I develop this, I will lean on Jacques Derrida's writing and thinking about drawing, since he makes the compelling but somewhat paradoxical claim that the definitive feature of drawing is its *rhetoric*. Rhetoric means the language of persuasion. More broadly, it can mean the formal study of discourse. When I describe the rhetorical force of drawing (and the dispositions and forms of attention that are sponsored by drawing) I mean the way it elicits, provokes and interacts with statements, postulations and questions—the way drawing *demands* writing. We see this in the subject position of 'Corson's Inlet', which predicates its mimeses negatively, that is, on what it *can't* draw. Rhetoric relates to language and abstraction. The other key determining force on that subject position is its surrender, or its 'availability', to the coming and going, the waxing and waning, of the demands made upon it by what it sees and what it therefore wants to question and express. I am going to call this rhythm. Rhythm always relates to the body.

This chapter will focus on a comparison between Jacques Derrida's *Memoirs of the Blind: The Self-Portrait and Other Ruins* (first published in French in 1990 as *Mémoires d'aveugle: L'autoportrait et autres ruines*) and Jean-Luc Nancy's *The Pleasure in Drawing* (first published in

French in 2007 as *Le Plaisir du dessin*). Furthermore, despite the rarefied circumstances of the art exhibitions that serve as the bases for these two texts, Derrida and Nancy are not motivated by connoisseurship: the claims they make apply equally to expert drawings as they do to children's drawings.

Much has been written on the complex proximities of these two thinkers, particularly the ways in which Nancy's thinking both enters and departs from the orbit of deconstruction.[1] That Derrida and Nancy alike turn towards abstracted accounts of drawing while curating exhibitions of graphic works remains an unexamined comparative encounter. In focusing on this, I am not just motivated by the intrinsic local value of reading these texts alongside each other in the context of a broader consideration of the overlapping or diverging contours of these two philosophical projects. I am motivated too by a demand of what I have referred to in the title as a poetics of drawing, which refers rather literally to the ways in which theories of drawing lend themselves to theories of poetry. Both Derridean and Nancean versions of drawing, I will argue, sponsor such a poetics, in different but complementary ways: Derrida with what he calls the 'rhetoric of the *trait*', and Nancy through an enigmatic consideration of the rhythm of drawing. My work here will be oriented towards developing these concepts.

In terms of the wider context of this comparison, the shift from drawing to poetry may seem an abrupt veer. But, I argue, drawing, the art of non-linguistic line-making and marking, is a privileged other of poetry, the art of lineated language.[2] If the history of modern poetry is, partially, the history of its migration, as a medium, from speech to paper, then it is too a history of its increasing proximity to the graphic arts.[3] This is not just a theoretical proposition: it is a demonstrable

1 For example, see James 2014.

2 I refer to drawing as an 'other' of poetry with Jahan Ramazani's *Poetry and its Others: News, Prayer, Song, and the Dialogue of Genres* in mind. Whereas Ramazani's study gives ways in which poetry enters into dialogue with other literary and verbal genres, I argue that the field of drawing represents a privileged other of poetry, and partly for the ways in which it *resists* the kind of dialogic engagement and appropriation that Ramazani, citing Bakhtin, charts in his book (Ramazani 2013). This, in turn, demands a consideration of the possible distinction between the dialogic and the ekphrastic, which is outside of my scope here.

3 The revolution of the drawn line associated with Cézanne (the shift from one-point linear perspective to a more spontaneous perceptual perspective)

preoccupation for poets, too. Yves Bonnefoy, for example, develops the analogy in the metaphor, not of the writing-pad, but of the common ground of the blank sheet:

> drawing is less defining contours, finding their truth, than venturing into that whiteness and discovering there the precarity of all that has been acquired [...] and thus drawing near to that reality-unity that language robs us of. *In this way, the drawing, the "great" drawing, will be poetry.* (Bonnefoy 1994, 15; emphasis mine)

Bonnefoy's projection of poetry as the apotheosis of drawing comes from his predication of those two forms not on their fulfillment of certain media-specific formal requisites and limits ('defining contours'), but instead on a common epistemological sensibility, anterior to the work, towards the withdrawal of received form.

This, in turn, recalls Walter Benjamin. As we discussed in the Introduction to the book, for Benjamin, 'pure drawing', in distinction to painting, depends upon leaving parts of its 'white ground' blank (Benjamin 1996, 83). The drawing *subjects* the 'area' it appropriates as a background, in the senses of both domination and constitution (it is exactly this dual sense that Derrida develops with his distinct but comparable term for the material support of the drawing, taken from Artaud: the '*subjectile*' [see Derrida 1994]). Time and again, one of the elements that draws philosophers, poets and literary theorists to the abstraction of a pure graphic art, is this interplay with, variously, the 'whiteness', the 'writing-pad', the '*subjectile*' or the 'background': the simultaneous ground and negation of form which it, not coincidentally, shares with writing in general and poetry in particular. Nancy and Derrida pursue their versions of drawing against this backdrop.

Mémoires d'Aveugle and *Le Plaisir Au Dessin*: The Exhibitions

In the case of both of these texts, it is necessary to bear in mind their geneses as extended catalog essays. I will, therefore, begin with a brief

was broadly contemporaneous with the revolution of the poetic line as a visual element associated with Mallarmé and Apollinaire. In each case, the line is recalibrated from being a received structural device to being a plastic, decomposable instrument of expression.

overview of the exhibitions. *Mémoires d'aveugle: L'autoportrait et autres ruines* was the name of the exhibition curated by Derrida at the Louvre in 1990 as part of the gallery's *Parti-pris* ('Taking Sides') series. Each exhibition in the series was curated by, as the catalog puts it, a 'personalit[y] known for their critical abilities' (MB vii). The idea was that each invited personality would take their pick from the Louvre's graphic arts collections to assemble a discursive exhibition, meditating on the 'argumentative value' of the selected works. Underpinning this format is the notion that drawing, as a field of conceptualization in visual art, may lend its generative potential to the theoretical treatise (Hubert Damisch's exhibition was entitled, appropriately, *Traité du trait*). It is perhaps owing to the precepts of the *Parti-pris* series that Derrida's book is so literally *thematic*: a treatise on drawing and blindness that finds its visual material, mainly, in drawings of the blind.[4] Of the works exhibited, of particular note are studies of the blind by Antoine Coypel, a series of searing self-portraits by Henri Fantin-Latour, and Joseph-Benoit Suvée's *Butades, or the Origin of Drawing* (1791).

Nancy, meanwhile, curated the exhibition *Le Plaisir au dessin* with Sylvie Ramond and Eric Pagliano at Lyon's Musée des Beaux-Arts in 2007. In contrast with Derrida's exhibition, the Lyon exhibition foregrounded the graphic act itself over possibilities of representation. In keeping with this, whereas Derrida thematizes drawings of the blind, Nancy thematizes drawings of the hand (but, as Nancy seems keen to point out in the exhibition press release, he eschewed, in his curation, any overall thematization).[5] A significant proportion of the drawings exhibited are autographic, scribbly and spontaneous: the first image is an untitled 1966 ink drawing by Joan Miró, composed of four rapid strokes of varying lengths, and a few spare blobby drops. There are, too, examples of Surrealist automatism, including by its most enthusiastic practitioner, André Masson. This is mentionable because Nancy's proposal that drawing constitutes the spontaneous and libidinal inauguration of form arguably finds its most apt artistic precedents in that practice.

4 A thematization that Derrida glosses with a distinction between the 'transcendental' (the impossibility of drawing) and the 'sacrificial' (thematic art, i.e. representing the blind, which makes that impossibility visible; which *marks* it) (see MB 41).

5 In the press dossier: '*Cette exposition n'est pas non plus proprement thématique*' (Nancy 2007, 6).

Neither thinker is invested in what art historian Benjamin Buchloh, in a significant essay, calls the 'diagrammatic' turn in drawing in the wake of Cubism (Buchloh 2006, 52). Here, Buchloh seeks to shift the critical focus away from the material support—undoubtedly a preoccupation in twentieth-century Western art—and towards other dialectical frontiers. If, as Buchloh argues, drawing conforms to a dialectic between 'the authentic corporeal trace and the externally established matrix' (Buchloh 2006, 52), then Nancy and Derrida alike dispense with the latter, as well as any other notion of extrinsic interaction or dialectic, for the sake of clearing the way for a unilateral philosophy of the line considered against nothing other than the plain sheet of paper, the material support, as a stand-in for ontological ground. Both, of course, are licensed to be tendentious by the constrained format in which their narratives of drawing take place: relatively small exhibitions drawn largely from museum collections of works on paper. Notwithstanding this, central to Buchloh's argument is the claim that the diagrammatic has been historically occluded in favor of, among other prominent, epistemic motifs, 'mimesis of libido' (Buchloh 2006, 52), a phrase which provides as good a description as any for what Nancy sets about recuperating for drawing in his essay. This is to say that, like Benjamin's, Nancy and Derrida's basis for thinking drawing is rather lacking in art-historical perspicacity, but in any case, they are less interested in drawing's place in visual art than they are in a fundamental and original relations to writing, language and signification.

Derrida and the Origin of Drawing

Derrida's writing on drawing orbits Pliny's myth of Butades, the same scene as that depicted in the Suvée painting. As Derrida will develop, this provides a model of the graphic line—or *trait*—as both a traced outline and the mark of an affect or intention. The Plinian origin of drawing is thus essentially and acutely melancholic, in the sense that, as Agamben succinctly defines it, 'melancholy offers the paradox of an intention to mourn that precedes and anticipates the loss of the object' (Agamben 1993, 20). Drawing thus becomes an anticipatory marking of melancholy that persists after the loss of the object.

Derrida's first encounter with the Plinian scene comes via his reading of Rousseau in *Of Grammatology*. As Derrida notices, Pliny lies behind Rousseau's aphorism, early in the *Essay on the Origin of Languages*, that '[l]ove […] is the inventor of drawing' (Rousseau 1998, 290). Rousseau's broader point, famously, is that gesture originates from need and language originates from passion.[6] Butades' daughter thus presents a kind of intermediate expression, between need and passion: neither pure gesture nor language, but a gestural inscription that, if not forming the basis of language, at least elicits or creates the conditions for imagined or supposed linguistic equivalents. Rousseau evokes this trajectory in a passage that is important for Derrida's reading: 'How she could say things to her beloved, who traced his shadow with such pleasure! What sounds might she use to work such magic! [*Quels sons eût-elle employés pour rendre ce mouvement de baguette?*]' (Rousseau 290, 6).[7]

As an indexical trace, drawing seems as indicative of the possibility of language as it is of the phenomenal appearance that it seeks, melancholically, to reproduce in outline. It is this twofold quality of the *trait* that Derrida lingers on, although, inevitably, it is less an indicative capacity than it is an indicative incapacity. Derrida writes at length about Rousseau's rendering of the Plinian scene as the 'origin of the sign', where the twofold incapacity is staged as the coincidence of the twofold activity of tracing and marking:[8]

> The movement of the magic wand [in French, *baguette*—i.e., stick, stylus] that traces with so much pleasure does not fall outside of the body. […] It is of course still an image which is traced at the tip of the wand [*au bout de la baguette*], but an image that is not completely separated from the person it represents […] The distance from the shadow or from the wand is almost nothing [*n'est presque*

6 The Plinian drawing, as an expression of passion that is *not* linguistic, therefore sits incongruously within Rousseau's theory—as Bernard Vouilloux points out: 'What is remarkable about this argument is that it maintains an apparently contradictory relationship with its context' (Vouilloux 1994, 175).

7 English translations of the passage in Rousseau tend to render *baguette*, which could just as well be translated as stick or stylus, as 'magic wand', as though to emphasize the virtual or subjunctive nature of the '*sons*'. I point this out because the translation of Rousseau appears to be the root of the misleading rendering, throughout Spivak's translations of *De la grammatologie*, of '*baguette*' as 'magic wand', which elides the literal or technical dimensions of drawing in favor of virtual dimensions.

8 Michael Newman explores the theoretical distinctions between tracing and marking throughout 'The Marks, Traces, and Gestures of Drawing' (Newman 2003).

> *rien*]. She who traces, holding, handling, now, the wand, is very close to touching what is very close to being the other it*self*, close by a minute difference [*à une infime différence*]; that small difference—visibility, spacing, death—is undoubtedly the origin of the sign and the breaking of immediacy; but it is in reducing it as much as possible that one marks the contours of signification. (Derrida 1976, 234)

The *trait* records, for Derrida, a fantasy of presence. Note that Derrida's language is not of negation, but of proximity and approximation, through the tactile figures of the tip of the *baguette* and the shadow (even the image is framed not in terms of visibility, but in terms of contiguity). Drawing, in the first instance, appears to represent the closest possible adequation of a fixing of presence. However, everything hinges on the mordant irony with which Derrida writes that the minute difference between tip and line, figure and shadow, is synonymous with nothing less than 'visibility, spacing, death', that is, the instantiation of difference itself, and the radical dissolution of wholeness that is necessary for signification. This is why drawing, for Derrida, cannot be considered akin to, say, a zero degree: while there is a scale of proximity between subject and object, there is no accompanying scale of signification: all graphic activity is equally implicated in the unlimited proliferation of supplementarity. The variable (and unpresentable) spacing between the drawer and the drawn is superseded by the invariability of spacing itself.

The possibility of 'marking' the 'contours of signification' (or the 'stroke' that opens up 'grammaticality', as Derrida puts it earlier) is distinct from the mimetic, metonymic proximity of tracing (Derrida 1976, 209). To mark implies a retrospective function, in the sense of commemoration (the French *marquer* shares this with the English verb). Whereas tracing originates from a will to reproduce the contours of a beheld object, *marking* unintentionally inscribes and commemorates an incipient formation of meaning-making *itself*, insofar as the intention to signify, rather than being realized as a presentation of the other, is realized as a kind of memorial of its own impossibility. In other words, the mark, intransitive, makes the origin of signification—the opening of form, situated here ambiguously between gesture and language, passion and need—*visible*. It abandons signification to visibility, in the same way that the drawing is an abandonment of gesture to the *trait*.

This abandonment is what Michael Newman, writing in a deconstructive mode, is developing when he formulates 'an undecidability of the relation between mark and signifier', which 'would open up the possibility of a continuity between the human and the non-human' (Newman 2003, 102). For Derrida in *Grammatology*, the significance of drawing is that the resistance to that continuity or undecidability is maintained from within by the same graphic gesture that surrenders to it. That is to say that when Derrida writes that 'Man *calls himself* man only by drawing limits excluding his other from the play of supplementarity' (Derrida 1976, 244), we should understand 'drawing' literally as much as figuratively.

I will move on to *Memoirs of the Blind*. What Derrida designates here as 'the rhetoric of the *trait*'—a rhetoric that is both proper to drawing and a product *of* it—is an expansion of the line of thought, in his reading of Rousseau, but rearticulating the deconstructive approach to graphism within the matrix of visibility, as opposed to that of contiguity. Appropriately for an exhibition catalog, the text foregrounds the act of looking. Returning to the Plinian origin, Derrida's reading of the scene is refracted not through Rousseau, but through Suvée's painting. In this reading, Butades' daughter tracing the shadow of her beloved becomes a scene of orphic aversion. Since Butades' daughter must avert her gaze from her beloved in order to trace his shadow, for Derrida, 'it is as if seeing were forbidden in order to draw, as if one drew only on the condition of not seeing, as if the drawing were a declaration of love destined for or suited to the invisibility of the other' (MB 49).

The drawing of Butades' daughter becomes an illustration of Derrida's central polemic, in *Memoirs*, that 'the heterogeneity between the thing drawn and the drawing *trait* remains abyssal' (MB 45). As an illustration of that thesis, it is, admittedly, a rather counterintuitive one, since the scene unavoidably presents the straightforward coincidence of the seen and the traced. Butades' daughter averts her eyes from her lover, but never loses sight of his shadow. The point, of course, is that there is necessarily always some displacement, in the same way that the logic of supplementarity ensures that any relation to the other cannot be extricated from an abyssal referral back to the self.[9] Derrida writes: 'Butades writes [*écrit*], and thus already loves in nostalgia' (MB 45).[10] She does not draw (*dessine*); she *writes*. if drawing proceeds as an anticipation of loss, its immediate replacement by writing takes place, in part,

9 As Michael Newman puts it in his sophisticated account of *Memoirs of the Blind*: 'there is no alterity without narcissism' (Newman 1994, 221).

10 Note that Derrida refers to Butades' daughter by the name of the father.

as an instant petrification of that anticipation into nostalgia (again, the commemoration of the mark).

Memoirs of the Blind tells various versions of this—drawing giving way to writing. Perhaps the most compelling of these events, which we touched upon in the Introduction to the book, is autobiographical. Referring to his boyhood jealousy of his brother's superior draughtsmanship, Derrida writes:

> I suffered seeing my brother's drawings on permanent display [...] As if, in place of drawing [...] I was called by another *trait*, this graphics of invisible words, this accord of time and voice that is called (the) word—or writing, scripture. A substitution, then, a clandestine exchange: one *trait* for the other, a *trait* for a *trait*. (MB 37)

Here, like Butades' daughter, Derrida writes in—and *as*—a nostalgia for drawing. His anecdote takes place on the same 'sacrificial' level as the portraits of blindness assembled for the exhibition, that is, it proffers a thematic representation of an unpresentable origin, an originary substitution in the metaphor of a volitional exchange. Note how, this time, the substitution of the *trait* is a passage of recourse from the visibility of the displayed drawings through to, via a renunciation of sightedness, writing as a graphic system whose object is essentially withdrawn.

Derrida characterizes this inextricable relation between drawing and writing, via the *trait*, as a rhetoric for perhaps two reasons. Rhetoric implies a sustained reliance on the substitutions of figural language as well as it implies a temporal movement of discursivity (the operative phrase being Derrida's 'accord of time and voice').[11] In these two senses, rhetoric, for Derrida, captures the quality of drawing as, itself, a figure of writing—its *trace*—and the quality of drawing as the ambivalent record of a discrete movement or gesture—its *mark*. To return to the question of non-human mark-making, in *Memoirs of the Blind*, it is precisely the rhetoric of drawing that distinguishes it from non-human marking, since drawing 'never goes without being articulated with articulation, without the order being given with words [...] Drawing

11 Derrida's gloss on the 'rhetoric of the *trait*': 'For is it not the withdrawal [*retrait*] of the line—that which draws the line back, draws it again [*retire*], at the very moment when the *trait* is drawn, when it draws away [*se tire*]—that which grants speech? [...] This question does not aim at restoring an authority of speech over sight, of word over drawing' (MB 56).

comes in the place of the name, which comes in the place of drawing: in order, like Butades, to hear oneself call the other or be called (by) the other' (MB 57). Drawing is 'articulated'—partially detached but conjoined—with articulation itself, that is, the nascent intent to signify. According to Derrida, drawing becomes less an art form than a form of address, or form *as* address: a form founded on the way in which it is co-formed with other modes of address. Here, the chiasmic relation or exchange that drawing occupies with naming—yet another graphic irruption—is a consequence of the status of drawing as, at once, the opening and abandonment (hence the 'ruin') of the possibility of address and, therefore, of an ethical encounter with the other.

The Rhythm of Drawing

Whereas Derrida broaches the domain of poetics through a shared 'graphics' of drawing and writing, Nancy modifies and extends a Heideggerian approach to drawing, inasmuch as his thought of drawing sponsors a thinking of the originary and formational movement that gives rise to all art media. Unlike Heidegger, he is, at the same time, concerned with thinking drawing *as such* (despite his reliance on figures of draughtsmanship, Heidegger omits the draughtsman from his roster of artists—not unlike Hegel's exclusion of drawing in his lectures on aesthetics, where painting is allied with *colore* only). Philosophical influence aside, *The Pleasure in Drawing* is an elaboration of a line of thought initiated by Nancy in *The Muses*, that is, defining the whole aesthetic realm according to a radical heterogeneity of arts that Nancy calls, characteristically, a '*singular plurality*' (Nancy 1996, 3). In organizing his graphic aesthetics around a Freudian principle of pleasure, Nancy rehabilitates the practical handbook cliché of drawing as a source of idle pleasure. To provide some context, the association between drawing and pleasure has significant antecedents in French art history, too; Joyce Bernstein Howell demonstrates, for example, that Eugène Delacroix established the precedent that practicing drawing can be a democratic source of pleasure for *anyone*, thereby breaking with the contemporary doxa that pleasure is experienced according to a strange polar logic, that is, either by viewers or by masters practicing their craft (see Bernstein Howell 2005, 232). That democratic ideal of availability remains present in Nancy's configuration of drawing as the humble essence of all artistic expression.

Nancy identifies the graphic impulse as the defining element of what he calls an essential 'gesture of art', where gesture might be understood as a single, unrepeatable, and necessarily somatic expression made from within a circumscribed field of possibility. As Ginette Michaud glosses it in her perceptive exposition of Nancy's text: 'drawing is the artistic gesture par excellence: an act, a passage, not as acting out, but as passage *of* the act itself, its on-the-spot actualization' (Michaud 2014, 96). Like Derrida, Nancy is drawn to drawing as an intimate performance of immediacy, as the locus of a contraction between subject and object, and as both art and act. But unlike Derrida's abyssal 'minute difference', at the tip of the stylus, Nancy's evocation of the drawing subject reproduces a version of sameness, the sameness of a body, guaranteed precisely by the technicity of the stylus. Drawing, he writes, offers 'an immanent *signifiance* [...] without the sign taking off toward the signified, but a sense that is offered right at the body [*à même le corps*]' (PD 39). Nancy is quick to clarify that his argument is not for a naive privileging of actual somatic presence: 'this gestural body is different from the organic body, without being a body without organs. Rather, it becomes the body-*organon* of art; and thus of the technique (*ars-techné*) that is in play' (PD 39). If Deleuze and Guarrati's concept of the body without organs is a *virtual* body, then Nancy's body-*organon* is distinguished as a *technical* body (the Greek *organon* referring both to the instrumentality of tools and the instrumentality of the vital organs), a body which produces and which is produced by—and which only ever exists in and as this simultaneity—a given work of art, irrespective of medium.

To a greater degree than Derrida, Nancy remains sensitive to the polysemy of the French word *dessin* as both *drawing* and *design*, and thus both form and concept. In this sense, he retains a fidelity to the Renaissance conception of *disegno*, according to which drawing was venerated as the twofold capacity of art to represent and to invent. The source of invention and creation, *disegno* was correlated with divinity; as David Rosand puts it, particularly in the case of Leonardo, '*disegno* comes to be recognized not only as the means of realizing ideas but as the very source of ideas itself' (Rosand 2002, 55). But when divorced from the religious faith in which the discourse of *disegno* is ultimately an investment, the co-determinacy of means and source, as with Nancy's body-*organon*, comes to resemble a lacuna or an event, an irruption of form, an 'opening'.

Indeed, *The Pleasure in Drawing* is, primarily, a treatise on form, where form is dynamized and temporalized in chiasmic relation with what Nancy refers to as 'force': 'the *formative force* of this very form [of drawing], or again, of the *form in its force* [...] is what constitutes the drawing of art or the art of drawing' (PD 12). All form, for Nancy, is perpetually *unfinished*: a discrete artistic form does not exist in phenomenal or aesthetic autonomy, but rather as a fleeting, fragile instance of a continual and inexhaustible emergence of sense. It is for this reason that Nancy locates a theoretical resonance in Freud's economic account of pleasure since, as he puts it, pleasure, whether libidinal or aesthetic 'comprises a renewed dynamic, revived by the desire to which it responds' (PD 17). That pleasure, and thus form, are generated by an inexhaustible cyclicality of desire and 'revival' provides the background for what Nancy will go on to call the 'rhythm' of drawing, where rhythm stands for an interruptive countermovement inherent to the formative force of drawing.

The triumvirate of rhythm, form and pleasure is well-trodden territory in the field of poetics. In his intervention into the theory of the lyric, Jonathan Culler argues that rhythm plays a supplementary role in lending the experience of reading lyric poetry a kind of embodied experience. 'Rhythm', he argues, 'gives lyric a somatic quality that novels and other extended forms lack—the visceral experience of rhythm linking it to the body—[...] and thus contributes to a different sort of pleasure' (Culler 2019, 22). While the specific kind of pleasure derived from reading poetry and 'experiencing' rhythm may be one of the criteria for a theory of lyric form, Nancy would have that pleasure, rhythm and form are connected in a more primary way. 'Rhythm', Nancy writes, prescriptively, 'whose double value of *scansion* and *schema* (*ruthmos* initially had a meaning close to "figure") could no doubt be brought to express a pulse of nascent form—should find its place in the analysis of drawing' (PD 50). In understanding *ruthmos* as a concatenation of scansion and *schema*, Nancy finds a succinct formulation for his account of graphic and aesthetic form, and one which inevitably relies for its expression on the language of poetics. Scansion, normally understood as the graphic representation of meter, becomes instead the graphic trace of rhythm itself; not the rhythm of phonetic patterns, but the rhythm of thinking and forming. Meanwhile *schema*, that is, form itself (and, in Kantian philosophy, the rule by which an intuition is correlated with an external object), comes to name the process or 'force' of formation implied by this graphic account of rhythm.

Nancy's recommendation in *The Pleasure in Drawing* of an association between drawing and rhythm develops some of his earlier work in philosophical poetics. In 'Taking Account of Poetry', collected in the 2006 volume *Multiple Arts: The Muses II*, Nancy suggests that poetry can help to uncover an 'articulation that precedes language', which 'no doubt functions as something akin to "rhythm", "cadence", "caesura", or "syncope" [...] and, at the same time, has the quality of what I would term, so as not to call it "figuration", an outline [*dessin*]' (Nancy 2006, 17). Here, Nancy anticipates the basic premise of *The Pleasure in Drawing*—an opening of sense and form that may be distinguished from linguistic structures of meaning-making and their discontents via an elaboration of the gestural, conceptual and formal qualities of drawing. Here, rhythm is allied with other terms from prosody, whose technical specificities are elided in favor of the essential way in which they each stand for an interruptive force that is necessarily both linguistic and extra-linguistic (the value of prosody for Nancy is that it places a focus on elements of speech that cut across phonetic units). Nancy goes on to extend the equivalence between rhythm and drawing in a later essay on Hölderlin, highlighting the way in which both are formed negatively: 'Rhythm is made of anti-rhythm, like the figure its outline' (Nancy 2018, 89). Crucially, the connection that Nancy draws between 'rhythm' and '*dessin*' cuts across temporal and spatial orders of form. Note, in comparison, the strikingly similar equivalence made by Ezra Pound in his *ABC of Reading*: 'Rhythm is a form cut into TIME, as a design is determined SPACE' (Pound 1934, 198).

Nancy's post-deconstructive rethinking of rhythm aims, precisely, to *re-temporalize* form, as well as it does to formalize temporality. Belonging as much to thinking as it does to the body, the generative and plural rhythm of drawing is Nancy's answer to Derrida's argument that drawing constitutes the abyssal instantiation of difference. Drawing, he writes, 'must be understood as engaging a rhythm, setting in play a beat, a differentiation, displacements, folds': between the arts, between bodies, between lines (PD 70).

Conclusion

I will work towards a conclusion by opening onto a broader consideration of how the two accounts of drawing may be put to use in a more direct analysis of poetic form—specifically, the formal unit of the line. In so doing, I am not aiming for a climactic synthesis—I hope I have already demonstrated how Derrida and Nancy's texts are theoretically distinct, and how, moreover, these texts instantiate broader differences between their thought. However, when it comes to the relation between graphic *trait* and poetic line, Derridean rhetoric and Nancean rhythm become complementary factors. As I have already suggested, a corollary of Derrida's notion of the rhetoric of the *trait* is that the irreducible possibility of the substitution of drawing by writing and vice versa is, in fact, a constitutive experience of both graphic modalities. To write is to mourn drawing, to draw is to mark possibilities of writing. Echoing his evocation of Butades' daughter writing in nostalgia, Derrida asks, 'Does one ever get over drawing, is one ever done mourning it?' (MB 39). The implication of this chronic mourning is that there remains a fundamental aesthetic question or motivation at the heart of writing. What I want to suggest is that poetry can provide a mode of writing that partakes in and formalizes this mourning (that, as it were, marks it) without overcoming it. But if we import the logic of the rhetoric of the *trait*, we might think of the form of the poem as an expression of the continuity, and thus a suspension, of what Derrida calls the 'clandestine exchange' of the graphic *trait* for the written line. Derrida writes that 'drawing always signals [...] toward the threshold where only the surroundings of the *trait* appear' (MB 54). The *trait* becomes something like the formless generator of form, the gesture that engenders form through what it excludes. The line break in the poem, meanwhile, performs an analogous function. Axiomatically, poetic form is negative, in that it derives not from the line but from the break. Poems may resist or subvert the principle of lineation, and may indeed jettison it altogether, but even in prose poems, as James Longenbach has argued, the line persists as a kind of phantom formal referent.[12] This, in turn, belongs to the same supplementary chain of negation that opposes writing to drawing in a dynamic of nostalgia or mourning. In other words, poetic lineation represents a flipside of Derrida's rhetoric of the *trait*, insofar as it is a disarticulation or decomposition of the *trait* that is inevitably articulated with it, and which inevitably refers back to it.

On the other hand, Nancy's account of rhythm foregrounds the way in which poems, like drawings, derive their organizing energy

12 On the prose poem, Longenbach argues that 'the absence of the line would not be interesting if we did not feel the possibility of its presence' (Longenbach 2008, 88), before demonstrating how lineation haunts John Ashbery's prose poem 'Retro'.

or 'formative force' from the dynamic accretion of finite lines. Nancy addresses the poetic line directly in an interview with Emmanuel Laugier, employing the distinctly Heideggerian metaphor of field-tilling to characterize the movements of what he refers to as verse: '*versus*, the reversal of the plough at the edge of the field and the verses as furrows that turn back when they reach the enclosure' (Nancy 2018, 114). For Nancy, the finitude of the line literally signifies our own finitude as mortals. Beyond the particularities of meter, we feel, and view, the rhythm of poetry as such: 'The verse allows death to be heard at the point of the break, the terminus of the line' (Nancy 2018, 115). This does not predicate the line on its verbal or syntactic qualities but, instead, on its nonverbal, non-syntactic qualities. To avail myself of one of the double-values that both Derrida and Nancy exploit in their respective essays—the French word *retrait*, which signifies withdrawal or retreat, as well as the re-inscription of the *trait* (PD 73)—the poetic line is a form of *retrait*. Enjambment enacts—or figures—the supersession of the *trait* by the poetic line, while at the same time re-inscribing the logic of the *trait* as a mark of finitude.

To return to the discussion I initiated in the introductory section of this essay, graphic and poetic line are, in a sense, antithetical. Lineated writing subsumes the graphic line and, conversely, the graphic line—Klee's 'active line on a walk, moving freely, without goal'—mocks, in its activity, the syntactic constraints of lineated writing (Klee 1953, 16). This, in turn, implies an expanded field, according to which poetry is no longer the opposite of prose—*drawing is.* Poetry, instead, occupies a position that is not quite intermediary, but is a mode of writing that interrupts, decomposes, and makes a virtue of linearization, and in so doing provides visual and rhythmic figurations of the kind of aspects of drawing that Derrida and Nancy both dwell on. Here, finally, 'rhetoric' and 'rhythm' can be re-appropriated to refer to the ways in which the poetic line functions as an ambiguously figurative unit: figurative, in the case of Derrida's rhetoric, of the continuity between drawing and writing; and conversely, in the case of Nancy's rhythm, of finitude—a finitude that is figured by the recurring termination of lines. In this sense, rhetoric and rhythm, continuity and finitude, correspond to the twofold movement of extension and interruption that defines poetic lineation.

CHAPTER SEVEN

Anne Carson: *Still Drawing*

Titles and Drama

Titles are supposed to convey a basic outline of the objects to which they refer. That's why it can be so perplexing when we struggle to see, or rationalize for ourselves, a clear connection between a title given by a child and the lines that they have drawn on a sheet of paper. In one psychological study, Paul Bloom and Lori Markson argue that 'it is hard to tell whether a child who names a picture "birdie" is actually viewing the picture as a representation of a bird, or is merely making a random comment' (Bloom and Markson 1998, 200).

This causal confusion connects to a much wider question about the relationship between works and their titles in general. *Moby-Dick: or, the Whale*, for example, is certainly a novel about a whale named Moby Dick, but names always occupy a spectrum with non-sequiturs, and titles of literary works (consider, for example, Wallace Stevens' absurdly named poem of desire and mortality, 'Le Monocle de Mon Oncle') can become a site for a very similar order of puzzlement that academic psychologists encounter the moment a two-year-old calls a distinctly unbirdlike scribble 'birdie'. Indeed, Bloom and Markson regard the child's act of naming their drawing as the mark of a particularly *aesthetic* impulse.[1] To bestow a title halos the drawing as a unique and proprietary object that is irreducible to whatever externality it might

1 They argue that three year olds and artists show the same 'metaphysical commitment' to their titles: 'When shown two of their own pictures that are virtually identical in form, children believe that the pictures should be treated differently and should get different names, much the same way as many artists

represent. In the Introduction to the book, we considered the tendency for some drawing children 'to declare completion' (Pinto et al. 2011, 236). Titles operate like declarations of completion. In fact, the title becomes a way of erecting a boundary between the integrity of the work and the world outside of it. In the context of literary objects, titles, as names which are given to works and which thereby constitute them as works, draw our attention to the creative agency of the writer as a distinct and biographical subject. The title is the social interface of the work; it is the only part of the work that is directly communicative.

In one of the substantial developmental studies of child drawing of the 1980s, Joseph Di Leo points out that pre-school children are likely to cycle through an array of titles, only settling arbitrarily ('as the figure is developed', he writes, 'it may undergo a series of appellations' [Di Leo 2013, 5]). As the social interface of the work (whether it's a drawing or a text), the title can also be the site of a performance (and, indeed, dissimulation). A title can be the verbal shorthand children (and authors) use to exhibit their works for our *immediate* consideration, as in the oral performance that accompanies a show-and-tell session. Howard Gardner identifies a sub-type of child drawers that he terms 'dramatists'. Dramatists, he says, 'offer names—perhaps funny or silly ones, sometimes related to events that have recently transpired, at other times inspired by familiar stories or even wholly imagined ones' (Gardner 1980, 48–49). Drawing, for these children, is pleasurable because it provides an occasion for extra-textual drama and demonstration. This drama begins with a riffing on the function of the name or the title. Transposed into the realm of poetry, Wallace Stevens and his 'Monocle', indeed, might be this kind of dramatist, saying, 'look: look at what I've *called* this poem!'.[2]

Can we say that Anne Carson also belongs to this category of dramatist? Her first collection of poetry—*Short Talks* (1992)—came into being by slowly taking the place of an unpublished set of drawings. *Short Talks* was, Carson says, 'a bunch of drawings which I put titles on, and then the titles got longer and longer' (see Brockes

and art connoisseurs distinguish [Duchamp's *Fountain* from an ordinary urinal]' (Bloom and Markson 1998, 203).

2 This is relevant for Helen Vendler's reading of Stevens as a poet of desire, whose 'strategies for freshness and originality are strategies of concealment, chiefly concealment of the lyric "I"' (Vendler 1984, 44).

2006).[3] At the risk of oversizing Carson's statement into another origin myth, and while also trying to resist too strict a linear chronology of artistic development, I *do* take it as a point of entry into framing the way Carson's poetry and prose consistently relate themselves to a favored practice of drawing that orbits around and informs an art of writing. From *Short Talks* to recent work *Wrong Norma* (2024), Carson continually comes back to drawing as a point of reference and contrast, and a source of dramatism. Carson's poetry is distinctive for its playful incorporations of other media and various genres. Of course, drawing is not the only 'other' of the Carsonian image-text: her work takes in the novelistic, the operatic, the theatrical, the essayistic, and playfully explores an astonishingly wide breadth of ideas and enthusiasms, from the classical to the contemporary. But drawing remains one of the original and organizing preoccupations of her work, and, I will argue, the preoccupation that most fully synthesizes and justifies the aesthetic stances, and the continuous formal play, that characterize it.

In a well-cited 2014 interview, Carson herself says that she 'had little interest in writing as a child but did drawings all the time and still seem to approach *writing as a very complicated, rule-bounded form of drawing*' (Constantine 2014, 37; emphasis mine). How, this chapter will ask, should we understand this peculiar kind of graphic displacement or substitution, and its subsequent turns and loops in subsequent works by Carson? What does it mean, from a developmental and literary perspective, to take seriously this idea that Carson's works are *still* drawings, or forms of drawing, continuous with the drawings of childhood? What kind of still-ness is this?

Short Talks is made up of brief prose poems called 'short talks'.[4] The form of the 'short talk' translates into a particular kind of performative

3 Readers might have encountered child artists whose spoken titles for their drawings spontaneously evolve into narrative or theoretical digressions, into short talks that outstrip their original graphic referents.

4 This is classic Carson. She has a tendency to coin new genres and forms, to categorize her works with provisional or repurposed labels (again, the proprietorial activity of the drawing dramatist). As well as the 'short talk', her work gives us a new poetic form that she calls 'tangos' (in *The Beauty of the Husband* 2001), and many other examples of idiosyncratic forms. Carson's experimentation with new generic coinages is, to my mind, akin to the child's act of naming and claiming 'completion' of their drawing: to claim completion is an ambivalent gesture since it is to say this is *mine*, while it is also to bequeath the text of the drawing to a world that might receive and make something of it.

or dramatic literary experience that plays with the desires, affects and abstractive energies of a drawing practice. 'Short Talk on the Rules of Perspective', for example, returns us to the familiar scene of Braque's atelier that we encountered in Chapter 4. 'Braque rejected perspective'. Carson writes, 'Why? Someone who spends his life drawing profiles will end up believing that man has one eye, Braque felt. Braque wanted to take full possession of objects' (Carson 2019, 43).

It is a prose poem about Cubism. When we think about connectivities between Cubism and the prose poem, we might well be reminded of Gertrude Stein. But Carson is doing something very different to Stein. She is using the linework (the playful interaction of sentences that are sometimes in harmony and sequence, and sometimes disruptive of harmony and sequence) afforded by the prose poem's elevation of syntax to sketch out a direct but impressionistic *reading* of Braque that questions itself as it asserts its descriptions. Note how it is a *sketch* of Braque too, insofar as it makes wholesale assertions about what Braque *felt*, what Braque *wanted*, a personal, internal construction of what 'Braque', as a word, refers to.

Several other poems in the collection thematize drawing and linework for similar ends: 'Short Talk on Housing', 'Short Talk on Major and Minor', 'Short Talk on the End', and most obviously 'Short Talk on His Draughtsmanship', which we will look at in more detail toward the end of this chapter. In the 'Short Talk on Reading', Carson takes us back to a childhood scene of reading *Madame Bovary* on a trip with her father: 'I glimpsed the stupendous clear-cut shoulders of the Rockies', she writes, 'from between paragraphs of *Madame Bovary* [...] Since those days I do not look at hair on female flesh without thinking, Deciduous?' (Carson 2019, 54). Here, Carson is staging an embodied experience of beholding the text and casting her eyes between the text and the world that is passing by outside of the text. This is what drawers do when they are drawing a still life, casting their eyes between the paper and the outside of the paper. As Derrida explores in *Memoirs*, mimetic drawing emerges directly out of a pendulum-like attention that swings back and forth between close observation and mark-making. As this 'short talk' suggests, Carson models her own theory of literary experience that shapes itself in the paper-space constructed by ludic expressivity that roves between the objects (usually two contrasting objects, as we will see) that command its attention. I will develop this, further in the chapter, by returning to Carson's book *Eros the Bittersweet: An Essay* (1986), where Carson comes closest to formulating a theory of literary experience based upon a private interaction with marks made and traced upon a page.

Elsewhere in this book, we have considered the ways in which child drawing opens onto speech and naming. A child draws a shrimp and says 'it's a shrimp!'; that's what Gardner calls a dramatist. By an analogous connection, Carson's work is full of erudite gags and punchline rhythms that work best delivered in front of an audience. I have been struck personally by how much Carson's readings feel like stand-up comedy. Her work is garrulous and warm. Now, in general, critical studies that address the *visual* dimensions of poetry (like the current study) often struggle to know what to make of the poetry's overriding historic oral and aural dimensions. This is also the case with Carson. But when we view the role of drawing in Carson's work through the framework of child drawing, and specifically against the concept of an extra-textual 'dramatism' that child drawing often involves, we are better equipped to understand better an original relationship between the page and the performance in Carson's poetics.

Men Who Draw: Hokusai contra Audubon

Men in the Off Hours (2000) is one of Carson's more eclectic, scrapbook-like collections, which experiments across a range of idiosyncratic genres, in particular its essays and poem-cycles that stage deliberately incongruous two-handed intertextual combinations (Virginia Woolf and Thucydides, Edward Hopper and St. Augustine). As ever, Carson uses the space of the page to theorize and develop her account of literary experience, the genesis of which we have already begun to trace in *Short Talks*, and which we will continue to trace further on through *Eros*.

But first, I will focus specifically on the two complementary poems from *Men in the Off Hours*, 'Hokusai' and 'Audubon', which present two contrasting images of draughtsmanship (specifically, as we will see, draughts-*man*-ship). 'Hokusai' is a lyrical portrait of the renowned Japanese painter and printmaker of the Edo period. Carson knows that in his later years, Hokusai produced studies of Chinese lions (*shishi*) every day, in what he believed was an apotropaic, life-lengthening routine. He called them his *Daily Exorcisms* (for more on this, see Coliron 2005, 224). We know Carson knows this, because in the poem, the aged Hokusai goes on making his drawing while *literal* lions jump and crash around outside his hut. 'I continue to draw / hoping for / a peaceful day' (Carson 2000, 16), Hokusai says.

Except for 'died', the figure of Hokusai commands only two verbs in this short poem: 'said' and 'made'. He says and he makes and he dies. Carson's Hokusai speaks economically of his drawings and his intentions in relation to them ('Time to do my drawings' [Carson 2000, 15]). The poem is a complex play with visual and verbal metaphors, since Carson literalizes and materializes Hokusai's lions in a carnivalesque ecology that envelopes the old printmaker, pointedly overspilling any arbitrary nature–culture demarcation (the lions are said to cross a 'snowy road', alighting on Hokusai's hut). This ecology is linked and networked via a profusion of causal actions: winds come 'gusting', and the lions come along like a kind of riotous plague: they 'swayed', 'leapt', 'crashed' and thudded' (Carson 2000, 15–16). There is a disproportion between the almost quantum dynamism of the clashing relations that are unfolding around Hokusai, and Hokusai himself, who is the still but displaced center of the poem, and who orients and girds himself by and through his drawing. So absurdly unconstrained is the movement of the lions that they are capable even of 'mauling stars' (Carson 2000, 15). Drawing offers a form of forbearance in the face of this chaos.

The key to reading the poem is at its most elliptical point, which is the riddle of its first two lines: 'Anger is a bitter lock. / But you can turn it' (Carson 2000, 15). What does it mean for a feeling, like anger, to be 'turned'? What kind of figure for the alteration of an affect is the *turning of a lock*? In fact: what does it even mean to turn a lock? Strictly speaking, locks aren't turned; keys are.

It is not the lock that can be turned, but anger. It can be turned, first of all, into a simple descriptive image like 'bitter lock' (metaphor as materialization and catharsis). The verb 'to turn' denotes both to transform and to change orientation, and here it is used intransitively. Anger can be altered in its orientation. Indeed, all affects are mutable orientations: simple descriptive images like 'bitter lock', like the act of drawing a lion, do not unlock or alter substantively, but they alter an orientation, they provide a new turn.

Turning a lock is a metonym for drawing a drawing, as a constraint on orientational movement (one turns a lock somewhere between one and three hundred and sixty degrees; one draws a drawing as much as the page allows). This is typical: Carson is often interested in limitations of movement and in the limited possibilities of linear reconfigurations. We see this elsewhere, for example, in her catechistic exegesis on Samuel

Beckett's pared-back play *Quad* in *Decreation* (2006): 'Clear marks', she writes, 'tilt and run on the plate never exasperated, never clumsy, never cruel' (Carson 2006, 119). And we also see it, in a different way, in the implicit constraints involved in her intertextual experiments. She limits her repertoire of reference and orientates among them as variously as she can. We see it here in the figure of the locked lock, turn-able by degrees. Another way of thinking about this: Carson works by demarcating what Gregory Bateson calls 'play frames' (Bateson 1985, 139). It is the playfulness of Carson's negotiations of literary experience in and as poems, essays, operas, and undefinable generic experiments that constantly gesture to an extra-literary outside, because play draws attention to itself as a suspension of some default state of affairs that exists outside of its demarcated space. The two-dimensional space of the page, and of the sheet of paper, is one particularly potent element that suggests this. In the case of Hokusai, drawing does nothing: it does not unlock, or reveal something behind the surface. But in its simplicity of expressive action, it re-orientates and turns. Hokusai sees the lions differently, and anger becomes something else, as he hopes for that peaceful day.

The poem 'Audubon' takes as its subject the nineteenth-century French-American ornithologist John James Audubon, who was most famous for his intricate hand-colored prints, published as *The Birds of America* (published as a series between 1827 and 1838). 'Audubon' begins in characteristic deadpan. 'Audubon', Carson writes, 'perfected a new way of drawing birds that he called his' (Carson 2000, 17). As Carson notes, the phrase 'drawn from nature', for Audubon, meant that he took the birds 'home to stuff and paint them' (Carson 2000, 17). Like 'Hokusai', the poem playfully traverses literal and figurative registers. Carson's Audubon is an unsophisticated literalist: he literally draws (he takes).

The contrast between Audubon and Hokusai is immediately apparent. For Hokusai, drawing is a retreat from, and ward against, a perceived naturalized violence that is conceptualized as encroaching upon cultural experience. For Audubon, what Carson calls drawing is itself an act of violence, an incorporative, murderous extraction from a field of nature into an arena of culture whose end is both epistemological and queasily decorative. This schematic contrast is, indeed, intended, and is thematized explicitly: Audubon's drawing, Carson writes, is 'the opposite of a peaceful day in Hokusai' (Carson 2000, 18).

As with 'Hokusai', the key to reading this poem lies in the movement of turning. In a subtle echo of the earlier poem, 'Audubon' repurposes the movement of turning to describe the experience of viewing one of Audubon's drawings (which are, in fact, not drawings, but vivid watercolors): 'Audubon colors dive in through your retina / [...] Until you turn away. /And you do turn away. /There is nothing to see' (Carson 2000, 17). Because of Carson's economy, we have to make an effort to tease out the logic of the poem. On one level, of course one does turn away from any textual experience. One always turns away from a book. But turning away here seems to be noteworthy because it is motivated by a lack of satisfaction, and perhaps an attendant sense of aversion or revulsion. Audubon's watercolors fail to satisfy, and they fail to satisfy presumably because they are the product of a violent manipulation of nature. They don't show birds, but birds as killed, stuffed and posed by an alleged naturalist, and so mutilated prior even to the act of visual mimesis.

But there is more going on here. The 'you' in this poem is a specific kind of readerly address; it is neither directive nor crudely universalizing, but it is Carson figuring her own, intimate and individual response to a reading of Audubon's *The Birds of America* in such a way that is opened up to a shared response, that is, which encourages readers to measure their own affective experiences of reading with Carson's. When Carson describes her own experiences of texts, while they are often couched in an imperative mode, she is not being prescriptive, but *demonstrative*. Carson's use of 'you' to refer to her own textual experience of Audubon's watercolors provides a kind of benchmark by which we might recognize or measure our own readerly habits and affective responses.

Now to the question of why Carson frames both Hokusai's lions (which were in some cases sketches, and in other cases paintings) and Audubon's watercolors as drawings. Neither are best or most accurately described as drawings. It is because drawing is a privileged form of visual expression in Carson's oeuvre, for two reasons. First, drawing, and the discourse of drawing, is the visual mode that is most intimately involved in the Carsonian image-text. Carson, as we have been discussing, is a drawer. But she is also characteristically taken with the origins and valences of words, and 'drawing' implies a movement, a movement of extraction and acquisition. Second, Carson joins the litany of artists and philosophers who reflexively regard drawing as being, if we can risk putting it this way, ontologically constitutive of the formal transactions and relations that occur between inner and outer experience when a visual representation is 'wrested' onto a surface (to use a Heideggerian word). Both 'Hokusai' and 'Audubon' explore variations on the Heideggerian notion of the rending of a relationship between 'world' (one's way of experiencing materiality and converting it into form), and 'earth' (the materiality in and among which one finds one's way).

Indeed, there is a real utility to the Heideggerian schema here, since we might characterize 'Hokusai' precisely as a poem of *world* (that is, understood as the opening up of an imaginative or aesthetic space that responds to felt material circumstances) and 'Audubon' as a poem of *earth* (understood as the crude manipulation of material circumstances that fails to achieve any imaginative or aesthetic conversion). With 'Hokusai', the creative and metaphoric work of drawing creates its own space of formal play and its own, self-impelling affect of hope (because it displaces and transforms the affects that inform it through the playful work it carries out). Hokusai creates a world of figures that offers recourse to his states of feeling. This is why one is able to 'turn' the lock, to turn *within*, to create new orientational states. With 'Audubon', one must turn *away*, because the work of drawing is corrupted by a crude and literalist violence; Audubon's work fails to transcend the circumstances of Audubon's killing and taxonomizing of real birds. Furthermore, to recall our earlier discussion of philosophical accounts of drawing as the imbrication of desire and theory, we observe that Hokusai represents drawing as *desire:* the desire for longevity, a desire for peace, whereas 'Audubon' represents drawing as theory, as observational abstraction. This observation is crucial for understanding where Carson finds her *self*, the self of her poetry, in relation to these two draughtsmen.

Two-handed comparisons allow Carson to mimic the pendulum-like attention of mimetic drawing. They also evoke an unconscious image of the two hands, holding up two objects and weighing them against each other. In the 'Note on Method' to her *Economy of the Unlost*, her comparative study of Simonides of Keos and Paul Celan, Carson writes: 'Attention is a task we share, you and I. To keep attention strong means to keep it from settling. Partly for this reason I have chosen to talk about two men at once' (Carson 1999, viii). Comparison is a means of agitating the attention, and appears to be a means too of evading a fixed subject position and instead *to share* that subject position with a reader who is following along and identifying in the back-and-forth movement between one object and another. But Carson reminds us too that textual comparison, and the forms of literary experience that produce it, are peculiarly embodied activities. Recall Kant on the notion of orientation, noting the felt difference between his left and right hands and how this felt difference extends into a sense of dimensional orientation (behind the comparison of two texts is the metonym of two hands).

A comparison of two figures like Hokusai and Audubon creates a nodal relation among an apprehending body and the textual coordinates that it has encountered. In *Men in the Off Hours*, Carson is interested in the gaps and interstices, the 'shadows' that occur in relation to the negotiation and co-ordination of diverse texts and authorships. These might be the feeling of dissatisfaction, the shortfalls of meaning, the readerly confusions that arise through reading and engaging with texts, but also the tensions that arise when a reading of one text recalls or inflects the reading of another. When it comes to the opposition between Hokusai and Audubon, Carson's sympathies are undoubtedly with Hokusai. But I want to avoid the language of competition here. Carson's tendentiousness, her preference for one writer over another, is never absolute or unqualified, and this, again, is one of the reasons for the privileged figurative position of drawing in her writing. Drawing is open to revision, to the addition of new lines, and it therefore provides Carson with a model of intertextual representation that eschews any fixing of value or hypostasis of preference. And it also enables Carson to figure her own yoking together of theory and desire in the same movement: the precision and lucidity of her interpretive insights and philosophical improvisations on moments of reading, and the way in which these insights and extrapolations are intimately interwoven with singular moments of readerly affection, sentiment or association.

Finally, Hokusai and Audubon are both men, and drawing is coded as a kind of male-claimed leisure activity (and, in relation to the 'on' activity of writing, for Carson drawing is especially conceptualized as something one does during the off hours). *Men in the Off Hours* begins with the prose poem essay 'Ordinary Time: Virginia Woolf and Thucydides on War', and it concludes by observing of Woolf's short story 'The Mark on the Wall' that '[e]ven in the off hours, men know marks' (Carson 2000, 7). We can certainly read a resonance here in the mark-making of men like Hokusai and Audubon, both of whom make marks in order to attain some kind of stable foothold in relation to epistemological uncertainty.

Carson's embrace of drawing, and her own practice of drawing, often stages itself as a feminist reclamation of drawing or mark-making from, at their worst, the violent epistemophilic and priapic instincts and tendencies of male graphism (we discussed these in Chapter 2). As

I noted earlier, Carson's oeuvre is full of draughts-*men*. *Economy of the Unlost*, for example, begins: 'Whether we are commending a mathematician for her proof or a *draughtsman for his use of line* [...], economy is a trope of intellectual, aesthetic and moral value' (Carson 1999, 3; emphasis mine).

In *Short Talks*, specifically in 'Short Talk on His Draughtsmanship' (and note how this first prominent reference to drawing in Carson's oeuvre is preceded by the male possessive), the draughtsman of Carson's talk uses drawing as a means of directing the female speaker of the poem, while also assuming a position of pedagogical mastery over and through the practice of drawing. He draws the speaker of the poem in order to instruct her on 'his draughtsmanship': 'Follow the lines, he would say, watch the surroundings' (Carson 2019, 32). But when '[d]escribing shadows'—that is, the *negative* areas of darkness cast by, and on, the body of the female subject—the draughtsman of the poem 'grew small, rascally' (Carson 2019, 32). That is how the poem mysteriously concludes. To grow both small and rascally is to appear diminished, but also to attempt to exercise one's power in a way commensurate with one's accepted diminishments. 'Rascally' makes a marked contrast with the self-possessed pedagogue that the draughtsman appears to be when the poem begins. Rascals are the opposite of teachers: the word derives from the old French *rascaille*, meaning rabble or mob.

Again, male draughtsmanship is linked to an effort to know and to control, in this case to know and to control the female speaker of the poem. There is a change in the draughtsman's behavior when describing shadows (and note that 'to describe' means both to draw and to represent verbally), because shadows, like the shadow in the myth of Butades, do not offer objectal material to be traced and delineated, but instead force one to confront the way in which objectal material is contingent upon its positional relations to sources of light and to other objects. Note too that if we take 'to describe' at its most literal denotation (*to outline*) then there is a tension here: shadows are sooner hatched or cross-hatched than they are outlined or described. The draughtsman is, perhaps, verbally describing because the objectal impulse of his draughtsmanship has reached a limit. He shifts into verbal description because he has reached the limit of his graphic abilities. This is yet another example in Carson's work of the threshold and mutual horizon between drawing and writing, couched in terms of patriarchal power.

Surface and Temporality

An expanding field of Carson scholarship has theorized and interpreted the intermedial / mixed media or 'inter-artistic' aspects of her work, including but not limited to its privileging of drawing. Among this field of scholarship, most critical approaches to the 'graphic nexus' between writing and drawing (as forms and as habits) tend to rely upon art-historical accounts of drawing as the primary means of constructing pictorial perspective (that is, as affording a particular and particularly refined perspective that the writer can simulate or deconstruct). In one probing article, Arturo Cisneros Poireth asks a very similar question to the one that I am posing in this chapter: 'How to read her poems as drawings? What kind of drawings are they?' (Cisneros Poireth 2022, 224). With a focus on *Men in the Off Hours*, Poireth's argument is that Carson's poetry 'emulates that of a draughtswoman and which is focussed on three actions: seeing, thinking, and translating', claiming that 'while [Carson's poems] are seeing they are also questioning visible appearances' (Cisneros Poireth 2022, 229). For Poireth, drawing provides a model for literary mimesis because it is produced from a reactive and engaged stance of situated interrogation that unfolds through time.

As Poireth astutely suggests, in Carson's work there is a consistent overscoring of the opaque and two-dimensional materiality of the page as the site of literary experience. 'The physicality of the poem', Poireth writes, 'is conveyed as an object or surface that leaves an impression on the mind of the reader' (Cisneros Poireth 2022, 223). Others too have noted the surficial quality of Carson's work. Helen Van Praet likens Carson's page to a screen and characterizes her work as 'fully exploit[ing]' the 'material—often visual—component of literature, which heightens an embodied reading process that encourages alternative, more affective forms of knowledge' (Van Praet 2023, 3). In an article on the *medium* of Carson's poetry, Al Bell reads *Autobiography of Red* as a poetic object that 'oscillates between a surface for the representation of sensations and a vehicle for their sharing' (Bell 2022, 1064).

Carson's work often offers textual surfaces that are self-consciously like drawings: as portable play surfaces that are exchanged and gifted, held and beheld, and commented upon. At its purest and most literal, we see this foregrounding of paper-bound materiality of literary experience in a text like Carson's 2021 *H of H Playbook*, an experimental reimagining of *Herakles*, which takes the form of a scrapbook and includes many drawings and collages. We could say, turning back to some of the lines of thought from Chapter 4, that *H of H Playbook* subjects the text of *Herakles* to the *atelier* process. Choice fragments of prose and verse are literally cut and pasted alongside drawings. But perhaps the most pertinent element of *H of H Playbook* is neither its fragments of language nor its drawings, but the way in which it is bookended, front and back, by three blank pages of varying widths. The first page in the sequence is half a page, appearing ripped; the second, three-quarters of a page, is also ripped; and the third, a full-length page with a clean edge (see Carson 2021a, front matter). This arrangement, resembling a staircase or a three-tiered threshold, elongates as one turns the pages, marking a physical route into and out of the book. With such a tactile device, Carson simply draws attention to the embodied act of reading, as a negotiation of and through material: page becomes paper.

As the blank pages at the start of the book get progressively wider, Carson prepares the reader, even before a written or drawn line has appeared, for a structural principle of linear progression. Three consecutive pages of increasing length is a wordless narrative in paper. The fact that the same structure repeats at the *end* of the text throws the self-containment of this linear, progressive structure into doubt. Carson wields the materiality of the text as a strategy against linear, temporal narrativization. In a reverse of the origin story of *Short Talks*, in Carson's recent prose piece 'Flaubert Again', the 'she' of the poem starts out trying to write a Flaubertian 'book about nothing', a 'story [...] just telling itself' (Carson 2024, 44) and ends up instead with 'sketches in a sketchbook' (Carson 2024, 47). When, in the introduction to *Short Talks*, Carson writes, somewhat elliptically, 'The marks construct an instant of nature gradually, without the boredom of a story. I emphasize this' (Carson 2019, 23), the incremental, paper-based nature of mark-making (drawing or poetry, or poetry as a form of drawing) is being opposed to the 'boredom' of narrativity. The pendulum is always swinging.

Elsewhere, studies of the relationship between Carson's writing process and its repressions and reflections of drawing frequently focus, unsurprisingly, on Carson's notably ekphrastic poem '*Seated Figure with Red Angle*' (1988) by Betty Goodwin'. The drawing by Goodwin that gives Carson's poem its title and object was one of a series that depict scenes of interrogation and torture as a response to South American dictatorships. The grammatical conceit of the poem is that it is comprised of a series of halted conditional sentences that forego an apodosis (in other words, a clause that begins with 'then'), for example; 'If you had the idea of interrogation' (Carson 2006, 97). Other critics have read this poem as an attempt at intermedial translation that does not just seek to find a poetic means of responding to and representing a *specific* artwork (i.e. Betty Goodwin's drawing), but a poetic means of finding a grammar that in some way translates the action and form of *drawing itself.* In an excellent article on what she calls Carson's 'radical ekphrasis', Monique Tschofen reads this grammar as 'in the spirit of drawing: exploratory, experimental, and like her grammatical form, conditional' (Tschofen 2013, 240). The poem thereby, she claims, 'enters into a relationship of reciprocity with the drawing to offer a new image *of thought*, an image of that which cannot be *pictured*, which it presents as gifts' (Tschofen 2013, 240). Elizabeth Sarah Coles, similarly, reads '*Seated Figure*' as 'coin[ing] a grammar of *pure interpretive energy* in the form of deliberately inconsequential, often counterintuitive perceptions' (Coles 2023, 137; emphasis mine).

'*Seated Figure*' indeed finds a distinctive, distilled syntax (in its distillation of a 'pure interpretive energy') for something that is by and large true of Carson's work taken as a whole, which is that she endeavors to *space* language on the page in a way that resists, again, the inherent narrativizing movement of writing in its linearity. By constructing a poem from a non-sequential set of conditional sentences that are all conditions without consequences, Carson achieves a dynamic stillness. Let's recall Tim Ingold's point that writing, as linearization, is the 'death of the line', a 'chain of point-to-point connections' in which 'there is neither life nor movement' (Ingold 2016, 155). Carson, I think, shares this intuition, and works to reverse that 'death' by restoring something of the play of the line in her writing. '*Seated Figure*' shows one of her strategies in doing this, by upsetting the linear flow of grammar.

In a 2003 interview, Carson describes the classical inflections of her approach to mimesis. What 'imitation is for the ancients', Carson argues, is 'a mirroring of the activity of the thought that you had at the time that you had it, and an attempt to make that activity happen again in the mind of the listener [...] Probably that's what I'm trying to do' (McNeilly 2003, 17). And while this is an ancient idea, it also has a lot in common with what Jonathan Culler describes as the 'modern proposal' of lyric as a practice of 'thought-writing' ('writing thoughts for readers to articulate') (Culler 2015, 18). But what kind of thinking, or thought-writing, do we find in the opening pages of *H of H Playbook* and the suspended conditionals of '*Seated Figure*'? I think of it as a dynamic of pendulum-like oscillation, whereby the proximity or continuity between writing and drawing is mirrored into the proximity between writer and reader, as we saw in *Men in the Off Hours*.

To elaborate on this, note the resonances between Carson's description of her approach to mimesis with what the Renaissance scholar David Rosand calls, in *Drawing Acts: Studies in Graphic Expression*, the 'gesture of drawing'. For Rosand, drawing—over and above other visual and plastic forms—'invites the participation of the viewer; indeed, it requires such an active response for the completion of realization of its significance' (Rosand 2002, 16). He continues: '[i]nteracting with the linear configuration of the drawing, the imagination of the viewer expresses itself in a corresponding mode' (Rosand 2002, 17). This is so similar to what Carson says about her own mimesis. The novel thing about Rosand's approach, and what it can help to teach us about Carson's art, is that it does not couch drawing in terms of perspective, but in terms of the phenomenological experience of viewing a drawing and the subtle modalities of identification that are activated by such experiences. When we view a drawing, we become aware of the temporality of its making, the traces of the gestures that produced it. Drawing, as a system of mimesis, recalls us to a phantom memory of the embodied duration of its expression.

How does this track into the literary experience of a Carson text? We can consider one brief example. When we read, in '*Seated Figure*', the consecutive incomplete conditional sentences: 'If objects are not solid / If objects are much too solid' (Carson 2006, 98), we enter a kind of 'interaction' with a 'linear configuration' (to use Rosand's terms). We track the swing between two contradictory and yet equivalent lines of thinking. The absence of an apodosis in each case means that the contradiction is not consummated but left in play.

In her recent book-length study of Carson, *Anne Carson: The Glass Essayist*, Elizabeth Sarah Coles makes a compelling argument for Carson's writing as a sophisticated, 'experimental mode of scholarship': 'a decades-long reckoning with the tasks, modes, and moods of the scholar and close reader' (Coles 2023, 3). Carson, Coles writes, is interested in exploring the 'unsanctioned emotional life of scholarship' (Coles 2023, 13), through a restlessly inventive approach to new forms that overwhelmingly take as their primary impulse the critical activity of reading. I find this persuasive, and it is not my intention, nor do I view it as logically necessary, to reject Coles' vision of Carson-the-scholar with a competing, and inevitably reductive, account of Carson-the-drawer.

These positions are far from mutually exclusive.[5] Scholarship and drawing, we should remember, are both ways of *studying*. We ought to understand the abstract sophistications of scholarship and the material, playful expressivity of drawing in Carson's work as two possible ways of engaging creatively with the field of objects, artifacts and references that fall into the sightlines of Carson's study.

The title of this chapter intends to activate a productive double valence. 'Still', from the Old English *stille* (unmoving, fixed) is both an adjective that means 'calm and quiet' and an adverb that means 'up to and including the present'. The phrase 'still drawing' might refer to the fact that *one drew in the past and still draws in the present*, or it might refer to the object of a drawn still life. Carson herself has written on the polysemy of 'stillness', in a 2021 *Critical Inquiry* essay called, precisely, 'Stillness'. 'There are many stillnesses' (Carson 2021b, 22), she writes. For Carson, stillness is something that needs to be cultivated, nurtured, worked on. Twice in the essay, Carson writes that '[s]tillness takes time' (Carson 2021b, 12). Reading John Cage, Carson explains that '[i]f, according to Cage, silence is what we're not noticing, can we say that silence *noticed* is stillness' (Carson 2021b, 12). Stillness is an intentional state that arises through a focusing of the attention. We are close to the idea of meditation here. But I focus on it because it relates to a cherished idea of Carson's. Simplicity, for Carson, is something that can take time and effort. In her 2023 essay on Twombly and Catullus, she writes something similar: Twombly's 'casualness is a fiction. I suspect every smear [...] arises from long concentration and complexity' (Carson 2023b, 3). I am not so sure of this—the famously frenetic swirls of Twombly's *Bacchus* series come to mind—and I think we should take it, indeed, as an example of Carson's exegetic eccentricity. Her 'scholarly' commentary is often against the grain, and willfully so; it makes a dramatic performance of its singularity. More to the point, Carson's statement discloses a wish to subvert the narrative myth that time brings with it greater sophistication, taxonomical diversification, more layers of meaning and, indeed, the kind of maturity and cultivation that we associate with critical scholarship in the arts. (Note how the blank pages at the end of *H of H Playbook*, and the unresolved conditionals

5 I do, however, wonder if Coles' emphasis on the scholarly performativity of Carson's writing downplays an ironic, sometimes parodically mannered, approach to academic writing.

of '*Seated Figure*', similarly revel in a particular kind of bathos that is aimed at resisting redemption, closure and climax).

As we will see, from *Short Talks* to *Wrong Norma*, Carson is consistently and radically unsure of the axiom that the passage of time (whether lived out, or played out, in the identifications of literary experience) brings with it clarity, completion, epiphany or epistemological mastery. Sometimes it results in a simple, kinetic swirl and sometimes in the vacancy of a blank page.

Drawing, Writing and Self-Identity: From *Eros* to *Wrong Norma*

Carson is a habitual drawer who is wary of drawing's self-disclosures. She is wary of what her hand has to say. Writing on drawing, writing next to drawing, as a kind of dramatism in the Gardnerian sense, offers a liminal space in which the self can be veiled in play. Carson's drawing relates to her writing as both an intimate *formal* other (sharing so much and yet being incomparable, in formal terms, with poetry) and a contiguous habitual practice.

We can learn much from the example of Cy Twombly. Like Carson, Twombly was a classicist. Like Carson, his version of mimesis is one that tries to convey an expressive spontaneity that is often indexed to acts of impassioned reading. Mary Jacobus writes beautifully about this aspect of Twombly in her brilliant *Reading Cy Twombly: Poetry in Paint* (2016). And like Carson, Twombly marked out a point of overlap between spontaneous visual production and the deep history of poetry and poems.

Twombly, as Carson knows, trained himself to draw with his other hand. As Mary Jacobus tells it: '[h]is military training proceeded side by side with a project to untrain his drawing hand as it began to trace—blindly and in darkness—the (in)direction of the libidinal unconscious' (Jacobus 2016, 107). In her Twombly essay, Carson writes 'I've always disliked my own hand. Its line seems self-insistent, self-exposing, a bit bathetic [...] You cannot get away from yourself in your own hand. And yet Cy Twombly does. He found his way to a hand that is no one's, or everyone's or mythic, or just a stain left behind' (Carson 2023b, 5). Clearly, Carson is speaking enviously of Twombly. She is also staging what the alienation of Twombly's line does to the drama of critical reading. It generates a set of equal options. It could be called this, *or* that, *or* this. This—let's call it undecidability—is appealing to Carson who habitually sees the world of textual experience as offering equally appealing abstractable and attention-grabbing objects. As with her Braque, her Twombly is *her Twombly*: an abstracted internal model. As I have suggested already, we see this elsewhere in Carson's work, for example in her celebrated 'The Glass Essay', where the life and work of Emily Bronte and her 'cold young soul' (Carson 1998b, 38) is turned into a playful set of propositions. Carson compresses authorships and artists down to Luquetian internal models to be selected from and expressively figured: this is one of the ways in which her style of criticism is in this way more akin to child drawing than it is to a traditional model academic scholarship.

My focus is to explore whether Carson is doing something akin to Twombly in her style of writing: that is, finding a way of getting away from her line, getting away from her hand, finding a way of *not-drawing*. Twombly, crucially, doesn't get away from his hand by renouncing drawing altogether. He still draws, but he finds a way of drawing and not drawing at the same time. Might we understand Carson's turn to writing (as a 'complicated form of drawing') intimately related to a practice of withdrawal or self-concealment? The best way to begin to answer this question is to turn to Carson's very first book, *Eros the Bittersweet: An Essay* (1986). *Eros* suggestively considers some concerns that Carson will carry with her and explore in almost everything she writes. Let's contextualize these first. Most important is the notion that classic literature as a canon yields a rich and fixed set of opening propositions, points of entry and sources of influence that we might return to again and again in our figuring out of what it is we are doing when we direct the attention of our bodies to the production of textual meaning. In *Autobiography of Red*, the Greek lyric poet Stesichorus, for example, is described as having 'released being' (Carson 1998a, 33) (another example of Carson's tendency to turn authors into internal figures about whom playful and often grand statements can be made). Classical texts offer epochal starting points.

But these starting points are, for Carson, phantasmatic. It is not that Carson subscribes to a conservative notion of the Western canon as something that begins with Homer and plays out all the way through to contemporary poetry. To stick with *Autobiography of Red*, Carson famously characterizes the three-millennium gap between the classical period and the modern period, between Homer and Gertrude Stein, as a 'difficult interval for a poet' (Carson 1998a, 3). 'Interval' is an instructive term here. Carson indexes a playful temporal deconstruction of the canon (the coexistence of the classical and the modern) to an equivalent deconstruction of graphic expression (the coexistence of drawing and writing). She does this by activating and inhabiting forms of the interstice, the interval, the in-between; what we might otherwise call the liminal zone, and what Carson herself thinks of as an interplay of 'edges' (Carson 2023a, 39) or boundaries. The conception of literary history as a 'difficult interval' also brings Carson into the conceptual harmony with Winnicott, for whom experience is an interplay of inner and outer edges and for whom life, itself, is a kind of 'difficult interval', unresolved between a point of origin and a point of destination, neither of which can ever be fully known or possessed (her penchant for two-handed comparisons, as with Audubon and Hokusai, is another form of staging difficult intervals, that is, intervals in reading).

Eros the Bittersweet is in part concerned precisely with what we might call the origins of embodied literary experience. It provides the foundations for a theory of self that endures implicitly throughout Carson's writing and bases that theory of self on a distinctly (though implicitly) Winnicottian account of boundaries and edges. From the very beginning, Carson is invested in ideas and figures of interval and edge, outline and inline. '[T]he boundaries of time and glance and I love you', Carson writes, 'are only aftershocks of the main, inevitable boundary that creates Eros: the boundary of flesh and self between you and me' (Carson 2023a, 30). Desire is *generated* by a boundary; the pronouns 'you' and 'me' are generated by a sense of differentiation felt along that line of difference. Identity belongs to the linear movement of identification. We are back, it seems, in the territory of the Plinian origin of drawing (it is in fact a surprise that this famous scene of melancholic desire does not feature in *Eros*). Carson's language here is deceptively simple. How can it be that 'flesh' and 'self', such philosophically separate terms, come to share a singular 'boundary'? Should it not be '*boundaries* of flesh and self'? In *Eros*, Carson is probing how 'flesh' and 'self' come to be in some way lined up or coordinated, through certain privileged experiences, such as the experience of desire and, also of course, the experience of reading.

The theory of a self in relation resonates, too, with the psychoanalytic account of lived experience as an experience of transition through, and adaptation to, an orientation among thresholds and outlines between inner and outer experience (or, indeed, self and flesh). 'The self', Carson writes, 'forms at the edge of desire, and a science of self arises in the effort to leave the self behind' (Carson 2023a, 39). Carson goes on to consider, crucially, how embodied experiences differ according to their modes of expression. She writes that '[a]n individual who lives in an oral culture uses his sense differently than one who lives in a literate culture' (43), which entails 'a different conception of his body and a different conception of his self' (Carson 2023a, 43). Again, here, Carson is interested in the interplay, as opposed to the identity, of body and self. The self is tied to the body because the only way of conducting a 'science of the self' is through the embodied experience of limits. When I doodle or journal on a notepad I am extending and expressing myself—or, well, my *self*—outwardly and across a surface, but I am also encountering an edge of my body as it interfaces with an object. When Carson distinguishes oral culture from literate culture it is not that she is simply relativizing different 'conceptions' of body and self, but that she wants to think about how our understanding of body and self might be quickened or loosened if we pay closer attention to the intervals, zones of transition or interplay, that intervene among these different modalities.

This plays out in the way that Carson imagines the transition from orality to literacy. Carson considers how learning to read and write requires a narrowing and delimiting of one's attention, conceived of as a property of both the body and the self. As a constraining of the body over a material surface, Carson's description of literacy recalls us to the childhood scene from Rilke's *The Notebook of Malte Laurids Brigge* that we considered in Chapter 2: '[a]s an individual reads and writes he gradually learns to close or inhibit the input of his senses [...] [h]e resists the environment outside him by distinguishing and controlling the one inside him' (Carson 2023a, 44). To imagine the event of the historical emergence of literate culture is to theorize the birth of literary experience. This is where Carson shifts from being a kind of literary historian to being an advocate for a conception of the kind of literary experience that she wants to engender and promote through her own writing. She wants literary experience, according again to a certain logic of 'mimesis' of graphic identification, to hearken back to this scene of acquisition where the self and the body come into a narrowed, tense overlap in a focused attention on the textual surface, which is where drawing (the line) gives way to writing (the letter), and where the text emerges from the world of which it is a part (as in the 'Short Talk on Reading'). Perhaps we might call this moment, to take a phrase from Carson's 'Flaubert Again', the 'childhood sublime' (Carson 2024, 45). Carson wants every reading experience to feel like that first experience of reading:

> We read too much, write too poorly and remember too little about the delightful discomfort of learning these skills for the first time. Think how much energy, time and emotion goes into that effort of learning: it absorbs years of your life and dominates your self-esteem; it informs much of your subsequent endeavor to grasp and communicate the world. Think of the beauty of letters, and of how it feels to come to know them. (Carson 2023a, 55)

To say that audiences 'read too much' seems an odd complaint for a professional writer. But Carson is calling for a more *writerly* reading, a form of reading—and therefore a form of text—that is better at engaging the active, creative and expressive impulses of readers. But it is also a more naive form of reading insofar as it yearns for a sense of freshness and discovery (recall the Whitmanian child) as opposed to lettered familiarity. She is calling, here, for the production of texts that are better—somehow better—at recalling readers to this threshold (we can, in fact, accurately call it another 'difficult interval') where line turns to letter, where drawing is regulated into writing, where learning becomes mastery.

In other words, we can read *Eros* as an advocacy, in advance, for the kind of texts that Carson was going to go on to put together. In structural terms—'[t]hink how much energy, time and emotion'—we should also recall Carson's writing on the time and effort it takes to realize a silence scored by John Cage, or a scribble made by Cy Twombly. The point of being recalled to the difficult interval between drawing and writing is that it roots identity in states of becoming and learning rather than in firm, consistent and stable states of mastery and accomplished knowledge, and it also roots identity in points of overlap between the sensorium of the body and the epistemology of the self ('the beauty of letters, and [...] how it *feels* to come to *know* them'). For Carson, literary experience recalls the ontogenetic acquisition of literacy, a sort of tussle with marks on a material support, the emergence of significance that is akin to the line becoming the letter, 'hand' becoming the standardization of a mnemonic system of writing. This (very graphological) conception of identity is far from the *sujet supposé savoir* of the critical reader that Carson affects elsewhere.

Now we will turn to some specific examples of how this interval of writing/drawing is thematized and accomplished in Carson's work, namely in *Wrong Norma* and, again, in *Short Talks*. *Wrong Norma* begins with the elliptical narrative prose piece '1 = 1', which was originally published in *The New Yorker* in 2016. This was in the wake of the 2015 European migrant crisis, when over one million refugees, mostly Syrians, sought refuge in Europe. In this piece, an unnamed woman, referred to only as 'she' (a characteristic self-veiling or fictioning), describes her routine, reflects on her selfishness, her love of lake-swimming, and a burgeoning awareness, filtered from 'the newspapers', of a deadly refugee crisis over the Atlantic. The only other person who features in the narrative, that is, *with whom she speaks*, is an eccentric neighbor, addressed as 'Comrade Chandler'. This figure appears to be a local outsider artist and he makes chalk drawings on the sidewalk outside the house they cohabit. Chandler's drawing is untutored and naive and appears motivated by an obscure inner impulse. 'His gaze is ahead and within', Carson writes (2024, 11). That is, his attention is wholly concentrated on this inner impulse *and* on its outward expression in his chalk drawings. Chandler, 'ahead and within', is a Winnicottian man-child, an absorbed drawer, who lives out the threshold between his inner world and the outer world, and thereby provides a pronounced foil for the 'she' of the poem who is working through the ethics of the disjunct between her own demarcated world of leisure and a distant world of profound suffering.

The tension of the piece is in the relationship between this figure of Chandler (and his drawings) and the woman's reckoning with the tensions between her love of water as a space of leisure and a growing but mediated awareness of the perils experienced by desperate others in waters elsewhere. 'She' speaks to Chandler as he draws. He speaks to himself:

> He returns to chalking. *Quickenough quickenough*, muttering to himself, and something something *buttended* something [...] *Long day, Chandler*, she says to the back of his head. He's moving down the sidewalk to mark out a new drawing. Red chalk in hand, it will be a fox, he likes a fox at the end of the day. (Carson 2024, 12)

The making of the drawing is, between Chandler and the unnamed woman, a scene of strange, strained sociability. At the margins of this act of graphic creation, in which Chandler is absorbed, he chatters absorbedly to himself, and the woman records him talking to himself, and talks to him while he talks to himself. This is far from a clean and clearcut conversational exchange (note that she is looking at the back of his head; this is not a face-to-face engagement), but the drawing intervenes, laterally or obliquely, between the woman and her neighbor in a way that makes words come out, both for Chandler as he chatters to himself, and for the 'she' of the poem as she records this chattering and attempts to engage him, with partial and fragmented success. They talk 'over many months, in broken bits [...] Conversation is precarious', Carson writes (2024, 11–12).

The drawing and the conversation around it allow the 'she' of the poem and Chandler to step to the mutual edge of their own inner worlds. There are multiple parallels to be drawn between Chandler's drawing and the woman's swimming, as leisure activities (Carson, generally, is often interested in drawing as a particular kind of leisure activity, and interested in the way it takes up time). We might make a parallel between Chandler's absorption in his act of making drawings and the woman's reflections on swimming (or 'balancing along in the water' [Carson 2024, 10]). She reflects on the kind of attention involved in staying afloat: 'An application of attention, at the same time autonomic, these modes being not exclusive of one another' (Carson 2024, 10). Both the woman's swimming and Chandler's drawing deconstruct a notion of pure intentionality by erasing this boundary between fully conscious 'attention' and unconscious automatism. This is revealing because it helps us to situate Carson's ideas around poetic figuration and narrative, and the often surprising and surreal turns her writing takes: neither autonomic nor intentional (in the phenomenological sense of being conscious *of*, which is what Carson means by the 'application of attention' here), but a blurring of these two, too-absolute, modes of being. '1=1' is characteristic for the way it implicitly theorizes the subjectivity of *writing* alongside, with, or in opposition to the model of drawing. It concludes with Chandler's fox. Chandler knocks on 'her' door, and they exchange words, face-to-face. 'The finished fox drawing is under a streetlamp. It glows. He has used some sort of phosphorescent chalk' (Carson 2024, 13). She likens the drawing to a lake, the kind of lake she likes to swim in. The piece concludes: 'The fox is stroking splashlessly forward. The fox does not fail' (Carson 2024, 13).

As we have already seen her do, Carson plays with the linear elasticity of syntax to mirror a graphic style. Whereas '*Seated Figure*' used a conditional grammar to reflect the tentative or interrogative quality of the sketch, the conclusion of '1 = 1' settles into a set of short and simple declarative statements kicked off with definite articles and determinate pronouns. 'Failure' appears to be a condition of time, which drawing evades. In a moment of symmetry and submerged resolution, this recalls the very first paragraph of '1 = 1', when the women reflects on wild swimming, and the need to 'keep finding' the current as one swims: 'You can fail it with each stroke', she writes. 'What does that mean, fail it?' (Carson 2024, 9). It is a curious question, made even more curious by its displaced resolution in the form of a luminescent drawing of a fox. The question 'What does that mean?' can be both semantic—what does this phrase *signify*, or denote?—and philosophical—what is the purpose, or the value, or the significance, of this failure? We might suppose here that Carson means the transitive sense of failing—as in, to disappoint, to let down, to desert. The movement of the water is failed. But 'failure', in this context, also has an ethical implication. 'To fail' is freighted with value-judgment: it is to let down *ethically*. What does it mean, literally, 'to fail' the water? And what are the ethical implications of this failing—what does it mean to let down a current, to fail to synchronize oneself with it, to be slightly out of sync and out of place?

The resolution of the fox drawing, which 'does not fail', encourages us to view the earlier question—'What does that mean, fail it?'—as an insoluble metalinguistic conundrum. The fox does not fail because it simply is a chalk drawing on the sidewalk, and so as a mode of expression it does not bring along with it the unanswerable questions, which in Carson's imagination are stubbornly attached to creative processes of verbal signification and narration, of both semantic and moral meaning. The drawing is immune to questions of meaning. But we should also remember who has produced the drawing. Comrade Chandler seems only to draw; he seems (he *seems*) untroubled by ethical and political questions, and fully absorbed in his day-to-day routine of drawing, chattering to himself. He represents political and social withdrawal, to the point that he barely exists among others ('Comrade', as an appellation, therefore takes on an ironic register): 'he seeps away, small tide of person, noticed as a retraction' (Carson 2024, 11). What I am trying to convey here is that, for Carson, the valorization of drawing is ambivalent, and it is melancholic. Carson's writings self-consciously *want* to be drawings, but also know they cannot, and must not, be drawings. They envy drawing. They *might have been* drawings, and are aware of this liminal, almost accidental status. This is in part because Carson herself is often concerned with the origins of writing. But they also know that, as writings, they *must* fail, they must enter the question of failure. Finally, it will serve us too to remember the conceit of *Small Talks* as dramatic responses to unpublished drawings: '1 = 1', as a verbal performance, is doing something similar in relation to the fox drawing.

Let's turn to another piece in *Wrong Norma*, 'The Visitors'. The drawing of a fox returns in this piece, unexpectedly and abruptly. It returns in the same way that, in *Interpretation of Dreams*, what Freud calls the remains of the day return in the manifest content of the dream. I think that is the point, because 'The Visitors' is, in part, about Freud: 'I'd like to draw Freud with his fox. I'm not good at wings. When not drawing I am incongruous (inappropriate, inapt, improper, incompatible, irreconcilable, inconsistent, unusual, strange, alien)' (Carson 2024, 128). We might be reminded of Gladman or Ammons on 'not drawing' (or not-drawing) here. The self or 'I' that writes itself coordinates itself in relation to the drawing that it is *not* doing. If we understand writing and drawing as mutual others or flipsides, then 'not drawing', here, does not just signify negation, but writing itself, writing as the negation of drawing. It is a self-referring piece of writing. We should note, too, that Chandler, a sort of quintessential drawer, for Carson, is described as a fluid 'small tide of a person', and is therefore exactly the opposite of incongruous.

To be incongruous is to be out of place, to stick out, to fail to agree or accord. In 'The Visitors', at the metalinguistic level, it is also ironically subject to an indefinite list of synonyms with which incongruous is congruent ('irreconcilable, inconsistent', etc.). Carson, earlier in the piece, calls Roget's lists of synonyms 'analogical children of slight difference (Carson 2024, 127). 'Incongruous', as a word, is incongruous because there is no congruence among synonyms, since all are 'children of slight difference'—that is, differences in etymology, connotative and even denotative differences, differences in historical and contemporary prevalence. Being in writing, that is, being a subject in writing, in the referring traces and etymological trails of language, is to be incongruous. Let's remember, too, what Carson describes in *Eros*: the threshold between drawing and literacy. 'I' is a figure of that threshold: a simple mark, a linear unit, that marks itself off, incongruously, as the sovereign marker of linguistic identity. The easiest way to read this is that Carson's not-drawing, that is, her writing, consistently valorizes and practices incongruity (such as the displaced fox!) to the point that, indeed, willed incongruity appears to provide a basis upon which to construct and assert the integrity of an 'I'. That incongruity is always aware of its congruence with drawing.

Conclusion

In this chapter, I have conducted a series of close readings across Carson's whole oeuvre to try to demonstrate that Carson herself, in implied and explicit ways, constructs and practices a theory of literary experience in relation to a drawing practice that begins, for Carson, in childhood. I will conclude by returning to the central premise of the book. Drawing and childhood are linked metonymically. By valorizing drawing (formally, expressively, affectively and thematically), Carson gestures towards the restless stillness of an inchoate lyric subjectivity that cannot be pinned down nor patronized, but which can, for example, declare its favorites and specialisms while considering or making out new potential areas of inquiry and absorption, and which always has available to itself the minor yet world-making possibilities of line-making and line-breaking.

Coda: *Traceability*

In the catalog essay to the 1938 *They Still Draw Pictures!* exhibition, Aldous Huxley writes that 'the majority of adults have grown, not up, but quite definitely down' (Huxley 1938, 5). Similarly, in the influential 1979 drawing manual *Drawing on the Right Side of the Brain*, Betty Edwards argues that 'almost all children draw freely and confidently for several years and then the ability seems to vanish' (Edwards 1999, 6).

Everyone seems to think that most adults gradually forget how to draw; Huxley and Edwards speak of it as an almost natural phenomenon. Of course, most adults find other means of occupying (or nullifying) their imaginations, not least of all the demands of a job. There is a whole other book to be written on how the commodification of labor and an increasingly marketized and technologized society forces subjects into 'growing down'. Herbert Marcuse's thesis in *One-Dimensional Man: Studies in the Ideology of Advanced Industrial Society* (1964)—to simplify—that imagination and critical thinking are suppressed in favor of conformity and productivity, and that '[t]he distinguishing feature of advanced industrial society is its effective suffocation of the needs which demand liberation [...] while it sustains and absolves the destructive power and repressive function of the affluent society' (Marcuse 1964, 7), is still a powerful version of this idea. In a certain Marxist-inflected tradition, drawing, conceived as synonymous with the creative production of a child yet to be compelled into a life of wage labor, takes on a utopian quality. At its most rhapsodical, Alain Badiou, for example, speaks of a 'politics of drawing' that might 'institute a new world' (Badiou 2014, 82).

Of course, the argument of this book has been that perhaps, in some cases, we don't stop drawing at all, but that what we do when we draw gets displaced into other activities, above all the activity of literary experience. I have avoided settling on a single explanation for what it is we are doing when we draw, and what it is we are doing when we read or write about drawings, because I don't believe there is a single explanation. In keeping with the formalist slant of my approach, in this Coda I am going to focus instead on how drawing is structurally aligned with forgetting: with 'vanishing', with absence, with memory as a surface trace rather than an etching. Drawing, I'll argue, is imagined as a scene of resistance not despite its disappearance, but because of it.

'Disappearance' is the word the art writer and novelist John Berger chooses in a 2004 letter to the art historian James Elkins. There, he describes a 'hunch' that 'drawing is a manual activity whose aim is to abolish a principle of Disappearance' (Berger 2007, 109). Without mentioning Pliny, Berger could, of course, be describing the myth of Butades. And while he is focusing on canonical works of art, I wonder if Berger's statement is equally applicable to the world of child drawing. First, I want to elaborate a conceptual field of 'traceability'. To be traceable is different from being visible. It is to be susceptible to an outline—to reduction, to demarcation. A body can be seen without being drawn, but to be drawn is to be fixed in a particular act of observation and rendered vulnerable to the line and what it figures. I will follow this idea through a comparative reading of Berger and the poet Jorie Graham.

In 1976, Berger writes an essay, 'Drawn to that Moment', about a life drawing he made of his late father. Jorie Graham writes a poem, 'Mother's Hands Drawing Me', about a life drawing made of her by her late mother. Neither Berger (as the subject of a drawing) nor Graham (as the object of a drawing) is writing explicitly about childhood in these pieces. Yet, they are reflections on being the child *of* someone, or, to use a more technical or theoretically specific term, they are reflections on filiation. This is significant from a psychoanalytically inclined perspective, where childhood is analyzed as the experience not simply of youth, but of being related to objects, elders, to caregivers, whether alive, dead, or dying, internal or external. The examples of Berger and Graham will show us how this notion of traceability—the susceptibility to being traced and tracked down—introduces an additional metonymic relation, between the tracing of the outline and the apprehension of a genealogical relation or a relation of hierarchal orientation.

Berger joins the likes of Marianne Moore, Renee Gladman, and others we have considered throughout this book as an avid drawer who writes reflexively, beautifully and authoritatively about the nature of drawing. In 'Drawn to that Moment', he examines a drawing that he made of his recently deceased father. He pins up the drawing in his house, and he describes it in terms that recall Proustian involuntary memory. 'Instead of marking the site of a departure', Berger writes, '[the drawing] began to mark the site of an arrival. The forms, drawn, filled out. The drawing became the immediate locus of my memories of my father [...] there was now a door through which moments of a life could enter' (Berger 2007, 28). Again, we are reminded of the drawing on the wall in the myth of Butades.

We have considered how children draw as a means of entering into dialogue with their parents and caregivers; we have seen how a drawing by a child can be theorized as the demarcation of a transitional field of play in which the child can begin to adapt themselves to the porous limits of their separation. Berger's essay reads as a poignant but logical extension of this psychoanalytic framing for two reasons. Firstly, as an adult, Berger uses drawing—a drawing of his father—as a means of setting out a zone in which the father is neither alive nor dead, but the drawing is a portal through which he can return, as memory. With the theory of child drawing, the textuality of the drawing requires the interaction, most typically, of a parent (or parent-figure or surrogate). Berger's essay becomes an extension of this kind of text, establishing the father as an absent interlocutor and witness.

For Berger, something about the tracing or outline of his father creates a space for his mind to step in and 'fill' the gaps. The traceability of the father's face is double-edged: one can remember the father, as a form, but at the same time one is reminded of everything that is excluded by this outlining. Berger frames graphic representation as an interrogative activity: '[a] drawing', he writes, '*slowly questions* an event's appearance and in doing so reminds us that appearances are always a construction with a history' (Berger 2007, 70; emphasis mine). Might we push this further and suggest that mimetic drawing puts one, indeed, in a thoroughgoing subject position of doubt? The act of observing and drawing an object or person from life involves a back-and-forth movement from eye to hand. (Derrida, as we saw, characteristically figures this movement between hand and eye as more of an insurmountable abyss.) During that back and forth, things may change in small or large ways, like creases in a person's face as their expression shifts. The caprices of the artist may shift too. To turn back to Berger's precise wording: drawings 'remind' us not of what they depict, but of the rule that the objects or phenomena that they depict are 'constructions[s] with history'.

If writing is a mnemonic practice, then drawing seems to operate at what we might call, rather awkwardly, a 'meta-mnemonic' level. By that, I simply mean that Berger's drawing of his father acts as a reminder of the poverty of the powers of memory and the limits of mnemonic capture when presented with the traceable histories that inform, and will continue to inform, appearances. Drawing can be meta-mnemonic in the way that it can stage and interrogate the conditions of memory—what gets remembered, what gets lost, what can or cannot be fixed in place. The traced outline of Berger's father on paper serves to remind him not of any *essential* filial connection to this man, but conversely of its lightness or 'disappearance'. There are circumstances in which this feeling might be as liberating as it is frightening or mournful. Here, we should recall Winnicott on string and squiggles and the general valence of lines as a means of regulating the ego's adaptation to its own independence and tracing out a 'denial of separation' with the mother. In Berger's case, the same principle is almost true—the drawing allows him to re-trace and remember a connection to his late father, but it has also taken on a much more melancholic grain. The lines act equally as a reminder of separation, of the formal fragility of the lines and strings that the child sets down and plays with.

Jorie Graham's 'Mother's Hands Drawing Me', which closes out her 2017 collection *Fast*, is a particularly moving counterpoint to Berger's narrative. It is equally and carefully concerned with thinking about the mode of observant attention peculiar to mimetic drawing. In the poem, Graham describes the discomfiting experience of observing herself being drawn by her aging, dying mother.[1] The poem is a remarkable example of poetic linework, finding a syntax and lineation for the slowly shuttling back and forth of a line drawing.[2]

First, the mother's drawing is presented as a terminal gesture, one

1 There is a longstanding association between drawing and senescence, which in turn is linked to the association between senescence and childhood (what Shakespeare called 'second childishness'). One of the most beautiful examples of this comes in the form of the conceptual artist Geta Brătescu's late drawings. Elsewhere, in her excellent book *The Primacy of Drawing*, Deanna Petherbridge charts what she calls 'the topos of the artist continuing to draw and to learn even as death approaches, as told by J.-A.-D. Ingres, Théodore Gericault, Gabriel de Saint-Aubin, Edgar Degas and others, and preserved in the photograph of Henri Matisse drawing with a stick from his sickbed' (Petherbridge 2010, 210).

2 In a 2018 interview with *Literary Hub*, Graham says 'when I was writing my

that runs against the grain of everything else her body is doing: 'Dying only mother's hands continue undying' (Graham 2017, 80). The speaker's experience of being drawn, and her awareness of her own traceability, meanwhile, is figured in vigorously physical terms. 'Drawn', here, means also drawn in the sense of drawing blood: 'what is this you drag / again today into non-being. Draw it. / The *me* who is not here. Who is the / ghost in this room. What am I that / is now drawn' (Graham 2017, 81). The drawing is somehow a kind of corporeal extraction. Being traced, the speaker feels less sure of herself, and less sure of who she is, leaving a sequence of weak and overlapping questions ('what', 'who', 'what') posed without question marks. It is as if the speaker cannot pose the questions to herself, because she is rendered less sure of any corresponding self that is able to answer. If Berger's drawing enacts a gentle questioning of appearances, Graham's speaker is so relentlessly questioned by the act of being drawn that she encounters a kind of crisis of her own self-appearance.[3]

The unpunctuated syntax of Graham's poem, dissolving the outward-turning apostrophe of its questions into paratactical clauses, is one of the ways in which Graham's poetic linework marks out a formal ekphrasis of drawing. A *process* of questioning is flattened into an unquestioning whole. The lines that compose a drawing, like the questions that compose the poem, are cumulative. To be subjected to, and interrogated by, the specific type of attention of the act of drawing is to be made uncommonly aware of the totality of one's traceability in time: both one's susceptibility to be traced as an outline, but also one's susceptibility to be traced back through a succession of consecutive moments.

It is an awareness of the fact, dramatized by the progressive back and forth of the drawer as they go from observation to demarcation ('looking up at what, / looking back down')—that, at bottom, one's entire social identity is contingent upon its amenability to an outline and a strangely corresponding filial order. The up-and-down movement of the attentive draughtsperson is unnervingly akin to that of the border agent, scanning the face, stamping the passport. With that awareness of the predication of

first book, I decided I had to draw each tiny thing I tried to describe in order to train my eye to see' (Graham 2023).

3 We should recall here that the ability to question, to doubt, is the foundation of Cartesian subjectivity. In Graham's poem, being traceable, being thereby questioned, subtly erases this Cartesian foundation.

the self within an externally imposed outline and traceable proportions, comes a keen sense that the self, itself, is something not just exogeneous, but hauntingly reduceable to two-dimensional form. Note the way the poem, here, marks and remarks itself into the present tense: 'today', 'now'. One only ever receives this exogenous identity in the amnesia of a present tense.

The mother is dying, and with her death will die the perceiving self that lends itself both to the drawing, and the drawing of identity that occurs with the act of the drawing. That is why, in Graham's poem, the sense of evacuation is so acute: 'You look back up, you take / my strangeness from me, you / machine me, you hatch me in' (Graham 2017, 91). Note the double valence of 'hatch': one 'hatches', as a kind of birth of emergence, but one is also *hatched in*, bounded by defining lines. Of course, the pathos of the poem is that the mother's drawing is proleptic of her dying. What does drawing have to do with death here? Perhaps the death of a parent marks the loss of a narcissistic relationship that provides the phantasmatic material support for considerable regions of individual identity that have been traced and retraced over the course of a life until that moment.

The poem's conclusion plays along the blurred zone between writing and drawing. Where the drawing forgets and expropriates, the writing of the poem serves to remember and to restore: 'as it / begins to take form there, in the not / being, there is *once* then there is the / big vocabulary, loosed, like / a jay's song thrown down when the / bird goes away' (Graham 2017, 84). Graham's lines call to mind the moment a drawing child becomes a writing child: the blossoming from the simple introductory adverb 'once' (the word children learn to use to initiate stories) into a whole 'big vocabulary'. A vocabulary is a sort of life. 'Vocabulary' is a term we use to refer to the total of what a person can speak. In *The Years*, Annie Ernaux reflects on this: 'Everything will be erased in a second. The dictionary of words amassed between cradle and deathbed, eliminated' (Ernaux 2008, 18). According to this logic, a vocabulary *is* the subject, the subject as an aggregate linguistic potentiality, as opposed to an easily traceable form.

In Graham's poem, the 'loosing' of a 'big vocabulary' refers both to the death of the mother, and the attendant 'elimination' of a vocabulary, as it does to the outpouring of words that the poem itself is as a coming to terms with that elimination. There is something haunting about this dual meaning. I agglomerate my vocabulary, which lives and dies with my body, from all the other finite bodies that taught me the words. I can let my vocabulary loose, and use it to express myself, but that expenditure is hauntingly close, *because* it's an expenditure, to the individual deaths that have made it possible. Circling around one another in the poem are the anticipated loss of a parent, the awareness of one's own traceable finitude as a body in space, and the relationship between words and lines.

Berger, too, is writing about his drawing as a way of letting loose a vocabulary in response to a mournful demand that is felt in the white spaces within and around the outlines. If we return to the comparison, Berger shows us how the linear form of a drawing, as an outlined transitional space between child and parent, can help to afford a grounding sense of a single, traceable person whose having been, and having been traceable, provides a kind of stabilizing solace for the beholder. Graham shows us the flipside: the destabilizing experience of finding oneself traced by the parent who is literally undergoing death. In both cases, drawing, like the drawing of Butades, becomes a means of remembering through forgetting. It outlines a loved one while also effacing their presence. And the *writing* of the drawing—the essay, the poem—serves to remember, to turn that forgetting outwards, fill in and make up for an anxiety of disappearance.

Berger's essay and Graham's poem are exemplary texts of child drawing. They are texts about drawing and texts about no longer drawing (but writing!), and they are texts about no longer being a child, but still being a child. They both respond with big vocabularies to individual drawings. They are variations of the child who draws an aquarium and says, 'this is a shrimp, this is a fish; and what is this?', or the child who comments on their friend's drawing and tries to draw the same thing, or something similar but their own. And they are reckonings with the ultimate loss of parents and forebears, and the structuring fantasies of parents and forebears, whose never-complete presences worry us into seeking solace in shareable stories and shapes. The language of such texts channels the language we acquire and test as children, as we learn to play and write and as we draw.

Bibliography

Agamben, Giorgio. *Infancy and History: The Destruction of Experience*. Translated by Liz Heron (London and New York: Verso 1993).

– *Means without End: Notes on Politics*. Translated by Vincenzo Binetti and Cesare Casarino (Minneapolis: University of Minnesota Press 2000).

– *Stanzas*. Translated by Ronald L. Martinez (Minneapolis: University of Minnesota Press 1993).

Alland Jr., Alexander. *Playing with Form: Children Draw in Six Cultures* (New York: Columbia University Press 1983).

Alloway, Lawrence. 'Sol LeWitt: Modules, Walls, Books'. In *Artforum* 13.8 (April 1975), pp. 38–43.

Ammons, A.R. *The Complete Poems of A.R. Ammons. Volume I. 1955–1977*. Edited by Robert M. West (New York and London: W.W. Norton and Company 2017a).

– *The Complete Poems of A.R. Ammons. Volume II. 1978–2005*. Edited by Robert M. West (New York and London: W.W. Norton and Company 2017b).

– *An Image for Longing: Selected Letters and Journals of A.R. Ammons, 1951–1974*. Edited by Kevin McGuirk (Victoria: ELS Editions 2013).

Anderson, Linda. *Elizabeth Bishop: Lines of Connection* (Edinburgh: Edinburgh University Press 2015).

– 'Visual Art'. In *Elizabeth Bishop in Context*. Edited by Angus Cleghorn and Jonathan Ellis (Cambridge: Cambridge University Press 2021), pp. 126–136.

Anning, Angela and Ring, Kathy. *Making Sense of Children's Drawings* (Maidenhead: Open University Press 2004).

Ariès, Philippe. *Centuries of Childhood: A Social History of Family Life*. Translated by Robert Baldick (New York: Vintage 1962).

Ashton, Dore. *Picasso on Art: A Selection of Views* (New York: Viking 1972).

Attridge, Derek. *The Singularity of Literature* (London and New York: Routledge 2004).

Ayman-Nolley, Saba. 'Vygotsky's Perspective on the Development of Imagination and Creativity'. In *Creativity Research Journal* 5.1 (1992), pp. 77–85.

Badiou, Alain. *The Age of the Poets: And Other Writings on Twentieth-Century Poetry and Prose.* Translated by Bruno Bosteels (New York: Verso 2014).

Barraza, Laura. 'Children's Drawings about the Environment'. In *Environmental Education Research* 5.1 (1999), pp. 49–66.

Bateson, Gregory. *Steps to an Ecology of Mind* (Chicago and London: University of Chicago Press 2000).

— 'A Theory of Play and Fantasy'. In *Semiotics: An Introductory Anthology.* Edited by Robert E. Ennis (Bloomington: Indiana University Press 1985), pp. 129–144.

Battles, Matthew. 'In Praise of Doodling'. In *The American Scholar* 73.4 (2004), pp. 105–108.

Baudelaire, Charles. *The Painter of Modern Life.* Translated by Patrick Edward Charvet (London: Penguin 2010).

Bearne, Eve and Kress, Gunther. 'Editorial'. In *Literacy* 35.3 (November 2001), pp. 89–93.

Beauchamp, George. 'What Is Graphology?' In *The Phrenological Journal and Science of Health* 122.1 (1906), pp. 11–12.

Bell, Al. 'Medium and Mediality in Anne Carson'. In *Textual Practice* 36.7 (2022), pp. 1050–1070.

Benjamin, Walter. *Selected Writings. Volume 1: 1913–1926.* Edited by Marcus Bullock and Michael W. Jennings (Cambridge and London: Belknap Press of Harvard University Press 1996).

Bennett, Jane. *Influx and Efflux: Writing Up with Walt Whitman* (Durham: Duke University Press 2020).

— *Vibrant Matter: A Political Ecology of Things* (Durham: Duke University Press 2010).

Berger, John. *Berger on Drawing* (Aghabullogue: Occasional Press 2007).

Bergson, Henri. *Matter and Memory.* Translated by Nancy Margaret Paul and W. Scott Palmer (London: George Allen and Unwin 191 1).

Bernstein Howell, Joyce. 'Eugène Delacroix's Review of Le Dessin sans maître and the Modernized Discourse of Drawing'. In *Word & Image* 21.3 (2005), pp. 223–243.

Bertrand, Melanie, Brooks, Maneka D. and Domínguez, Ashley D. 'Challenging Adultism: Centering Youth as Educational Decision Makers'. In *Urban Education* 58.10 (2020), pp. 2570–2597.

Bishop, Elizabeth. *Poems* (London: Chatto & Windus 2011).

Bloom, Paul and Markson, Lori. 'Intention and Analogy in Children's Naming of Pictorial Representations'. In *Psychological Science* 9.3 (1998), pp. 200–204.

Bonnefoy, Yves. 'Overture: The Narrow Path toward the Whole'. In *Yale French Studies* 84 (1994), pp. 13–16.

Braster, Sjaak and del Pozo Andrés, Maria del Mar. 'Education and the Children's Colonies in the Spanish Civil War (1936–1939): The Images of the Community Ideal'. In *Paedagogica Historica* 51.4 (2015), pp. 455–477.

Breton, André. 'Artistic Genesis and Perspective of Surrealism'. In *Surrealism and Painting*. Translated by Simon Watson Taylor (New York: Harper and Row 1972).

— 'Words without Wrinkles'. In *The Lost Steps*. Translated by Mark Polizzotti (Lincoln and London: University of Nebraska Press 1996).

Brinkman, Bartholomew. *Poetic Modernism in the Culture of Mass Print* (Baltimore: Johns Hopkins University Press 2017).

Brockes, Emma. 'Magical Thinking'. *The Guardian*, 30 Dec 2006, https://www.theguardian.com/books/2006/dec/30/featuresreviews.guardianreview7. Accessed 19 Jul 2025.

Brooks, Peter. 'Freud's Masterplot'. In *Yale French Studies* 55/56 (1977), pp. 280–300.

Brown, Andrew. *Roland Barthes: The Figures of Writing* (Oxford: Clarendon Press 1992).

Bruns, Gerald L. 'Francis Ponge on the Rue de la Chaussée'. In *Comparative Literature* 53.3 (Summer 2001), pp. 193–213.

Bryson, Norman. 'A Walk for a Walk's Sake'. In *The Stage of Drawing – Gesture and Act: Selected from the Tate Collection* (London: Tate Publications 2003), pp. 149–158.

Buchloh, Benjamin H.D. 'Hesse's Endgame: Facing the Diagram'. In *Eva Hesse Drawing*. Edited by Catherine de Zegher (New York: The Drawing Center 2006), pp. 117–150.

Butler, Judith. *Gender Trouble* (New York: Routledge 1990).

Carson, Anne. *Autobiography of Red: A Novel in Verse* (London: Jonathan Cape 1998a).

— *The Beauty of the Husband: A Fictional Essay in 29 Tangos* (London: Cape Poetry 2001).

— 'Cy Twombly: A Rustle of Catullus'. In *Arion: A Journal of the Humanities and the Classics* 30.3 (Winter 2023b), pp. 1–12.

— *Decreation: Poetry, Essays, Opera* (London: Jonathan Cape 2006).

— *Economy of the Unlost (Reading Simonides of Keos with Paul Celan)* (Princeton: Princeton University Press 1999).

— *Eros the Bittersweet: An Essay* (Princeton and Oxford: Princeton University Press 2023a).

— *Glass and God* (London: Jonathan Cape 1998b).

— *H of H Playbook* (London: Jonathan Cape 2021a).

— *Men in the Off Hours* (New York: Vintage 2000).
— *Short Talks* (London: Brick Books 2019).
— 'Stillness'. In *Critical Inquiry* 48.1 (2021b), pp. 1–22.
— *Wrong Norma* (London: Jonathan Cape 2024).
Cavé, Marie Elisabeth. *Le Dessin sans maître, méthode pour apprendre à dessiner de mémoire* (Paris: Susse frères 1850).
Chodorow, Nancy. *The Reproduction of Mothering* (Berkeley: University of California Press 1978).
Cisneros Poireth, Arturo. 'Rendering Visible Through Language: Writing Drawings and the Literary Portrait in Anne Carson's *Men in the Off Hours*'. In *Word & Image* 38.3 (2022), pp. 223–236.
Coles, Elizabeth Sarah. *Anne Carson: The Glass Essayist* (Oxford: Oxford University Press 2023).
Coliron, Margaret. 'Lions, Witches, and Happy Old Men: Some Parallels Between Balinese and Japanese Ritual Masks'. In *Asian Theatre Journal* 22.2 (Autumn 2005), pp. 227–248.
Constantine, Peter. 'Ancient Worlds, Modern Words: A Conversation with Anne Carson'. In *World Literature Today* (January–February 2014), pp. 36–37.
Costello, Bonnie. *Marianne Moore: Imaginary Possessions* (Cambridge and London: Harvard University Press 1981).
Cox, Maureen. *Children's Drawings of the Human Figure* (London: Psychology Press 2013).
Crary, Jonathan. *Suspensions of Perception: Attention, Spectacle and Modern Culture* (Cambridge, MA: MIT Press 1999).
Creeley, Robert. *A Quick Graph: Collected Notes & Essays*. Edited by Donald Allen (San Francisco: Four Seasons Foundation 1970).
Culler, Jonathan. *Theory of the Lyric* (Cambridge and London: Harvard University Press 2015).
— 'Why Rhythm'. In *Critical Rhythm*. Edited by Ben Glaser and Jonathan Culler (New York: Fordham University Press 2019), pp. 21–39.
Cusset, François. *French Theory: How Foucault, Derrida, Delueze and Co. Transformed the Intellectual Life of the United States* (Minneapolis: University of Minnesota Press 2008).
Davis, Whitney. 'Sigmund Freud's Drawing of the Dream of the Wolves'. In *Oxford Art Journal* 15.2 (1992), pp. 70–87.
De Man, Paul. 'Sign and Symbol in Hegel's "Aesthetics"'. In *Critical Inquiry* 8.4 (Summer 1982), pp. 761–775.
Delacroix, Eugène. *The Journal of Eugène Delacroix*. Edited by Hubert Wellington and translated by Lucy Norton. 3rd edition (London: Phaidon 1995).

Deguara, Jo and Nutbrown, Cathy. 'Signs, Symbols, and Schemas: Understanding Meaning in a Child's Drawings'. In *International Journal of Early Years Education* 21.1 (2018), pp. 4–23.

Derrida, Jacques. 'Maddening the Subjectile'. In *Yale French Studies* 84 (1994), pp. 154–171.

— *Memoirs of the Blind: The Self-Portrait and Other Ruins*. Translated by Pascale-Anne Brault and Michael B. Naas (Chicago: University of Chicago Press 1993).

— *Of Grammatology*. Translated by Gayatri Chakravorty Spivak (Baltimore: Johns Hopkins University Press 1976).

— 'Paper or Myself, You Know… (New Speculations on a Luxury of the Poor)'. In *Paragraph* 21.1 (March 1998), pp. 1–27.

Di Leo, Joseph H. *Interpreting Children's Drawings* (New York: Routledge 2013).

Dubuffet, Jean. 'On Drawing: Selections from Letters and Other Writings'. Translated by Richard Howard. In *Dubuffet – Drawings 1935–1962*. Edited by Isabelle Dervaux (London: Thames and Hudson 2016), pp. 43–71.

Dworkin, Craig. *No Medium* (Boston: MIT Press 2015).

— *Radium of the Word: A Poetics of Materiality* (Chicago and London: University of Chicago Press 2020).

Dyer, Hannah, Sinclair-Palm, Julia, Joynt, Chase, Yeo, Miranda and Tait, Calla. 'Aesthetic Expressions of Queer Kinship in Children's Drawings'. In *Journal of Canadian Studies/Revue d'études canadiennes* 54.2 (2020), pp. 526–543.

Edelman, Lee. *No Future: Queer Theory and the Death Drive* (Durham and London: Duke University Press 2004).

Edwards, Betty. *Drawing on the Right Side of the Brain*. Revised edition (New York: Tarcher/Putnam 1999).

Embree, Lester. 'Merleau-Ponty's Examination of Gestalt Psychology'. In *Research in Phenomenology* 10 (1980), pp. 89–121.

Epstein, Andrew. *Attention Equals Life: The Pursuit of the Everyday in Contemporary Poetry and Culture* (Oxford: Oxford University Press 2016).

— '"The Rhapsody of Things as They Are": Stevens, Francis Ponge and the Impossible Everyday'. In *The Wallace Stevens Journal* 36.1 (Spring 2012), pp. 47–77.

Erkkila, Betsy. *Walt Whitman Among the French: Poet and Myth* (Princeton: Princeton University Press 1980).

Ernaux, Annie. *The Years*. Translated by Alison L. Strayer (London: Fitzcarraldo Editions 2008).

Esdale, Logan. 'Gertrude Stein's Twin'. In *Textual Practice* 25.11 (2011), pp. 989–1014.

Farhi, Nina. 'Psychotherapy and the Squiggle Game: A Sophisticated Game of Hide and Seek'. In *Squiggles and Spaces: Revisiting the Work of D.W. Winnicott. II*. Edited by Mario Bertolini, Andreas Giannakoulas and Max Hernandez (London: Whurr Publishers 2001), pp. 65–75.

Fineberg, Jonathan. *The Innocent Eye: Children's Art and the Modern Artist* (Princeton: Princeton University Press 1997).

Fisher, Jean. 'On Drawing'. In *The Stage of Drawing – Gesture and Act: Selected from the Tate Collection* (London: Tate Pulications 2003), pp. 217–226.

Fleming, Juliet. *Cultural Graphology: Writing After Derrida* (Chicago and London: University of Chicago Press 2016).

Focillon, Henri. *The Life of Forms in Art*. Translated by Charles Beecher Hogan and George Kubler (New Haven: Yale University Press 1942).

Freeman, Norman. *Strategies of Representation in Young Children: Analysis of Spatial Skills and Drawing Processes* (London: Academic Press 1980).

Freud, Sigmund. *Beyond the Pleasure Principle*. Translated by Caroline Jane Mary Hubback (London: International Psychoanalytical Press 1922).

– *The Problem of Anxiety*. Translated by Henry Alden Bunker (New York: Psychoanalytic Quarterly Press and W. W. Norton 1936).

– *The Standard Edition of the Complete Psychological Works of Sigmund Freud. Volume XVII*. Translated by James Strachey (London: The Hogarth Press and the Institute of Psychoanalysis 1918).

– *Three Essays on the Theory of Sexuality: The 1905 Edition*. Translated by Ulrike Kistner (London: Verso 2016).

Fry, Roger. 'Children's Drawings'. In *The Burlington Magazine* 30.171 (June 1917).

Gallop, Jane. *Reading Lacan* (Ithaca: Cornell University Press 1985).

Gardner, Howard. *Artful Scribbles: The Significance of Child Drawing* (New York: Basic Books 1980).

Geissmann, Claudine and Pierre. *A History of Child Psychoanalysis* (New York and London: Routledge 1998).

Geist, Anthony L. and Carroll, Peter N. *They Still Draw Pictures: Children's Art in Wartime from the Spanish Civil War to Kosovo* (Urbana and Chicago: University of Illinois Press 2002).

Gibbs Jr., Raymond W. 'Embodied Dynamics in Literary Experience'. In *Cognitive Literary Science: Dialogues Between Literature and Cognition*. Edited by Michael Burke and Emily T. Troscianko (Oxford: Oxford University Press 2017), pp. 219–238.

Gladman, Renee. *Calamities* (Seattle and New York: Wave Books 2016).

– *Plans for Sentences* (Seattle and New York: Wave Books 2022).

Goethe, Johann Wolfgang von. *Theory of Colours*. Translated by Charles Lock Eastlake (London: John Murray 1840).

Gombrich, E.H. *Art and Illusion: A Study in the Psychology of Pictorial Representation* (London: Phaidon 1977).

Gordon, Jan. *A Step-Ladder to Painting* (London: Faber 1934).

Gould, Thomas. 'The Hatred of Speech and the Poetics of Silence'. In *Silence and Its Derivatives: Conversations Across Disciplines*. Edited by Mahshid Mayar and Marion Schulte (Cham: Palgrave MacMillan 2022), pp. 199–213.

— 'Legerdemain/Gaucherie: Doodle Theory with Barthes and Beckett'. In *Paragraph* 45.2 (2022), pp. 233–247.

Graham, Jorie. *Fast* (Manchester: Carcanet 2017).

— 'In Conversation with Jorie Graham'. *Literary Hub*, 13 Feb 2023, https://lithub.com/in-conversation-with-jorie-graham. Accessed 16 Jul 2025.

Green, Christopher. 'Joan Miró and the Infantile Image'. In *Discovering Child Art: Essays on Childhood, Primitivism, and Modernism*. Edited by Jonathan Fineberg (Princeton: Princeton University Press 1998), pp. 210–234.

Greene, Robert W. *Six French Poets of Our Time: A Critical and Historical Study* (Princeton: Princeton University Press 1979).

Gregory, Elizabeth. *Apparition of Splendor: Marianne Moore Performing Democracy Through Celebrity, 1952–1970* (Newark: University of Delaware Press 2021).

Gubar, Susan. '"The Blank Page" and the Issues of Female Creativity'. In *Critical Inquiry* 8.2 (Winter 1981), pp. 243–263.

Gumbrecht, Hans Ulrich. 'Forum: On Presence'. In *History and Theory* 45 (October 2006), pp. 317–327.

Guston, Philip. *I Paint What I Want to See* (London: Penguin 2022).

Haidt, Jonathan. *The Anxious Generation: How the Great Rewiring of Childhood is Causing an Epidemic of Mental Illness* (New York: Penguin 2024).

Halton-Hernandez, Emilia. 'The Milner Method: Marion Milner and Alison Bechdel's Autobiographical Cures'. In *Life Writing* 18.2 (2021), pp. 243–260.

Harris, Paul L. *Children's Imagination* (Cambridge: Cambridge University Press 2022).

Hartman, Saidiya. 'Intimate History, Radical Narrative'. In *The Journal of African American History* 106.1 (2021), pp. 127–135.

Hegel, Georg Wilhelm Friedrich. *Aesthetics: Lectures on Fine Art. Volume II*. Translated by Thomas Malcolm Knox (Oxford: Oxford University Press 1974).

— *Introductory Lectures on Aesthetics*. Translated by Bernard Bosanquet (London: Penguin 2004).

— *Phenomenology of Spirit*. Translated by A.V. Miller (Oxford: Oxford University Press 1977).

Heidegger, Martin. *Basic Writings*. Translated by David Farrell Krell (Abingdon: Routledge 2011).

– *Gesamtausgabe, Band 5: Holzwege* (Frankfurt am Main: Vittorio Klostermann 1977).
– *Parmenides.* Translated by André Schuwer and Richard Rojcewicz (Bloomington: Indiana University Press 1992).
– *Poetry, Language, Thought.* Translated by Albert Hofstadter (New York: Harper Perennial 2013).
Heuving, Jeanne. *Omissions Are Not Accidents: Gender in the Art of Marianne Moore* (Detroit: Wayne State University Press 1992).
Holder, Alan. *A.R. Ammons* (Boston: Twayne 1978).
Holmboe, Rye Dag. 'A Line Around a Think'. In *Critical Quarterly* 63.4 (2021), pp. 51–72.
Hopperstad, Marit H. 'How Children Make Meaning Through Drawing and Play'. In *Visual Communication* 7.1 (2008), pp. 77–96.
Hubert, Renée Riese. 'The Postmodern Line and the Postmodern Page'. In *The Line in Postmodern Poetry.* Edited by Robert Frank and Henry Sayre (Urbana and Chicago: University of Illinois Press 1988), pp. 132–151.
Huxley, Aldous. 'Introduction'. In *They Still Draw Pictures! A Collection of 60 Drawings Made by Spanish Children During the War* (New York: Spanish Child Welfare Association of America 1938), pp. 4–8.
Ingold, Tim. *Lines: A Brief History* (London: Routledge 2016).
Irigaray, Luce. *Speculum of the Other Woman.* Translated by Gillian Gill (Ithaca: Cornell University Press 1985).
Jackson, Virginia. *Dickinson's Misery: A Theory of Lyric Reading* (Princeton: Princeton University Press 2005).
Jacobus, Mary. *The Poetics of Psychoanalysis: In the Wake of Klein* (Oxford: Oxford University Press 2005).
– *Reading Cy Twombly: Poetry in Paint* (Princeton: Princeton University Press 2016).
Jacoby, Joachim. 'Raphael: Draughtsman and Storyteller'. In *Raphael: Drawings.* Edited by Joachim Jacoby and Martin Sonnabend (Munich: Hirmer Verlag 2012), pp. 4–34.
James, Ian. 'Differing on Difference'. In *Nancy Now.* Edited by Verena Conley and Irving Goh (Cambridge: Polity 2014), pp. 110–126.
Jolley, Richard. *Children and Pictures: Drawing and Understanding* (Chichester: Blackwell 2010).
Kant, Immanuel. *Religion within the Boundaries of Mere Reason and Other Writings* (Cambridge: Cambridge Texts in the History of Philosophy 2018).
Kittler, Friedrich A. *Gramophone, Film, Typewriter* (Stanford: Stanford University Press 1999).
Klee, Paul. *Notebooks, Vol. 1: The Thinking Eye.* Translated by Heinz Norden and edited by Jürg Spiller (Woodstock: The Overlook Press 1992a).

— *Pedagogical Sketchbook*. Translated by Sibyl Moholy-Nagy (London: Faber 1953).
Klein, Melanie. *Love, Guilt and Reparation and Other Works 1921–1945* (London: Vintage 1998a).
— *Narrative of a Child Analysis* (London: Vintage 1998b).
— 'The Psychoanalytic Play Technique'. In *American Journal of Orthopsychiatry* 25.2 (1955), pp. 223–237.
Krčma, Ed. *Drawing Time: Trace, Materiality and the Body in Drawing After 1940* (PhD thesis, University College London 2007).
Kristeva, Julia. *Powers of Horror: An Essay on Abjection*. Translated by Leon S. Roudiez (New York: Columbia University Press 1982).
Laubender, Carolyn. 'Empires of Mind: Postcolonial Cartographies of "The Empire" in Melanie Klein's Narrative of a Child Analysis'. In *Psychoanalysis, Culture and Society* 26 (2021), pp. 323–344.
Leach, Edmund. *Culture and Communication: The Logic by Which Symbols Are Connected. An Introduction to the Use of Structuralist Analysis in Social Anthropology* (Cambridge: Cambridge University Press 1976).
Levine, Caroline. *Forms: Whole, Rhythm, Hierarchy, Network* (Princeton and Oxford: Princeton University Press 2015).
Levrero, Mario. *Empty Words*. Translated by Annie McDermott (Sheffield: And Other Stories 2019).
Lewis, Vicky. 'Young Children's Painting of the Sky and the Ground'. In *International Journal of Behavioural Development* 13.1 (1990), pp. 49–65.
Lichtenstein, Jacqueline. 'Up Close, From Afar: The Subject's Distance from Representation'. In *Qui Parle* 4.1 (Fall 1990), pp. 98–116.
Longenbach, James. *The Art of the Poetic Line* (Saint Paul: Graywolf 2008).
Longobardi, Claudio, Quaglia, Rocco and Iotti, Nathalie O. 'Reconsidering the Scribbling Stage of Drawing: A New Perspective on Toddlers' Representational Processes'. In *Frontiers in Psychology* 6.1227 (2015), pp. 1–9.
Luquet, Georges-Henri. *Children's Drawings*. Translated by Alan Costall (London: Free Association Books 2001).
Lyotard, Jean-François. *The Inhuman: Reflections on Time*. Translated by Geoffrey Bennington and Rachel Bowlby (Cambridge: Polity Press 1991).
Makisa, Hidemoto. 'Clinical Practice with a Child's Drawings from Kleinian and Lacanian Perspectives'. In *British Journal of Psychotherapy* 29.3 (2013), pp. 358–372.
Malchiodi, Cathy A. *Understanding Children's Drawings* (New York and London: The Guilford Press 1998).
Marcuse, Herbert. *One-Dimensional Man: Studies in the Ideology of Advanced Industrial Society* (Boston: Beacon Press 1964).
Martens, Lorna. *The Promise of Memory: Childhood Recollection and Its Objects in Literary Modernism* (Cambridge: Harvard University Press 2011).

Matthews, Gareth B. *The Philosophy of Childhood* (Cambridge and London: Harvard University Press 1994).

McCumber, John. 'Introduction: Transforming Thought'. In *Endings: Questions of Memory in Hegel and Heidegger*. Edited by Rebecca Comay and John McCumber (Evanston: Northwestern University Press 1999), pp. 1–26.

McLaughlin, Emily. 'How to Think Like a Plant? Ponge, Jaccotte, Guillevic'. In *What Forms Can Do: The Work of Form in 20th- and 21st-Century French Literature and Thought*. Edited by Patrick Crowley and Shirley Jordan (Liverpool: Liverpool University Press 2020), pp. 237–254.

McNeilly, Kevin. 'Gifts and Questions: An Interview with Anne Carson'. In *Canadian Literature* 176 (Spring 2003), pp. 12–25.

Merleau-Ponty, Maurice. *Child Psychology and Pedagogy: The Sorbonne Lectures 1949–1952*. Translated by Talia Welsh (Evanston: Northwestern University Press 2010).

– *Phenomenology of Perception*. Translated by Colin Smith (London: Routledge Classics 2002).

Michaud, Ginette. 'Extended Drawing'. In *Nancy Now*. Edited by Verena Conley and Irving Goh (Cambridge: Polity 2014), pp. 90–109.

Miller, J. Hillis. *Ariadne's Thread* (New Haven and London: Yale University Press 1992).

Milner, Marion. *Bothered by Alligators* (London and New York: Routledge 2012).

– *On Not Being Able to Paint* (London and New York: Routledge 2010).

Mitchell, Juliet. *Psychoanalysis and Feminism* (New York: Pantheon Books 1974).

Mitchell, W.J.T. *Iconology: Image, Text, Ideology* (Chicago: University of Chicago Press 1986).

– *Picture Theory: Essays on Verbal and Visual Representation* (Chicago and London: University of Chicago Press 1994).

Moore, Marianne. *Complete Poems of Marianne Moore* (New York: Penguin 1987).

Morgenstern, Sophie. 'Le Symbolisme et la valeur psychanalytique des dessins infantiles'. In *Revue Française de Psychanalyse* 11.1 (1939), pp. 39–48.

– 'Un cas de Mutism Psychogène'. In *Revue Française de Psychanalyse* 1.3 (1927), pp. 492–504.

Nancy, Jean-Luc. *Expectation: Philosophy, Literature*. Translated by Robert Bononno (New York: Fordham University Press 2018).

– 'Introduction à l'exposition'. In *Le Plaisir au dessin: Dossier de presse* (Lyon: Musée des Beaux-Arts de Lyon 2007), pp. 6–9.

– *Multiple Arts: The Muses II*. Edited by Simon Sparks (Stanford: Stanford University Press 2006).

– *The Muses*. Translated by Peggy Kamuf (Stanford: Stanford University Press 1996).

– *The Pleasure in Drawing*. Translated by Philip Armstrong (New York: Fordham University Press 2009).

Newman, Mark. 'The Marks, Traces, and Gestures of Drawing'. In *The Stage of Drawing – Gesture and Act: Selected from the Tate Collection* (London: Tate Publications 2003), pp. 93–108.

Newman, Michael. 'Derrida and the Scene of Drawing'. In *Research in Phenomenology* 24.1 (1994), pp. 218–234.

Nowell Smith, David. *Sounding/Silence: Martin Heidegger at the Limits of Poetics* (New York: Fordham University Press 2013).

O'Connor, Brian. 'The Death Drive as Existence without Tension'. In *Psychoanalytic Review* 103.3 (2016), pp. 423–443.

Peale, Rembrandt. *Graphics: A Manual of Drawing and Writing, for the Use of Schools and Families* (New York: JP Peaslee 1835).

Perloff, Marjorie. *The Poetics of Indeterminacy: Rimbaud to Cage* (Princeton: Princeton University Press 1981).

Petherbridge, Deanna. *The Primacy of Drawing: Histories and Theories of Practice* (New Haven and London: Yale University Press 2010).

Phillips, Adam. *D.W. Winnicott* (London: Fontana 1988).

Pignot, Manon. *La guerre des crayons: quand les petits Parisiens dessinaient la Grande Guerre* (Paris: Parigramme 2004).

Pinto, Giuliana, Accorti Gamannossi, Beatrice and Cameron, Catherine Ann. 'From Scribble to Meanings: Social Interaction in Different Cultures and the Emergence of Young Children's Early Drawing'. In *Early Child Development and Care* 181.4 (2011), pp. 425–444.

Pippin, Robert B. *Hegel and the Philosophy of Pictorial Modernism* (Chicago and London: University of Chicago Press 2014).

Pliny the Elder. *Natural History. Vol. IX, Books 33–35*. Translated by H. Rackham (Cambridge: Harvard University Press 1952).

Ponge, Francis. *Œuvres complètes*, Vol. 1 (Paris: Gallimard 1999).

– *Œuvres complètes*, Vol. 2 (Paris: Gallimard 2002).

– *The Voice of Things*. Translated and edited by Beth Archer (New York: McGraw-Hill 1972).

Pound, Ezra. *ABC of Reading* (New York: New Directions 1934).

Prinz, Jesse J. 'Foreword: Hand Manifesto'. In *The Hand, an Organ of the Mind: What the Manual Tells the Mental*. Edited by Zdravko Radman (Cambridge, MA: MIT Press 2013), pp. ix–xvii.

Quirk, Tom. *Bergson and American Culture* (Chapel Hill: University of North Carolina Press 1988).

Ramazani, Jahan. *Poetry and Its Others: News, Prayer, Song, and the Dialogue of Genres* (Chicago and London: University of Chicago Press 2013).

Reid, Martine. 'Editor's Preface: Legible/Visible'. Translated by Nigel Turner. In *Yale French Studies* 84 (1994), pp. 1–12.

Rilke, Rainer Maria. *The Notebooks of Malte Laurids Brigge*. Translated and edited by Michael Hulse (London: Penguin 2009).

Robinson, Jenefer. 'Expression and Expressiveness in Art'. In *Postgraduate Journal of Aesthetics* 4.2 (August 2007), pp. 19–41.

Roque, Georges. 'Writing/Drawing/Color'. Translated by Caroline Weber. In *Yale French Studies* 84 (1994), pp. 43–62.

Rosand, David. *Drawing Acts: Studies in Graphic Expression and Representation* (Cambridge: Cambridge University Press 2002).

Rose, Bernice. *A Century of Modern Drawing from the Museum of Modern Art* (New York: MoMA 1982).

Rose, Jacqueline. 'The Case of Peter Pan'. In *The Children's Culture Reader*. Edited by Henry Jenkins (New York: NYU Press 1998), pp. 95–109.

— *Sexuality in the Field of Vision* (London: Verso 1986).

Roskill, Mark. *Dolce's 'Aretino' and Venetian Art Theory of the Cinquecento* (New York: New York University Press 1968).

Rousseau, Jean-Jacques. *The Collected Writings of Rousseau: Volume 7 – Essay on the Origin of Languages and Writings Related to Music*. Translated by John T. Scott (Hanover: University Press of New England 1998).

Rudnytsky, Peter L. 'Introduction'. In *Transitional Objects and Potential Spaces: Literary Uses of D.W. Winnicott*. Edited by Peter L. Rudnytsky (New York: Columbia University Press 1993), pp. i–xxii.

Ruskin, John. *The Elements of Drawing* (New York: Dover Publications 1971).

Samuels, Peggy Anne. *Deep Skin: Elizabeth Bishop and Visual Art* (Ithaca: Cornell University Press 2010).

Schelling, Friedrich Wilhelm Joseph. *The Philosophy of Art*. Translated by Douglas W. Stott (Minneapolis: University of Minnesota Press 1989).

Schopenhauer, Arthur. *On Vision and Colors: An Essay*. Translated by E.F.J. Payne. Edited with an Introduction by David E. Cartwright (Oxford and Providence, RI: Berg 1994).

Schwenger, Peter. *Asemic: The Art of Writing* (Minneapolis: University of Minnesota Press 2019).

Sherados, Benjamin. 'Merleau-Ponty's Immanent Critique of Gestalt Theory'. In *Human Studies* 40.2 (2017), pp. 191–215.

Shockley, Evie. 'On Seeing and Reading the "Nothing": Poetry and Blackness Visualized'. In *New Literary History* 50.4 (Autumn 2019), pp. 499–528.

Sky, Jeanette. 'Myths of Innocence and Imagination: The Case of the Fairy Tale'. In *Literature and Theology* 16.4 (December 2002), pp. 363–376.

Spitz, Ellen Handler. 'Picturing the Child's Inner World of Fantasy: On the Dialectic of Word and Image'. In *Transitional Objects and Potential Spaces: Literary Uses of D.W. Winnicott*. Edited by Peter L. Rudnytsky (New York: Columbia University Press 1993), pp. 258–272.

Stevens, Wallace. 'From the "Adagia"'. In *Poetry* 90.1 (April 1957), pp. 40–44.

Stockton, Kathryn Bond. *The Queer Child, or Growing Sideways in the Twentieth Century* (Durham and London: Duke University Press 2009).

Tarn Steiner, Deborah. *Images in the Mind: Statues in Archaic and Classical Literature and Thought* (Princeton and Oxford: Princeton University Press 2001).

Taussig, Michael. *I Swear I Saw This: Drawings in Fieldwork Notebooks, Namely My Own* (Chicago: University of Chicago Press 2011).

Teitelbaum, Stefanie. 'Do I Have to Draw You a Picture? Sigmund Freud, Imagery, and the Wolf-Man's Drawing'. In *Psychoanalytic Inquiry* 36.8 (2016), pp. 633–643.

Tisseron, Serge. 'All Writing is Drawing: The Spatial Development of the Manuscript'. In *Yale French Studies* 84 (1994), pp. 29–42.

Toku, Masami. 'Cross-Cultural Analysis of Artistic Development: Drawing by Japanese and U.S. Children'. In *Visual Arts Research* 27.1 (2001), pp. 46–59.

Tschofen, Monique. 'Drawing Out a New Image of Thought: Anne Carson's Radical Ekphrasis'. In *Word & Image* 29.2 (2013), pp. 233–243.

Turner, Dianne. 'Exhibitions of Children's Art'. In *Working Papers in Art Education* 7.1 (1988), pp. 44–59.

Turner, John. 'Wordsworth and Winnicott in the Area of Play'. In *Transitional Objects and Potential Spaces: Literary Uses of D.W. Winnicott*. Edited by Peter L. Rudnytsky (New York: Columbia University Press 1993), pp. 161–188.

Tyson, Helen. '"Forebodings about Fascism": Marion Milner and Virginia Woolf'. In *Feminist Modernist Studies* 4.1 (2020), pp. 1–21.

UNRWA. *Hear Their Voices: The Lasting Trauma in the Drawings of Three Palestine Refugee Siblings in Gaza*. https://www.unrwa.org/newsroom/features/heartheirvoices-lasting-trauma-drawings-three-palestine-refugee-siblings-gaza . Accessed 17 Jul 2025.

Van Praet, Helena. 'Touching the Screen: On Visual Textuality and Knowledge Construction in Anne Carson's Poetry'. In *Textual Practice* (2023), https://doi.org/10.1080/0950236X.2023.2259354.

Vendler, Helen. *Wallace Stevens: Words Chosen Out of Desire* (Knoxville: University of Tennessee Press 1984).

Viñao, Antonio. 'Politics, Education and Pedagogy: Ruptures, Continuities and Discontinuities (Spain 1936–1939)'. In *Paedagogica Historica* 51 (2015), pp. 405–417.

Vouilloux, Bernard. 'Drawing Between the Eye and Hand: (On Rousseau)'. Translated by Christine Cano and Peter Hallward. In *Yale French Studies* 84 (1994), pp. 175–197.

Vygotsky, Lev. 'Thinking and Speech'. In *The Collected Works of L.S. Vygotsky. Volume 1: Problems of General Psychology, Including the Volume 'Thinking and Speech'*. Edited by Robert W. Rieber and Aaron S. Carton and translated by Norris Minick (New York: Plenum Press 1987), pp. 39–285.

Whaite, Clarence. 'Introduction'. In *1961 International Exhibition of Children's Art*. Exhibition Catalogue. 21 October to 17 November 1961 (London: South London Art Gallery 1961).

Whitman, Walt. *Leaves of Grass* (Oxford: Oxford University Press 2008).

Winner, Ellen. 'The Origins and Ends of Giftedness'. In *American Psychologist* 55.1 (2000), pp. 159–169.

Winnicott, D.W. *Home Is Where We Start From* (London: Penguin 1990).

— *Playing and Reality* (London and New York: Routledge 1971).

— 'Psychoses and Child Care'. In *Through Paediatrics to Psycho-Analysis* (London: The Hogarth Press 1975), pp. 219–228.

— 'The Squiggle Game'. In *The Collected Works of D.W. Winnicott: Volume 8, 1967–1968*. Edited by Lesley Caldwell and Helen Taylor Robinson (Oxford: Oxford University Press 2016), pp. 413–440.

— 'String: A Technique of Communication'. In *The International Psycho-analytical Library* 64 (1965), pp. 153–157.

Wittmann, Barbara. 'Drawing Cure: Children's Drawings as a Psychoanalytic Instrument'. In *Configurations* 18.3 (2010), pp. 251–272.

— 'A Neolithic Childhood: Children's Drawings as Prehistoric Sources'. In *Res: Anthropology and Aesthetics* 63.1 (2013), pp. 125–142.

Wölfflin, Heinrich. *Principles of Art History: The Problem of the Development of Style in Early Modern Art*. Translated by Jonathan Blower (Los Angeles: Getty Publications 2015).

Ziarek, Krzysztof. *Language After Heidegger* (Bloomington: Indiana University Press 2013).

Žižek, Slavoj. *Looking Awry: An Introduction to Jacques Lacan through Popular Culture* (Cambridge: MIT Press 1991).

Index

Printed and bound by CPI Group (UK) Ltd, Croydon, CR0 4YY

14/10/2026

14981780-0003